# Taiwan Travel Guide

## Information Tourism

Author
Ibrahim Lloyd.

First Printed: 2019.

**Publisher**:
SONITTEC LTD
College House, 2nd
Floor
17 King Edwards
Road,
Ruislip
London
HA4 7AE.

# Table of Content

# Summary

## Wonderful Benefits of Traveling

If there was one piece of advice I have for people today to experience more joy in life, it is to travel more. I don't mean taking vacations or going on pre-planning trips, I mean making the journey out to somewhere you've never gone before with an open schedule, to let life show you what opportunities were waiting for you that you couldn't have even imaged before.

Traveling is wonderful in many ways. It captures us with a sense of wanderlust and has us longing for more destinations to visit, cultures to experience, food to eat, and people to meet. As amazing as traveling is, most of us think we need to wait until our later years to really explore a lot of the world. I want to inspire you to travel more now and I will do that by sharing 9 wonderful benefits of traveling so you can take the leap of faith you've been waiting for.

You'll find a new purpose

To travel is to take a journey into yourself.

Traveling is an amazingly underrated investment in yourself. As you travel you're exposed to more new people, cultures, and lifestyles than you are living in your homeland all the time. With all the newness in your life, you're also opened to new insights, ways of seeing the world and living, which often gives people a new purpose for their lives. If you're feeling stuck on what your purpose is, what you want to do with your life, the career or educational path you want to pursue, go travel...you might just be surprised about what you discover as a new sense of life purpose and direction.

You'll appreciate your home more

All travel has it's advantages. If the passenger visits better countries, he may learn to improve his own. And if fortune carries him to worse, he may learn to enjoy it.

When we spend time away from home, especially in a place where we don't have the same luxuries readily available to us...like a village in Fiji that runs without electricity...we become more aware and appreciative for the luxuries we have back at home. I remember a time where I visited my cousin in Argentina after she'd been living there for about a year. I was visiting her around Christmas time and brought her the new Harry Potter book along with some basic goods that you can find almost anywhere in Los Angeles. She was over joyous and filled with gratitude, like she just got the greatest gift in the world. In other parts of the world, like India and Ethiopia, people don't have as much access to clean drinking water...especially from what's readily available on tap. Traveling through areas like that really make us appreciate what we do have, and often can spark the movement of something to support people living there experience a greater quality of life.

You'll realize that your home is more than just where you grew up

No one realizes how beautiful it is to travel until he comes home and rests his head on his old, familiar pillow.

The more we travel, the more we realize that our home is so much more than the town, city, state and even country that we've grown up in; we realize that our home is the world, this planet, and we become more conscious of how we can harmoniously live and support one another. And in that knowingness and state of consciousness, people like those supporting the movement of charity:water come into fruition.

You'll realize how little you actually knew about the world

The world is a book, and those who do not travel read only one page

There's concept, and then there's experience. When we travel, we may notice that some of the things we've heard about the world end up being very different than what we were indoctrinated and conditioned to believe. Many of the initial myths that get dispelled are often about traveling itself. Where you once may have thought it was too expensive and dangerous, you may realize how you can actually save more on your lifestyle expenses traveling the world than you do living at home. You may also realize how kind and friendly strangers can be, and how they are even willing to take care of you with a place to sleep at night. Beyond that, you have the whole world to learn about with every place you discover, every person you meet and every culture you experience.

You'll realize that we all share similar needs

Travel is fatal to prejudice, bigotry, and narrow-mindedness.

Tony Robbins has said many times that no matter what your background is, all human beings share 6 common needs. As you travel more, you notice the truth of this even more...and as that happens, you are more adept in being able to relate to people regardless of their background.

You'll realize that it's extremely easy to make friends

A journey is best measured in friends, rather than miles.

One of the first things I learned from traveling solo is how easy it is to make friends. Something magical happens in how people can show up more raw and real when they're out of their conditioned environment and open to express themselves without feeling judged. That rawness and realness ends up inspiring others to be authentic, and that's how you can become best friends with people when you've only known them for a few hours.

You'll experience the interconnectedness of humanity

Perhaps travel cannot prevent bigotry, but by demonstrating all peoples cry, laugh, eat, worry, and die, it can introduce the idea that if we try and understand each other, we may even become friends.

Just as we notice how we share similar needs, how our perspective of our home expands, and how we become close friends with others from different backgrounds and cultures, we begin to realize how we are all connected. This state of awareness is a jump in consciousness, and what I mean by that is in the way we perceive the world, the life experience and ourselves. Ken Wilber speaks about consciousness as spiral dynamics, each level of consciousness inclusive of the one previous. I feel that traveling often helps people experience a world-centric view of consciousness, and some even on that's integrated...able to see, understand and accept all states of consciousness, and utilizing the gifts of whatever is best and most appropriate in the moment.

You'll experience serendipity and synchronicity

Traveling is one of the easiest ways to become aware of the magic that weaves all of creation together through serendipity and synchronicity with perfect timing.

Serendipity: luck that takes the form of finding valuable or pleasant things that are not looked for. And here's Synchronicity: coincidence of events that appear meaningfully related but do not seem to be causally connected

I'm going to share one story of how I experienced serendipity and synchronicity in Spain. It was early in the morning and it was time for me to return the motorcycle my friend had rented with me yesterday. She left very early in the morning on a flight home so it was my responsibility to return it. I woke up to a beautiful sunny morning in Spain and went out to the street to start the motorcycle. I started to drive, forgetting that the chain was left on the wheel. Having no previous experience with motorcycles, I realized I was in a predicament. Two minutes later, a car drove and parked behind me. I had a feeling that someone in that vehicle knew how to fix motorcycles and was going to help me remove the chain so I could return the motorcycle. As they got out, I spoke to them in Spanish, telling them what happened. One of them motioned the other to go on. He mentioned they were mechanics and here for a job, and that he could help me get the chain off...and he did. I thanked him and he seemed gratified to help a fellow soul on their way. In that moment, I realized that no matter what...the world is here to support me, which leads us to the last benefit of traveling.

You'll realize life is a wonderful gift

Life is either a daring adventure or nothing.

“Twenty years from now you will be more disappointed by the things that you didn’t do than by the ones you did do. So throw off the bowlines. Sail away from the safe harbor. Catch the trade winds in your sails. Explore. Dream. Discover.” Mark Twain

Life is a wonderful gift. It really is, and as we travel and experience more of the world and life, we often become overwhelmed with gratitude and appreciation for all the beautiful moments we enjoyed and people we’ve shared them with. More often than not, this is a realization that we can experience and take action from now while we’re still alive with energy rather than stacking up regrets by the time we’re on our death bed. Rather than waiting until you’re saying “I wish I had”, live so you can say “I’m glad I did”.

# Introduction

When the Portuguese named the main island of Taiwan Ilha Formosa, which means "Beautiful Island" in 1544, they provided an apt summary of the area that became Taiwan. Stunning mountains, rivers and gorges, giant trees, colorful blossoms, and tropical reefs in blue-green seas all contribute to the beauty of the island. Today, these natural attractions are complemented by modern cities, with the country attracting an increasing number of Asian tourists, as well as those from beyond the region.

While parts of modern Taiwan are full of factories and office blocks at odds with the nation's reputation for beauty, there are some wonders of modern architecture, significant monuments, and historic buildings and temples which give the cities an appeal of their own. Taipei is by far Taiwan's largest city and is home to the bulk of Taiwan's famous tourist attractions, museums, and art galleries, while all the major cities are known for excellent food and shopping. The rural areas of Taiwan are the most beautiful, with mountains like the Wulai and gorges such as Taroko attracting hikers, photographers, climbers, and romantics.

The many hotels in Taiwan range from considerably down-market backpacker hostels to five-star resorts. Some international hotel chains such as Hyatt operate in Taiwan, but tend to charge more than local hotels. Visitors should be aware that in Taiwan motels are much like the Japanese 'love hotels' and refer to places where couples can hole up for anywhere from one hour to a few days. For ease of travel, it is a good idea to research and book hotels in advance, but be aware that many hotels will have an English and a Chinese name that bear no relation to one-another, so it is a good idea to have the Chinese name written down for dealing with taxi drivers or getting directions.

All kinds of food including Western food and fast food are available in Taiwan but the real culinary joy of visiting Taiwan is the opportunity to try the local food, which is varied, interesting, and delicious. Taiwan's confusing history has lead to an ongoing ambiguity about the political status of Taiwan. Aside from this, the Taiwanese have a strong regional identity, characterized by distinctive traditions, foods, festivals, crafts, and habits.

Diverse Taiwan is not yet seeing the visitor numbers of other Asian hot spots such as Singapore, but its mix of natural and urban attractions ensure great potential for excursions from its pulsating cities. A favorite here are hot springs, with Taiwan a popular choice, while national parks and even aboriginal villages provide worthy distractions from the glass-and-steel architectural wonders of Taipei.

The country has a marine tropical climate, and thus experiences a lot of rain throughout the year. The rainy seasons last from January to March and June to September, with some areas getting prolonged storms known as plume rains in May. But the weather turns around and warms up between June and September - but the humidity also spikes, making Taiwan hot and muggy almost everywhere. The winters last from October to December and can, conversely, get pretty cold. Despite the humidity and heat, summer is the most popular time to visit Taiwan, because the weather is most predictable and at its nicest.

Taiwan has three international airports, with Taiwan Taoyuan International Airport being the main arrival point for most overseas tourists. Trains are a popular way of getting around Taiwan, particularly some of the more scenic routes such as the one along the east coast or the one that goes through the Central Mountains.

# Taiwan History

Farmers from mainland China settled in Taiwan about 4,000 years ago and are believed to be the ancestors of today's Taiwanese aborigines. The islands of Taiwan were ruled by various tribes, whose hostility repelled invaders and traders for centuries. During the 13th century, Han Chinese began settling the Penghu islands.

The Dutch East India Company failed in an attempt to set up an outpost on the Penghu Islands due to intervention by Ming authorities in 1622. Fort Zeelandia was established on Tayouan islet off Anping, Tainan by the Company in 1624. At that time, the area was populated by a variety of tribal settlements, each with their own chief, some of which had fallen under Dutch control by the 1650s. The Spanish conquered northern Taiwan in 1626, and set up forts and colonies which lasted until 1642, when Dutch forces captured the area.

The Dutch were defeated in 1666 by loyalist, Koxinga (Zheng Chenggong), fleeing the fall of the Ming Dynasty. Koxinga and his heirs ruled the renamed Kingdom of Tungning until 1682, regularly raiding the coast of mainland China.

Quing Dynasty forces captured Taiwan in 1683 and absorbed it into the Fujian province. During this time, Fujian immigrants moved to Taiwan and there was regular conflict amongst Chinese from different regions as well as with local aborigines. The Qing created Taiwan as a separate province in 1885, with Taipei as the capital. A process of modernization followed which saw the construction of Taiwan's first railway and the introduction of a postal service.

The Japanese gained control of Taiwan and Penghu as a result of the 1894-1895 First Sino-Japanese War. The Japanese industrialized the islands, extending the railways, implementing sanitation systems and introducing formal education. Production of the main crops of rice and sugar cane increased to the point that Taiwan was world's seventh largest rice producer by 1939. The Japanese marginalized and persecuted the Taiwanese and aborigines. They instigated a deliberate campaign in 1935m to teach the subjects of the Japanese Empire to see themselves as Japanese, with some success. During World War II, tens of thousands of Taiwanese served in the Japanese military. Japan used Taiwan as base for naval and air campaigns throughout to war, which, along with industrial targets, made Taiwan an object for regular and heavy Allied bombing.

In October 1945, the Japanese surrendered Taiwan to the Republic of China (ROC) troops. The ROC considered the turnover of Taiwan to be completed from that time, while the Allies considered it to be a military occupation of a place under Japanese sovereignty until Japan renounced all claim in 1952.

The ROC administration was not popular in Taiwan which, along with economic issues, led to great unrest in Taiwan during 1947. At the same time, the Chinese Civil War between Nationalists (Kuomintang) and Communists was in progress on mainland China, from which the Communists emerged victorious to form the People's Republic of China (POC) in 1949.

The defeated ROC Government and some two million soldiers, Kuomintang party members, intellectuals, and elite businesspeople evacuated to Taiwan, taking mainland China's gold reserves with them and making Taipei the temporary capital.

From then onwards, the territories under Kuomintang ROC control were reduced to Taiwan and a few other islands. Despite this, the ROC continued to claim the right to rule all China, including mainland China, Outer Mongolia and Taiwan. By contrast, the Communists of mainland China claimed that the ROC was extinct and that there was only one China, which included Taiwan.

The ROC declared martial law in 1949, which was used to suppress political oppositions and lasted until 1987. A one party policy prevailed and anyone perceived to be pro-communist or anti-nationalist was subjected to persecution, which could include, amongst other horrors, imprisonment, torture and death.

Throughout the 1950s, the ROC government constructed military fortifications across Taiwan, as well as the Central Cross-Island Highway. The Chinese civil war continued throughout this time, with sporadic unpublicized clashes and raids. 1958 saw the establishment of Nike-Hercules missile in Taiwan, which were not deactivated until 1997, when they were replaced by new systems.

Technological innovation and industrialization allowed Taiwan to recognize rapid economic growth during the 1960s and '70s, even while the ROC maintained an authoritarian, single-party rule. This growth, along with American support, allowed Taiwan to establish fiscal independence from mainland China. Anti-communist ideals left most Western nations to consider the ROC to be China's sole legitimate governing body during the Cold War. After the Cold War, this recognition largely switched to the PRC while Taiwan retained a status as an independent territory known as the Republic of China.

A quashed pro-democracy protest in 1979, united Taiwanese opposition forces to push for reform. The Government began to enact a process of liberalization from about 1984. The first official opposition party, the Democratic Progressive Party (DPP), was allowed to form in 1986 and martial law was lifted in 1987.

The first ethnically Taiwanese president of the ROC succeeded the presidency in 1988, following the death of the original incumbent. Democratization continued, including a policy of increased localization, which promoted Taiwanese culture and history rather than pan-Chinese identity. The bans using Taiwanese Hokkien language in schools and the media were removed. In 1991, government officials who had held positions without re-election since 1947 were forced to resign.

The president was re-elected in 1996, in what was the first democratic election in the history of the ROC. In 2000, DPP representative Chen Shui-bian, was the first elected non-KMT President. He was re-elected in 2004. Today, the politics of Taiwan are polarized between the Pan-blue Coalition, who favor Chinese reunification and the Pan-Green Coalition, which prefers the prospect of an independent Taiwan. To this day most countries do not recognize the sovereign state of ROC, mainly due to pressure from China, so it remains in diplomatic limbo, with trade missions around the world rather than embassies, but still asserts a measure of authority.

In 2007, the ruling DPP formally asserted a separate identity from China. In 2008, elections returned control to the KMT, with presidential stated aims of increased economic growth and better ties with the PRC.

**Culture**

Taiwan has a well formed regional identity, separate from mainland China, made from a blend of ideas and traditions brought by the various people who settled the region. The Taiwanese are a hardworking, family oriented, polite and pragmatic people, known for hospitality. Food plays a large part in Taiwanese culture with many activities and even festivals centered around food based traditions.

Religion and superstition also shape the Taiwanese culture with Buddhist, Taoist, indigenous, and folk traditions blending into a fascinating and colorful mosaic of temples, shrines, festivals, art, poetry, proverbs, and habits.

# The People

## The friendly people of Taiwan

Taiwan has a population of 23 million. The larger part of the country's inhabitants are the descendants of immigrants from the various provinces of mainland China, but in particular from the southeastern coastal provinces: Fujian and Guangdong.

Because the different ethnic groups have fairly well integrated, differences that originally existed between people from different provinces have gradually disappeared. Nearly 500,000 indigenous people, the original inhabitants of Taiwan, still live here; they are into 16 different tribes, namely Amis, Atayal, Paiwan, Bunun, Puyuma, Rukai, Tsou, Saisiyat, Yami, Thao, Kavalan, Truku, Sakizaya, Sediq ,Kanakanavu ,and Hla'alua.

## Language

The official language of Taiwan is Mandarin Chinese; but because many Taiwanese are of southern Fujianese descent, Minnan (the Southern Min dialect or Heluo) is also widely spoken. The smaller groups of Hakka people and indigenous tribes have also preserved their own languages. Many elderly people can also speak some Japanese, as they were subjected to Japanese education before Taiwan was returned to Chinese rule in 1945 after the Japanese occupation, which lasted for half a century.

The most popular foreign language in Taiwan is English, which is part of the regular school curriculum. However, for your own convenience, when taking a taxi in Taiwan, it is advisable to prepare a note with your destination written in Chinese to show the taxi driver.

Taiwan is also the ideal place to learn Chinese. There are numerous language schools that offer Chinese classes, ranging from hourly-based classes to recognized university programs. Many foreigners from Europe and the United States, as well as other areas, come to Taiwan to spend their holidays, or one or two years, studying Chinese.

# Religion

### Origin of Temples in Taiwan

During the Qing Dynasty, plenty of people from Zhangzhou and Quanzhou in China came to Taiwan via boat trips. The Taiwan Strait was known for malicious winds and waves back then.

Thus, the immigrants often carried deity statues, incense, and ashes of incense with them, thinking that these would keep them safe. "Mazu" was the most popular deity because she is the goddess of the seas. People liked to place a statue of Mazu on a boat, so that they might have a safe journey.

In the early days of settlement, because medicine was rare, whenever a disease broke out, many people died. Therefore, people also worshipped the deity of plague - "Wangye." Wangye was also known as "Thousand-year God" or "Thousand-year Governor," with many different family names. Since Wangye can expel plague, people think that it can also keep people healthy. As the immigrant villages thrived, believers built all sorts of temples to thank gods for their protection. And Mazu and Wangye expanded to be the two most powerful folk beliefs in Taiwan. In fact, in those times, temples often provided moral teachings and urgent financial aids to locals, in addition to being religious centers.

# About Taipei and the Prople

## There is no other city in the world like Taipei.

The statement may sound like some banal utterance headlining a paid tourism advert or the first sentence in the fiftieth edition of some travel guide; however, I mean it when I say that of the many places I have visited around the world, there is *no other place* with a similar feeling.

The city is a living concoction of seemingly contradictory qualities. All around Taipei, you can find international luxury brands, local mom and pop's restaurants that have been in business for decades, chic coffee shops tucked away in 2-meter wide alleyways, Japanese izakaya bars, pocket parks, timeless-looking temples in the shadow of glass high rises, and neon-lit night markets accompanied with wafts of fragrant street snacks. Row upon row of orderly, square city blocks are cut into fragments by a jigsaw of alleyways where even Google Maps cannot help you. And even these quiet neighborhood alleyways, reminiscent of the 1950s, are then juxtaposed by a hypermodern metro system — arguably one of the best in the world — that moves millions of people a day from one side of the city to another. Thus, Taipei is paradoxically a comforting, chaotic, convenient, confounding, and orderly place.

But having now lived in the city twice for unfortunately brief durations, I have been itching to understand just how Taipei came to be Taipei. Luckily enough, I worked for the city government over the summer of 2018, so that gave me just the opportunity I was looking for to dig into the city's story.

## Tracing Threads: Back to the Beginning

Anyone who has visited before knows that Taipei is nestled in a wet and humid basin surrounded by rainforest-covered mountains. The basin, which now contains the urban conglomeration of both Taipei and New Taipei City, was once submerged beneath a vast, shallow lake. Imperial documents from the Ming Dynasty report that the lake was formed from an earthquake, which disrupted the flow of the region's rivers. According to a contemporary folk historian, the lake was so vast that if a person were to stand on the shoreline, the far shore would not be visible.

The Ketagalan tribe, an Austronesian people that migrated to Taiwan before recorded history, had settled near the lake shore and remained active in the area until Han settlers began to crowd them out. Settlers from the Fujian Province in China established trading posts and fishing villages across the island starting in the seventeenth century, although most of the Chinese settlements were initially concentrated in flat plain of the south, including the island's administrative capital of Tainan. A few settlements dotted the modern capital region, including the ports of Tamsui (淡水) and Keelung, then colloquially referred to as in Southern Min).

During the turbulent seventeenth century, first the Spanish and then the Dutch attempted to wrest control of the island from the Han settlers (who were occupiers themselves). The European colonial powers constructed forts within a stone's throw of the island's coastal settlements, including in Tamsui and Keelung; however, their activity being so close to China's doorstep drew the ire of both the waning Ming Dynasty loyalists and the newly-ascendant Qing Dynasty. A military intervention from the general Koxinga combined with persistent raids from the indigenous peoples of Taiwan thwarted European colonial ambitions; however, the independent island was subsequently settled by Koxinga's forces and later centralized and incorporated into Chinese imperial administration.

By the nineteenth century, the aforementioned shallow lake had long ago drained. In its stead flowed the wide and meandering Tamsui River. The river originated in mountains to the south and wound its way to the Pacific in the north. On its banks grew two towns that would eventually be known as the oldest neighborhoods of Taipei City: *Banka* and *Twatutia*.

These sleepy farming villages literally translates as "big rice paddy jar") were tiny and of little note, remaining backwater settlements of a wild frontier for years and years. After the conclusion of the Opium Wars, however, the villages' statuses forever changed: Taiwan was fortuitously opened to foreign trade. A thriving tea export business picked up steam in Twatutia, with dozens of tea shops opening along the riverfront. After significant growth, both in terms of population and in wealth, the two towns were merged into a single polity in 1875. This administrative decision came on the heels of the Qing establishing a new town due east of Banka called *Chengnei*, or "inside walls"). The new city center's name was derived from the construction of city walls to protect the area from the increasing threat of foreign attacks. They proved to be the last city walls constructed in Imperial China. While the walls no longer exist today, the old city gates are still visible in Taipei to this day.

## Reorganization and the Birth of Taipei

In 1887, the Qing Empire reorganized the political boundaries of Taiwan by separating the island from the mainland Fujian Province. At the same time, the administrative center of Taiwan was shifted from the sunny, cultural hub of Tainan in the south to the wet, muddy walled town of Chengnei in the north. The walled town was rechristened as Taipei, "Tai(wan) North").

The decision perplexed many not just in retrospect, but contemporaneously. Tainan was by far the largest settlement on the island, with an imposing Dutch-constructed fort acting as existing coastal defense. Taipei had experienced a flurry of construction in the past decade, such as the first incarnation of the Taipei Confucius Temple, a *yamen* (a residence for imperial bureaucrats) and the beginnings of a train line to Keelung, but was in the peripheral hinterlands when compared to Tainan. Contrary to first appearance, the government's decision was quite rational. Qing supremacy in the region was weakening and raids from pirates and European powers were taking their toll on Taiwan. Situated in the flat coastlands, Tainan was subject to frequent attack. Taipei, however, surrounded on all sides by mountains save for coastal access to the northwest and northeast, was substantially easier to defend. There was also ample undeveloped land surrounding the walled city.

Humorously though, the government actually intended the move to Taipei to be a temporary one. The Qing originally sought to construct a permanent provincial capital near modern-day Taichung (台中) due to its central location on the island, but the plan never had time to come to fruition. Less than a decade after Taipei was declared the 'interim' provincial capital of Taiwan, the island came under the occupation of the Japanese Empire.

At the conclusion of the First Sino-Japanese War in 1895, the Qing Empire was forced to cede Taiwan along with Penghu and other territories to the victorious Japanese. This surrender proved to not pass peacefully. While the island was on the fringes of the Chinese Empire, the Han citizens were not in support of the treaty's provisions and local officials immediately moved to found the short-lived Republic of Formosa. This triggered a Japanese invasion and bitter fighting swept the island. The provincial capital, although threatened by the very militia that was formed to protect it, was spared from much of the war's violence.

## Colonial Taipei, a Japanese Legacy

If you visit the Taipei neighborhood of *Ximending* ("ding" is a Chinese translation of the Japanese character for "district"), you may feel as though you have stepped through a portal into the heart of Tokyo or Osaka. Giant electronic screens cover multiple stories of high-rise malls. Adverts for clothing lines and upcoming films tower over you as you walk through the streets. All around you, vendors are selling Japanese snacks, clothes, anime movies, magazines, books, and other pop cultural items. This commercial center may feel a bit out of place considering the quiet mid-century neighborhoods that border it; but with a clear lens to the past, it is apparent why there is such a heavy Japanese cultural presence in Taipei.

For fifty years, Japan directly ruled Taiwan. The colonial power left a tremendous mark on the country's culture, physical appearance, and especially its spatial layout. This legacy is felt the strongest in Taipei.

Taipei was in its infancy when the Japanese declared it their colonial capital of Taiwan; thus, it was the beneficiary of a substantial amount of investment and planning from the industrializing nation. Japan's government, influenced by its contemporary European colonial rivals, had embraced European ideas of urban planning. Upon seizing control of Taiwan, the burgeoning Japanese Empire immediately began a construction frenzy in Taipei. The Office of the Governor-General of Taiwan (now the Presidential Office Building), the Red House Theatre, the Taiwan High Court, and the Public Hall were all Japanese architectural contributions to the city. The treelined route along Zhongshan Road to a former shrine (now the site of the Grand Hotel that hosts both local and foreign dignitaries) was a complete mirror of Tokyo's Omotesandō Avenue, which led to the Meiji Jingu. Many of the ordinary residential and commercial structures built during this time were Japanese style one-to-two-stories, with brick and mortar exteriors. Street fronts were adorned with shaded arcades, formed by high archways and colonnades. These covered sidewalks became a staple of Taipei, and are present throughout a majority of Taipei's boulevards and avenues. The Japanese also imported a Western-style grid street plan that has been continued in the city's planning to this day, along with initiating Taipei's (and Taiwan's) railway network.

By the turn of the twentieth century, Taipei had been utterly transformed. It surpassed Tainan to be the largest city on the island. Even though there still were residents alive that could remember Taipei as two sleepy fishing villages, that past was now unrecognizable as the city had tripled in size. The most integral part of Taipei's urban fabric shifted from the Tamsui River inland to the east. Having long outgrown its walls, the Japanese decided to demolish the old structures in 1907 as part of a series of new urban plans, yet they identified *Chengnei* and its surroundings as the city center. A checkerboard grid road network was built out as far as the contemporary Zhongshan and Da'an districts; although at the time, these districts were not densely infilled as they are today, but merely a few commercial streets mixed with agrarian residential farmland.

In 1938, the city annexed additional lands to the east (seen in green on the map above). The then-undeveloped marshland, covered in bogs, bushes and mushy earth, is now home to Taipei 101 and other high-rises of the Xinyi district.

## The Nationalists

In August 1945, Japan relinquished governance of Taiwan to the Republic of China as a part of its defeat in the Second World War. Unfortunately, the relationship between the city and its new government soured quickly.

Before becoming a colony of Japan, the peoples of Taiwan were a curious amalgam of Southern Min and Hakka settlers, along with dozens of indigenous tribes. It could be said that the island's society then was rather analogous to the early days of the English colonies in North America: specifically, while Taiwan was on the frontier of Chinese cultural influence, a Mandarin-speaking person visiting from Beijing would have found the inhabitants of Taiwan to be utterly alien, especially those of an indigenous background that spoke non-Sino-Tibetan languages and practiced non-Chinese religions.

Years spent as Japanese colony further transformed the Taiwanese people (in fact, it was during this period of occupation when "Taiwanese" as a sole identity truly began to solidify). Decade after decade of celebrating Japanese holidays and festivals, learning the Japanese language in schools along with the standard curriculum taught in the Japanese homeland, consuming Japanese products, and living amongst Japanese immigrants remolded the local cultures significantly. Even considering the reactionary events that followed the collapse of the colonial government, the Land of the Rising Sun's influence can be easily observed in contemporary Taiwanese culture (ranging from the omnipresence of bento boxes as a lunchtime meal to the loud cries of "welcome!" that greets guests when they enter a store).

Considering these facts helps provide context to the impending clash that occurred when Taiwan was "recovered" by the Republic of China. In his book *Taipei: City of Displacements*, Professor Joseph R. Allen provides a summary of the differences in attitude between the Chinese officials and the local Taiwanese:

"In policy and personality, the Chinese government regarded the Taiwanese, especially the Japanese-educated elite, with deep suspicion and distrust ... While the Nationalist forces expected to be seen as comrades who had suffered through a horrendous war on the continent against the Japanese, the Taiwanese elites expected to be treated as an educated class who had gained experience and insight into the modern world during fifty years of Japanese rule," (Allen, 9).

The social division between the continental government and the island's people soon enough grew to a chasm. In its first year controlling the island, the Nationalists forcibly repatriated ninety percent of Taiwan's Japanese population. This policy ripped families from their homes and disrupted entire neighborhoods of Taipei. Subsequent seizures of property and heavy-handed treatment of local vendors sparked a civil uprising that began February 27, 1947. Violence swept Taipei the following day (known to history as the "February 28 Incident") as mainland Chinese officials were indiscriminately targeted and lynched. The Nationalists responded to the event with extreme force as the military swept into Taipei and other cities across the island. In the period of Taiwanese history known as the "White Terror", thousands of local Taiwanese went missing, were imprisoned, or were killed. Whether all targets of government violence were participants in the civil uprising or not, approximately 10,000 lives were taken.

## From Provincial Capital to National Capital

Tensions were high in Taipei following the February 28 Incident; however, the citizens of Taipei were certainly not prepared for the events of 1949. Just a mere four years after the conclusion of World War II, the entire governing apparatus of the Republic of China suddenly descended upon Taipei, declaring martial law over the island as they came. The Chinese Civil War, having been on hiatus during the events of World War II, concluded with the Communist's seizure of all Nationalist mainland holdings. Mao Zedong declared the establishment of the People's Republic of China on October 1, 1949, shortly after Chiang Kai-shek's Nationalist government fled to Taiwan.

This political earthquake which rocked Taipei was accompanied by the mass immigration of over two million Chinese wartime refugees. Doctors, lawyers, professors, soldiers, and anyone remotely associated with the Nationalist Party fled to the political safety of Taiwan, with a significant share of the refugees settling in Taipei. This dramatic migration occurred within a year's time and its effects on the city were both consequential and irreversible.

Taipei's posh colonial character and economic status was altered by the sudden need to accommodate millions of refugees. While the upper echelon of the government settled into the former Japanese colonial estates, a majority of the migrants were poor soldiers who could not afford either new or existing housing. The Nationalist government turned a blind eye to the rapidly-constructed military housing units that began to crowd unused lots of land. These informal settlements were also consequently constructed with low quality materials, a fact that would come back to haunt Taipei in the following decades.

The Nationalist government's actions following the move did not ameliorate the chasm. Declaring Taipei the 'temporary capital' of their state, the Republic of China initiated plans for recovering their mainland territories and directed all resources towards that aim. Although it had just been elevated in status from a provincial seat to a national capital, Taipei was severely underfunded and its planning during this period of history was largely ignored. The government's actions indicated to the pre-war, local Taiwanese that they were not invested in the well-being of Taipei. To rectify what the government saw as a perversion of Chinese culture, the Nationalists also banned Taiwanese Southern Min and Japanese from both the schools and streets of Taipei, along with greater Taiwan. In its stead, Mandarin Chinese (referred to as, or "guoyu") was imported and mandated as the only official language. For a time, Taiwanese culture, along with the language of its people, was silenced.

The fortunes of Taipei were not all sour. The city exploded in physical growth during the 1950s, but without much oversight or direction when compared to the Japanese colonial period. Development continued to shoot eastward as more and more farms were consumed by urban blocks. Many of Taipei's apartments that were built during this period had similar design: four-story structures with two apartments per floor. These structures were copy-and-pasted across the new urban landscape, intercut by a maze of alleyways. Larger corridors were packed with small businesses on the ground floors with residential uses above. This era also saw the proliferation of sidewalk arcades, which provided shelter to pedestrians during rain showers. While it was chaotic growth, it proved to be practical and to the benefit of the city come the turn of the twenty-first century.

## Becoming a Tiger

The 1960s brought the beginning of what became the "Taiwan Economic Miracle", or a massive expansion of the manufacturing, fabrics, and electronics industries. The citizens of Taipei experienced a dramatic increase in quality of life, as Taiwan suddenly contained a middle-class majority (even today as income inequality is on the rise in countries with 'developed' economies, Taiwan has one of the highest income equality index scores in all of Asia).

Taipei's increasing wealth and access to education, along with the Nationalist's loss of international political recognition as "China" in the 1970s led to a period of aggressive cultural production, both internally and externally-speaking. Still under martial law, Taipei was swept in waves of popular protests. Indigenous rights, gender equality, the recognition of same-sex love, and environmentalism were are subjects of varying degrees of public discourse. The latter demand was the first to gain traction, as city planning began to incorporate the practice of green space place-making. While the the 1950s and early 1960s had been a period of haphazard growth and urban infill, there were pockets of land within the city blocks that the government transformed into small parks and courtyards. These small parks were progenitors to two massive green space projects that transformed Taipei's landscape: the Chiang Kai-shek Memorial Hall and the Da'an Forest Park

Taipei thus entered the 1980s on the verge of yet another transformation, arguably the forth in its short one hundred-year life. Although this time, the change would produce the Taipei that is recognizable today.

## From a Chinese Dictatorship to a Taiwanese Republic

Taipei's most recent metamorphosis came with the lifting of martial law in 1987 along with the democratization and the "Taiwanization" of the government. The tensions that existed between the post-war mainland immigrants, who had dominated the central government since 1949, and the local Taiwanese dissipated as the former were absorbed into the latter. In the midst of this incorporation, the newly-liberalized government turned its full attention to domestic concerns such as improving the conditions of Taipei. The government also relaxed its strangle-hold over the press and fully tolerated public demonstrations. The reform led to a whole new period of urban planning—a period marked by an involved and engaged city government.

One of the most visible changes that came about after the end of the dictatorship was the creation of monumental public spaces. For being a capital city and a growing regional economic hub, Taipei lacked many of the symbolic structures that adorned cities of rival size. Clusters of sub-standard military housing and informal settlements that rested atop state-owned land were thus controversially raised and replaced with massive public parks. The two crown jewels of the government were the previously-mentioned Chiang Kai-shek Memorial Hall (opened in 1980) and Da'an Forest Park (opened in 1994). Taipei's most famous landmark, however, was yet to be built.

The groundwork for that landmark was initiated contemporaneously with Taipei's public space projects. Deciding that the shopping strips that lined Taipei's busiest corridors were not adequate to serve as a commercial hub for the city, the government created the Xinyi Special District in 1981. Xinyi, once boggy fields, now was on the periphery of Taipei and a prime location for creating a new administrative hub and central business district (CBD). Taipei urban planners took inspiration from their city's design successes, along with American-style CBDs, to produce a district boasting shopping malls, high-rise hotels, and office spaces. A new city hall was constructed following the initial popularity of Xinyi and opened in 1993. And in 2004, the iconic Taipei 101 super-tall skyscraper opened its doors to the public. At 1,647 feet (509.2 m), the building was the tallest skyscraper in the world until the end of the decade and continues to be the most recognized symbol of Taiwan.

The final puzzle piece needed to understand how contemporary Taipei came to be is not visible even from the heights of Taipei 101; however, carrying over 2.1 million passengers a day, the Taipei Metro axiomatically collapsed travel distances and rearranged the spatial patterns of Taipei. The third-rail system first opened with the Brown Line in 1996, and was followed by the Red, Green, Orange, and Blue lines, respectively. In 2018, the MRT system covered 84.9 miles (136.6 km) of the Taipei metropolitan area, with an additional five new lines plus an expansion of the Red Line in the works. Upon completion, the approved expansion will bring the total system coverage up to 126.1 miles (203 km).

The MRT's effect on Taipei and the surrounding neighborhoods of New Taipei City was multifaceted and monumental. Before the MRT's introduction to the city, surface traffic was considerably heavier. Cars and scooters formerly clogged the narrow roads, suffocating the city's air and causing jams reminiscent of an American city's rush hour; but what was before a thirty-minute drive in congestion now become a nine minute ride on the MRT. Extremely short headways guaranteed consistent service, and that reliability led to a mass exodus from driving cars. The share of cars on the roads of Taipei fell from 24% in

2000 to 14% by 2010. Meanwhile, the ease of access that the MRT provided opened up news areas in the Taipei region that were formerly remote, such as Tamsui, or that were declining, such as Ximending.

## Taipei History

Evidence of human life on Taiwan dates back to between five and ten thousand years ago. Not much is known about the origins of Taiwan's earliest inhabitants except that their language bears more similarity to Indonesian than any of the languages from China. The island enjoyed relatively anonymity until 1206 when Ghengis Khan named Taiwan a protectorate of the newly established Yuan Dynasty. However, the Emperor had little interest in the island and it once again slipped into anonymity.

Taiwan remained a quiet backwater until the 17th century when it became caught in both Chinese and colonial politics. The first note of Taiwan came in the form of a diary entry from a passage of Portuguese ship passing off the coast in 1517. Moved by the beauty of the island, the writer named it "Ilha Formosa" (or beautiful island). To this day, Formosa has remained a popular second name for Taiwan. In 1624, a Dutch contingent landed in southern Taiwan as part of their effort to bolster their presence in Asia and began the first colonial occupation of island by building a fort at the site of modern day

Tainan. The island was then populated by a mixture of the early inhabitants and a small number of Chinese fishermen who had emigrated from the nearby province of Fujian.

Two years later, the Spanish (also known as the red beards) followed challenged the Dutch presence by claiming Dan Shui in northern Taiwan in 1626 and constructing Fort San Domingo. The Dutch, however, were not ready to share their conquest, and managed to evict the Spanish colonialist in 1641. The Dutch reign was not destined to last however, for in 1661, Koxinga (Cheng Cheng-kung) came upon the scene.

Koxinga was formerly the son of a powerful merchant in southern China loyal to the Ming Dynasty. Following the collapse of the Ming Empire, Koxinga refused to pledge loyalty to the Qing Dynasty and was forced to flee China. Taking his army of over 30,000 men, Koxinaga decided to make Taiwan his base of operations for continuing his war against the Qing. After evicting the Dutch, Koxinaga resumed his war against the Qing. However, in 1682 the Qing (Manchus) captured Taiwan and made it into a county of Fujian province. In 1885, following a brief (1884-1885) occupation of northern Taiwan by the French, the island became an independent province of China.

Taiwan was not destined to maintain its new status as a province for long, however. In 1895, as part of the Treaty of Shimonoseki, Taiwan was handed over to Japan in perpetuity as an end to the Sino-

Japanese War. After quashing a short-lived civilian revolt aimed at creating Asia's first republic (the Formosan Republic), the new Japanese rulers began a series of major construction projects to integrate Taiwan into the Japanese colonial economy. The remaining aboriginal tribes were gradually forced up into Taiwan's central mountains as the commercially important coastal plains became increasingly developed. The Japanese began systematically building up a network of roads, railroads, hospitals, and teacher's universities around Taiwan. Agricultural holdings were consolidated and massive sugar cane plantations established around the island. The Japanese ruled the island until the end of World War II when the 1945 Yalta Conference returned Taiwan once again into the hands of China.

Returning Taiwan to the Chinese government was not simple, however, since China was in the midst of a civil war. In 1912, the Qing Dynasty had been overthrown and the Republic of China established by the political leader Sun Yat-sen. From 1912 through the end of World War II, China was in political turmoil as the Nationalists (Kuomingtang, or KMT) under Chiang Kai-Shek waged war with the Communists under Mao Tse-dong. During the same period, the Japanese also invaded Northern China. In 1945, when Taiwan was returned, the civil war in China was still raging.

Chiang Kai-shek, busy in the mainland, sent Governor Chen-yi to Taiwan to maintain order. Famed for his greed and inability to rule,

Chen-yi was disliked by local Taiwanese. On February 28, 1947, the culmination of this disapproval came with a Taiwanese protest now known as the 2-28 Massacre during which the KMT killed tens of thousands of civilians. In 1949, it became clear that the war on the mainland was lost and Chiang Kai-shek fled with over one million Mainland Chinese (more than half of which were military) to Taiwan. The KMT became the local government, and one year later, under Chiang's orders, Chen-yi was executed. The KMT established martial law in Taiwan that was to last for another 40 years.

The KMT retreat to Taiwan was much like Koxinga's retreat over three hundred years earlier. The idea was to use the island as a base until recapture of the mainland was possible. In the years that followed, despite regular skirmishes with mainland Chinese forces, the KMT never did mount the major offensive. In 1971, a major political defeat was handed to Taiwan when it lost its seat in the United Nation. Chiang Kai-shek passed away in 1975.

In 1978, Chiang's son, Chiang Ching-kuo was elected in an uncontested race to the position of president. Unlike his father, Chiang Ching-kuo believed that the future of the KMT lay in developing local roots, and under his administration a gradual relaxation of the political began. The thaw continued until 1986, when Chiang allowed the formation of the first opposition party - Democratic Progressive Party (DPP).

Following the establishment of the DPP, Taiwan's politics began to undergo a rapid transformation. Martial Law ended in 1987 and citizens were allowed to send and receive mainland Chinese mail as well as request mainland travel permits for the first time since the 1940's. In 1988, Chiang Ching-kuo died and vice president Lee Deng-hui began the island's first native-born president. Lee immediately undertook a massive reform of the KMT and was reelected President in 1996 with 54% of the votes. The end of the century also marked the end of the KMT's 40 year rule as DPP candidate Chen Shui-bian was elected President on March 18th, 2000.

## Places inside Taipei

Taipei, the political and financial center of Taiwan, is the island's most populous city. Taipei originated as a small trading port over two hundred years ago before becoming the administrative capital for the island under the Qing Dynasty. During the last few decades there has been tremendous growth in the city. Even as recently as thirty years ago, the city was still dotted with rice paddies. Now a sprawling metropolis, Taipei is best suited for those who do not mind the hustle and bustle of life in the big city.

### Bei Tou (Peitou)

Located in the northwestern part of Taipei, Bei Tou is famous for its sulfur springs, spas, and hotels. One of the more popular sulfur pits is called Hell Valley, where the Taiwanese like to go to boil eggs in the naturally boiling water. Bei Tou, located in the middle of a small mountain range, is connected to Wellington Heights and Yang Ming Shan by public transport. Yang Ming Shan National Park (much of which is located in the Bei Tou District) is a good place to go hiking and get away from the commotion of the city.

**Shi Lin (Shihlin)**

The Shi Lin district covers both banks of the Keelung River and spills into the surrounding mountains. Shi Lin is best known for hosting Taipei's largest night market, the Shihlin Night Market. Once the sun goes down, residents and tourists throng to the area squeezing amongst street vendors and food stalls. A little to the north of the night market, one can find the more peaceful Tian Mu area which features a large expatriate community and several of Taipei's international schools. Mostly due to the heavy expatriate presence, a wide variety of foreign foods can be found in Tian Mu's restaurants and grocery stores. The Chinese Culture and Movie Center and the world-renowned National Palace Museum are also both located within this district.

**Da Tong (Tatung)**

The Da Tong District was once home to European merchants who settled here to trade with the Taiwanese. Walk through the old lanes of this district, and you will find numerous tea companies, a few

European-style buildings, and several temples including the famous Confucius Temple and Bao An Temple. Perhaps the most popular attraction here is Di Hua Street , one of Taipei's main trading centers during the 1800s. Today, Di Hua Street is still lined with traditional merchant shops selling dried goods and herbal medicines. The area becomes packed around Chinese New Year as many Taipei residents buy goods in preparation for the holidays. Nearby, you'll also find the somewhat decaying Yuan Huan Market, a round market situated in the middle of a traffic circle that was once the most popular place in Taipei for late night snacks.

**Zhong Shan (Chungshan)**

Running through the center of the district is Zhong Shan North Road which serves as the dividing line for the city's eastern and western halves. Zhong Shan was once the commercial center for Taipei, but many offices have gradually been shifting to the eastern part of the city. Now the area is better known for its shops (mostly bridal shops and a sprinkling of antiques/folk crafts) and the combat zone, host to one of Taipei's densest concentrations of bars. The area also has the dubious fortune of being home to one of the major red light districts. The district does also have several cultural offerings including the Taipei Fine Arts Museum, Lin An Tai House, the Grand Hotel, Xing Tian Temple and the Taipei Children's Recreation Center.

**Song Shan (Sungshan)**

Home to Taipei's central business district and the headquarters of many local and multinational companies, this is one of Taipei's most international districts. Attracted by the international and sophisticated local clientele, numerous restaurants offering various foreign cuisine have opened in the streets and alleys off of Dun Hua North Road and Min Sheng East Road. To the north, the Sungshan Domestic Airport provides a gateway to Taiwan's major cities and outlying islands. For expatriate residents and visitors, the area is also important as the home of numerous American banking centers, including Citibank, American Express, and Bank of America. In addition, the Magnolia Hotel, Hard Rock Cafe, the Taipei Municipal Stadium, the Asiaworld Shopping Center, Chang Gun Memorial Hospital, and the Adventist Hospital are also located on Dun Hua North Road.

**Wan Hua**

The oldest district in Taipei, Wan Hua was once a thriving port. Conveniently located on the Dan Shui River, this area was built up by Fukianese merchants from Mainland China who traded in camphor and tea. Religion played a major role in the lives of these Chinese settlers who built numerous temples in the area. Present-day temples in the Wan Hua district include the Lungshan Temple (Taipei's oldest temple), Ching Shui Yan Temple, and Ching Shan Temple. Other main attractions in this area are the popular Xi Men Ding shopping and movie district, Hua Xi Street (better known as Snake Alley), and Taipei's Youth Park.

**Zhong Zheng (Chungcheng)**

The political center of Taipei City, the Zhong Zheng District is home to numerous government offices, parks, and museums. The 2-28 Memorial Peace Park, Taiwan Provincial Museum, Botanical Gardens, Chang Foundation Museum, and the Presidential Building are all located in Zhong Zheng. Perhaps best known is the massive Chiang Kai-Shek Memorial Hall that also houses the National Theater and National Concert Hall. The memorial truly comes alive on the weekends as families bring children out to rollerblade and fly kites, marching bands use the space to practice, and elderly residents relax in shaded hallways while practicing Chinese opera.

**Da An (Ta An)**

Da An District, located in downtown Taipei, is a mix of residential and commercial housing. Zhong Xiao East Road, Section 4 is the most popular shopping strip in Da An (and Taipei for that matter) and includes numerous boutiques, coffee shops, KTVs as well as the Sogo Department Store. Running parallel to Zhong Xiao is the beautiful tree-lined Ren Ai Road. The Da An district has a thriving night life and many late-night restaurants, bars, and clubs can be found in this area.

**Xin Yi (Hsinyi)**

Mainly a residential and commercial district, Xin Yi is home to the Sun

Yat-sen Memorial Hall, Taipei World Trade Center, Grand Hyatt Taipei, Mitsukoshi and New York, New York department stores, and the new Warner Village movie complex. Over the last 100 years, Taipei City has been expanding eastwards towards the mountains and the Xin Yi District marks the newest edge of the city's development. As recently as a few years ago, the neighborhood around Warner Village was primarily empty lots. Today, the district is seeing increasing traffic thanks to the draw of the newer developments mentioned above, the many new corporate headquarters and office buildings, in addition, the increasing number of people moving to new residential developments at the edge of the mountains bordering the district.

**Nei Hu, Wen Shan, Nan Gang**

These three outlying districts are less populated than the city center and are great places to visit to get away from the bustle of Taipei. A hilly area, Nei Hou is popular with hikers and outdoors lovers. It is also possible to see a bit of culture as well by hiking up to the Pi Shan Temple. Wen Shan is best known for the numerous tea houses dotting the hills in the Mu Cha area. However, the district also offers the Taipei City Zoo and the Chang Shan Temple. Primarily an industrial area, Nan Gang is home to the Academia Sinica, the leading academic research institute in Taiwan.

**Surrounding areas - Dan Shui, Keelung, Wu Lai**

North of Taipei and accessible on the MRT line is the old fishing village of Dan Shui. Once a main port, Dan Shui is where the Spanish landed when they arrived on Taiwan. Fort San Domingo is one of the few remaining relics from this period of Taiwanese history. Traveling east along the coastal highway will lead you to the northern seaport of Keelung. Well known for its food and numerous temples, many residents of Taipei head to Keelung on the weekends for a change of scenery and a meal at its famous night market. Just south of Taipei is the mountain village of Wu Lai, home to a large population of aborigines from the Atayal tribe. Make sure to try the local cuisine as some of the vegetables served in the Wulai restaurants are only found locally. Wulai is also a popular point for hiking and mountain biking.

# Kaohsiung

Kaohsiung City, the second largest city in Taiwan, is comprised of eleven districts; each with its own unique character.

**Qi Jin (Chi Chin)**

Qi Jin Island is one of the oldest districts in Kaohsiung. Together with Gu Shan, Yen Cheng, and Zuo Ying, it forms what is commonly called the "old city". The first signs of permanent residents on the island can be traced back to the 17th century. These early settlers were fishermen who saw the island as the ideal place from which to launch their fishing boats. Not much has changed: Today the island still retains much of the charm of a sleepy fishing village despite the fact that it now forms part of a bustling city.

Three-wheeled carts, once common all over Asia but now largely a thing of the past, are still a familiar sight here. The island is home to one of the oldest temples in the Kaohsiung area: the Matsu Temple (also known as the Tien Hou Kung Temple) is dedicated, appropriately, to the patron goddess of fishermen. The temple dates back to the late 1600s. The popular Qi Jin Beach runs along the west coast of the island. The Qi Jin Lighthouse and Qi Jin Seashore Park can also be found here-testament to the nautical origins of the local population.

**Yan Cheng (Yencheng)**

Yan Cheng is the original downtown area of Kaohsiung. In spite of the shift in focus to the east bank of the Love River, this district has remained a popular hangout because of the many restaurants, pubs and nightclubs in the area. Yan Cheng has a reputation for being a bit rowdy because it is frequented by sailors from nearby Kaohsiung Harbour: This district never sleeps! It is full of interesting people and interesting little shops selling everything from souvenirs to hard-to-come-by imported foodstuffs.

**Gu Shan (Kushan)**

This district is dominated by the beautiful vista of Shoushan Mountain, which is also called Longevity Mountain. The mountain is home to hundreds of indigenous Taiwanese monkeys who roam freely around

Shoushan Park. It is also the home of many other animals in the Shoushan Zoo. It is in this district that much of the upgrading initiated during the Japanese Occupation took place-such as the extensive development of the harbour facilities. Chungshan University sits at the foot of the mountain with the Hsitzu Bay Beach forming part of its pretty campus. But not everything in Gu Shan is modern: This district has its roots and memories firmly anchored in the past as local monuments such as the Yuanheng Temple and the Martyrs' Shrine will testify. The Former British Consulate, the first foreign consulate in Taiwan and now a history museum, is also found in this district.

**Zuo Ying (Tsoying)**

Zuo Ying is full of reminders of Taiwan's history: Remains of the military fortress established in the mid-1600s are dotted around the area. Today the district still has a distinct military flavour-not surprising with the large Navy Harbour situated here. The most popular attraction in Zuo Ying, however, is the Lotus Lake scenic area. The Confucius Temple can be found on the shores of the lake-the largest temple in Taiwan dedicated to the great sage. The lake is also the site of the Dragon and Tiger Pagodas as well as the Spring and Autumn Pavilions.

**Downtown**

The downtown area is comprised of the districts of Xin Xing, Chian Jin and Ling Ya. It is the area where the pulse of Kaohsiung beats the strongest; where old meets new and East and West exist side by side.

**Xin Xing (Hsinhsing)**

Xin Xing is the heart of the city in more ways than one. Situated roughly in the middle of Kaohsiung, this district has numerous bars and nightclubs, as well as interesting little shops catering to the teen and young twenties crowd. This district is always humming day or night. One of the most popular attractions is the Liu He Night Market, a shopping paradise for locals and tourists alike. The Xin Xing Market on Nan Hua Road is a great place to shop for inexpensive clothing or to go to watch the crowds.

**Qian Jin (Chienchin)**

The Love River borders this district on the west with the Shoushan Mountain rising in the background. With such a setting it is not surprising that Qian Jin is home to some of the best hotels in Kaohsiung. It is also a good place to go shopping as both the Tali Department Store and the Hanshin Department Store are situated here. If you are in the mood for a spot of sightseeing, this district boasts the Holy Rosary Cathedral, as well as superb views from the banks and bridges of the Love River. Alternatively, you can relax under the trees in Rotary Park - Kaohsiung's own "Central Park".

**Ling Ya (Lingya)**

Ling Ya forms the bulk of the downtown area and is known for its wide variety of restaurants, bars and nightclubs, as well as many of the top hotels in the city. It is a shopper's dream because of the many department stores, smaller specialty stores and souvenir shops in the area. You can also find the Garbage Market (don't be mislead by the name-the produce sold is of the very best quality) and Flower Market here. The district is home to Kaohsiung's tallest building, the Tuntex T&C Towers. The view over the city and harbour from the top of this building is breathtaking. Ling Ya is also the cultural heart of Kaohsiung: the Chiang Kai Shek Cultural Center has many exhibition galleries as well as performance halls where all sorts of artistic productions, from opera to contemporary dance, take place regularly.

**The City Outskirts**

Four districts lie on the outskirts of Kaohsiung, namely San Min, Nan Zi, Qian Zhen and Xiao Gang. These areas tend to be predominantly residential or industrial in nature.

**San Min (San Ming)**

San Min is a popular residential district because it is a little quieter than the downtown area, but is still close enough to be infected with the vibe of the city. San Min is also the market district: in addition to the big food markets on San Feng Zhong Street and at the intersection of Min Zu and Shi Chuan Roads, San Min is also the site of the Jade Market. Situated on Shi Chuan Road, this is the best place to shop for souvenirs and to take in some local culture at the same time. This district will also find favour with museum lovers as both the Kaohsiung Museum of Fine Arts and the National Museum of Science and Technology are in this area. If architecture is your passion, take a trip to the Grand 50 Tower. This impressive, beautifully designed building has become a trademark feature of the San Min District.

### Nan Zi (Nantze)

Nan Zi is the most northerly-situated district in Kaohsiung. It is in equal parts a residential district and industrial area. The export processing zones are situated here. It is possible to shop at the export processing factories for inexpensive items of all descriptions, but you must present your passport if you wish to make a purchase.

### Qian Zhen (Chien Chen)

Qian Zhen is situated to the south of the city's downtown area. This is a district dominated by the fishing industry. Qian Jin Fishing Harbour is very pretty at night when the lights from the fishing boats sparkle across the water.

### Xiao Gang (Hsiaokang)

This is the most southerly of Kaohsiung's eleven districts and the first place visitors see because it is home to the Kaohsiung International Airport. The area is heavily industrialized, but Kaohsiung Park near the airport goes some way to inject a bit of greenery into the otherwise grey, man-made landscape

# Travel and Tourism

Taiwan boasts a number of high-profile attractions, such as Sun Moon Lake, Alishan, Kenting, and the National Palace Museum. Yet enormous tourism potential also exists in the country's unique small towns. To encourage local governments to develop their tourism resources, the Taiwan Tourism Bureau has selected 10 distinctive townships and city districts with tourism appeal, visitor-friendly environments, and other qualities suited for international marketing, with future promotions focused on encouraging visitors to experience in-depth Taiwan's small town charm.

The themes for each of the ten designated townships and districts are: "Matsu Culture" (Dajia District, Taichung City), "A Presidential Town" (Daxi District, Taoyuan City), "Small Town Elegance" (Beitou District, Taipei City), "Namesake of Taiwan" (Anping District, Tainan City), "Old World Charm in Houpu" (Jincheng Township, Kinmen County), "Hakka Beauty and Hospitality" (Meinong District, Kaohsiung City), "Craftsmanship, Cuisine, and Historic Sites" (Lugang Township, Changhua County), "Railway Impressions and Cycling Excursions" (Jiji

Township, Nantou County), "Gold Mines of Discovery in Shuinandong, Jinguashi, and Jiufen" (Ruifang District, New Taipei City), "LOHAS Life at the Jiaoxi Hot Springs" (Jiaoxi Township, Yilan County), "Taiwan's Wood Sculpture Capital" (Sanyi Township, Miaoli County), "Fragrant Tea, Dairy and Hot Springs" (Ruisui Township, Hualien), and "Fashion Central" (Xinyi District, Taipei City). Among the ten, Sanyi was voted as the "Most Locally Distinctive Small Town"; Ruisui was picked as the "Cleanest Tourism Town"; and Xinyi took the crown as the "District with the Most International Tourism Potential." All of these destinations invite you to visit and discover the small-town fun and beauty of Taiwan.

Daxi District, Taoyuan City: A Presidential Town

Daxi is closely linked to the history and memory of Chiang Kai-shek and Chiang Ching-kuo, former presidents of the ROC, with a trove of stories waiting to be discovered. For the traveler, this picturesque, centuries-old town offers historic buildings, trails, cultural activities, wood sculpture, and delicious food. It also offers the perfect blend of natural beauty and modern amenities for relaxation. Daxi has been a hub for travelers for over a century. It is the origination point of the Northern Cross-island Highway. Setting out from Daxi, travelers can experience a variety of scenic attractions and tribal culture. It is also highly accessible for international travelers. The 2011 Michelin Guide gave Daxi a two-star (Recommended) rating and a two-page introduction. Ready to go? Join us, and create lasting memories in Daxi.

Sanyi Township, Miaoli County: Taiwan's Wood Sculpture Capital

Miaoli has been dedicating efforts to tourism marketing with an aim to create new business opportunities and put the county on the global map. This campaign involves the promotion of seven major tourist routes and three major routes tailored for international visitors. The county is also marketing Sanyi Township as a center for wood sculpture and a new hub for international travel in Taiwan. In addition to its wood sculpture industry, Sanyi has convenient transportation links, world-renowned scenic spots, a variety of tourist attractions, and warm hospitality. The township is also investing heavily to develop the local tourism industry to international standards, while continuing to preserve and innovate on its tourism appeal as a unique destination for wood sculpture industry-based tourism.

Anping District, Tainan City: Namesake of Taiwan

In earlier times, Anping was known as "Dayuan," the origin of the name "Taiwan." It is known not only for its deep culture and history, but also for its sunsets, nightlife, beautiful natural scenery, ocean activities, and delicious cuisine.

Anping abounds with historic sites—Anping Fort, the Eternal Golden Castle, and Anping Tree House are a few of its major attractions. Other points of interest include the Old Julius Mannich Merchant House, Haishan Hostel, Tait & Co. Merchant House and Anping Minor Artillery Fort. These historical sites reflect the history and architectural styles of the Dutch occupation, Cheng Cheng-kung (Koxinga) period, Qing administration, and Japanese colonial era, embodying more than 300 years of quintessential history in Taiwan.

No visit to Anping is complete without trying the amazing array of delicious local foods—shrimp cakes, bean curd pudding, candied fruit, shrimp rolls, oyster rolls, fish ball soup, and oyster pancakes, for a start. The shops around Yanping Old Street are good places to find distinctive mementos and gifts—no one leaves Yanping empty-handed!

Dajia District, Taichung City: Matsu Culture

Dajia brings together a unique mix of natural assets—the Dajia River, Da'an River, and Tiezhen Mountain among them, with other attractions, such as the Craftsman's Hometown recreational farm area, Songbo Harbor, distinctive folk ceremonies, and a rich local history and culture. Zhenlan Temple, built on present-day Dajia Street by early Han Chinese settlers, hosts the Dajia Matsu pilgrimage activity each March. More than one million people join this annual event, ranking the festival among the top-three religious celebrations in the world. Living history can be experienced at the Chastity Arch, which recounts the story of the frail sister who saved the townspeople, and

Wenchang Temple, built with funding by the local gentry to support education. Dajia is also famous for its specialty farm products, including award-winning premium rice, certified high-quality bitter gourd, Welsh onions, and square watermelon. Jian Well (Sword Well), built on Tiezhen Mountain during Koxinga's administration of Taiwan, the historic Rinan Railway Station and Da'an River Bridge, and locally-produced hats, mats, and pastries are other worthwhile attractions for local and foreign visitors alike, inviting you to discover the deep history and warm hospitality of Dajia.

Jincheng Township, Kinmen County: Old World Charm in Houpu

Houpu has a history dating back six or seven hundred years. It is the political and economic center of Kinmen and home to numerous legends and historic sites. The cultural legacy of the town combines southern Fujianese and overseas Chinese influences, as well as traces of its battlefield history. To walk its streets is to take a journey back in time.

Houpu is also well positioned geographically, weaving together the river, sea, harbor, and town into the rhythm of life. Visitors can explore the scenic lakes and hills or relax by the sea and watch the birds riding the waves. A simple elegance, beauty and human warmth all contribute to the lasting impression one invariably brings home from a journey to Houpu.

## Meinong District, Kaohsiung City: Hakka Beauty and Hospitality

Meinong is a small southern Hakka community with plenty of visual charm. Meinong came out on top in the "Land of Smiles" internet survey jointly conducted by CommonWealth magazine and the Taiwan Tourism Bureau. Its vibrant Hakka culture, rustic landscape, and simple, sincere residents make it a popular destination for visitors who want to experience the richness of the Hakka culture and way of life.

## Yilan County: LOHAS Life at the Jiaoxi Hot Springs

Jiaoxi is home to the only flatland hot springs in Taiwan. In addition to its convenient transportation links and abundant natural charms, the township offers a visitor-friendly environment with high-quality tourism attractions, services and facilities. A local commitment to tourism development has further raised Jiaoxi's profile as one of Taiwan's premier visitor destinations.

## Jiji Township, Nantou County: Railway Impressions and Cycling Excursions

Few things can lighten the spirits like a leisurely bicycle ride along the sun-splashed Jiji Green Tunnel. The railway and beautiful farmland accompany you along the way; and the ever-changing tapestry of Jiji Township's scenic charms unfold as you pedal along, showing one why this area is one of Taiwan's premier visitor destinations.

For those weary of the noise and stress of the city, Jiji offers a small-town escape into a world where life slows down and the soothing influence of nature is everywhere present.

Jiji's allures are multidimensional, from its historic railway station to natural landscape, cuisine to local specialty items. All of these elements form together to create a place of natural richness and cultural depth and place Jiji Township in a unique position on Taiwan's tourism map. Board a train or set out on a bike, however you explore, Jiji is sure to win your heart.

Ruifang District, New Taipei City: Gold Mines of Discovery in Shuinandong, Jinguashi, and Jiufen

Shuinandong, Jinguashi, and Jiufen are former mining towns in Ruifang District, New Taipei City. The three towns present living records of the history and culture of Taiwan's mining industry, each one distinguished by the different mining methods they adopted: the simple charm of Shuinandong; the tranquility of Jinguashi; and the traces of the miners' nightlife in Jiufen. Though the gold mines are now closed, these towns continue to exert an allure that attracts visitors to visit and dream.

In Shuinandong, the abandoned "13-Level Smelter" evokes the image of Pompeii. The Yin Yang Sea, with its yellow and blue waters, and the beautiful Golden Waterfall are other attractions here. Jinguashi is a quiet hillside town. And along the old lanes of bustling Jiufen, one can find gold mines of history and culture. Together, these areas offer welcome comfort to the road-weary traveler and provide plenty of food for thought.

Beitou District, Taipei City: Small Town Elegance

Featured in the Travel section of the The New York Times online edition, Beitou a hot spring escape with abundant natural, cultural and historical attractions, as well as convenient rapid transit access, making it one of Taipei's premier tourism destinations.

Beitou District encompasses the Beitou Hot Springs, Yangmingshan National Park, and the Guandu scenic area. The Beitou Hot Spring Museum, Taiwan Folk Arts Museum, and Plum Garden are a few of the many points cultural and historic interest here. Distinctive hot spring hotels, Taiwan's first green library building, and the hot-spring themed MRT train art are other attractions here. In 2011, Beitou was ranked as a three-star tourist attraction in the Michelin Green Guide. Fox News also gave a thumbs-up to this very special tourism district.

Xinyi District, Taipei City: Fashion Central

Xinyi is a one-of-a-kind tourism area in Taiwan. A product of urban planning, it is the center of fashion and a place where Taipei's future is being created. The district has convenient transportation links to other parts of the city and region. The stores here sell the world's best brands. Xinyi is also home to Taiwan biggest bookstore chain, Eslite and the international landmark Taipei 101 building. Four Four South Village (a restored military dependents housing complex), Songshan Cultural and Creative Park, an internationally-renowned Michelin star restaurant, eye-catching buildings and installation art, and the annual Taipei New Year Eve Party all further add to the sparkle of Xinyi District.

For shopping, entertainment and delicious cuisine to art, culture and international MICE facilities, Xinyi District serves up the best of Taiwan.

Ruisui Township, Hualien County: Fragrant Tea, Dairy and Hot Springs

Ruisui Township boasts a wide range of specialty products, cultural attractions, and some of eastern Taiwan's best tourism resources, with something sure to satisfy every visitor desire.

Ruisui is also an ideal place to enjoy the leisurely pace of life on Taiwan's East Coast. In an area defined by a mere 135-km circumference, one can enjoy delicious dairy, coffee, tea, and other beverages, take a healthy hot spring excursion, savor a spectrum of specialty cuisine, experience small town life, or go on an exciting whitewater rafting adventure. Local and Hakka ceremonies and stirring percussion performances at the Drum King Competition further add to the township's unique tourism appeal. In addition to its cultural allures, Ruisui presents the beauty of nature in its full charm, setting the perfect stage for a leisurely escape to Taiwan's East Coast.

Lugang Township, Changhua County: Craftsmanship, Cuisine, and Historic Sites

Lugang was the economic and transport hub of central Taiwan in earlier times. The saying "first Tainan, second Lugang and third Mengjia (today Wanhua District in Taipei)," illustrates the high position of the town in its glory days.

In addition to being the early cultural capital of Taiwan, Lugang was also a commercially prosperous area. During the Qing period, the town was an important trading port, bringing all types of products to the town and fueling Lugang's economic rise. Lugang was also unrivaled for its high cuisine and a diversity of local snack foods reflecting its broad immigrant mix. Delicious seafood, baked goods, and distinctive street food are part of Lugang's signature appeal. This diverse food culture, along with historic sites, scenic attractions, beautiful craftsmanship, make Lugang a destination as rewarding to the eyes and mind as it is to the palate.

Visit Lugang and discover why it shares a spot with Taichung City and Nantou County among Taiwan's must-see "Golden Triangle" tourism destinations.

# Attractions

## Accessible Travel

Yehliu Geopark

TEL: +886-2-2492-2016 (Yehliu Visitor Center)

Address: No 167-1, Gangdong Rd., Yehliu Village, Wanli District, New Taipei City

Yehliu is a cape of about 1,700 meters long formed by Datun Mountain reaching into the sea. When overlooked from above, the place is like a giant turtle submerging into the sea. Thus, it is also called "Yehliu Turtle." Because the rock layer of seashore contains sandstone of limestone texture and it is subject to sea erosion, weathering and earth movements, there is particular scenery consisting of sea trenches/holes, candle shaped rocks, and pot shaped rocks. The place is divided into three sections.

The first section has rocks like Queen's Head, Fairy's Shoe and Candle. The second section has rocks like Bean Curd, Dragon Head. The third section has sea-eroded caves, seal shaped rock, etc. The place is suitable for geological study and field research. In addition, there is a statue of Lin Tien Jane in commemoration of the person's bravery of scarifying own live for saving others. The monument describes in details the touching story.

There is a marine world in Yehliu. The marine world is the first marine center in the country for exhibition of ocean evolution. It has the best sightseeing tunnel under sea, showing about 200 rare fish species and marine lives. The area of marine live specimen demonstrates many specimens of precious marine mammals and fish. It is very educational. There are excellent shows of whales, dolphins and seals, such as diving, ballet on water and other talent shows. There is a stadium with 3,500 seats. On holidays, the place attracts many visitors for the show. When you visit Yehliu, don't forget to visit sea world and feel the marine wanders.

## Maolin National Scenic Area - Xinwei Visitor Center

TEL: +886-7-687-1234

Address: No.171, Xinwei, Liugui Dist., Kaohsiung City

The Maolin Scenic Area covers the townships of Maolin and Liugui in Kaohsiung County, as well as parts of the administrative areas of Sandimen Township in Pingtung County. The Maolin Scenic Area has many scenic spots, such as the Baolai Hot Spring, Bulao Hot Spring, Shiba Luoshan Mountain (Luohanshan), Meiya Valley Fall, Longtou Mountain, and Maolin Valley. Scenic resources near the Shiba Luoshan Mountain (Luohanshan) Reservation Area and the Meiya Valley, tourists can often see Formosan Macaque, squirrels, Varicorhinus barbatulus, and Taiwan blue magpies. All of them are precious resources in the Maolin Scenic Area.

The state-owned forest in this area is another natural feature. The artistic side of the Maolin Scenic Area includes tunnels, temples, suspension bridges and aborigine cultures. Maolin, Wan Mountain (Wanshan), and Duona in Maolin Townships are reserved for aborigines. It is the home of the Rukai Tribe. The Rukai Tribe is famous for its slate houses. At present about 30 slate houses are being preserved in the Duona village of the Maolin Township, making it the largest collection of preserved slate houses in Taiwan. The Liugui Tunnel, consisting of six parts, is the only highway tunnel in southern Taiwan. Because of its views, the Liugui Tunnel has become a famous scenic spot. The Maolin Scenic Area has beautiful scenery and a lot of well-known Buddhist temples, such as the Miaotong and Miaocueng temples. The Maolin Scenic Area has many suspension bridges, the Duona Suspension Bridge being famous for its length.

## Guguan Hot Springs

TEL: +886-4-2595-1496

Address: Sec. 1, Dongguan Rd., Bo'ai Village, Heping District, Taichung City

Guguan is located in Bo'ai Village of Heping District of Taichung City. The altitude is 800 meters. It is next to Dajia River. It is a standard valley. The place is called Guguan because the Central Cross-Island Highway cuts across the valley and it looks like a guarded entrance. It is at the meeting points of Central Cross-Island Highway eastbound and westbound. It is also the center of Central Cross-Island touring route.

The place is famous for hot springs and country items. The hot springs in Guguan were first discovered by Atayal Tribe back in 1907. The quality of hot spring is good and the hot springs have been well renowned since the age of Japanese colonization. The hot springs are carbonic acid springs and the temperature is about 48 degrees Celsius. The hot springs are mild and are good for spa. Hotels in the region are equipped with hot spring spa facilities. The place is surrounded by clear creeks and dense forestry. Visitors can go camping, swimming and fishing. The scenery along the road is beautiful and there are many attractions. Spring and autumn are Guguan's most beautiful seasons. There are splendor cherry blossoms and maple trees for viewing. After enjoying the hot spring spa and the mountain view, one may further try the trout dish. What a pleasure!

## Dongshan (Dong Mountain) River Water Park

TEL: +886-3-950-2097

Address: No.2, Sec. 2, Qinhe Rd., Wujie Township, Yilan County

The Dongshan (Dong Mountain) River is only 24 kilometers long, but it is the fifth-longest stream in Yilan. A multi-purpose riverside recreation area has been planned along its course to provide for sports, leisure, and recreation activities divided into upstream, midstream, and downstream sections, each of which exhibits a different recreational character into what, it is hoped, will make the river into an outdoor water park.

The most important recreational site on the river is the Dongshan (Dong Mountain) River Water Park, which has been designed to rebuild the natural relationship between man and water. This park simulates the natural landscapes and incorporates elements of the native culture of Lanyang for example, there is a water stage, five conical stone towers built of pebbles, and Turtle Island, which rises from the sea off the Yilan coast, bring the landmark of Lanyang into the park, seemingly without thought.

The banks of the Dongshan (Dong Mountain) River are claimed by legend to be protected by a green dragon and a yellow dragon, and for this reason undulations and curves are built of pebbles along the river's banks to simulate dragons' scales, with pottery tile inlays of green and blue, and orange and yellow, adding to the characters of the two different types of dragon. Interesting mosaic pictures masterpieces executed by the children of Lanyang embellish the dragon-skin steps.

Today, the annual Dragon Boat races, international scholastic rowing championships, and international toy festival are all held in the Dongshan (Dong Mountain) River Park. For the Qixi Chinese Lovers' Day, and magpie bridge (by which, according to Chinese traditional, two legendary lovers are allowed to meet once a year) is built to add to the park's romantic atmosphere. Over the past few years, the

Dongshan (Dong Mountain) River Water Park has become one of the hottest tourist destinations in Taiwan.

The Dongshan (Dong Mountain) River attracts large numbers of visitors to its famous scenery. Qinshui Park, located along the banks of the river, is especially popular for its outdoor stage shows, shallow pools where visitors can wade in the water, and deeper areas where they can row boats. Green and yellow ceramic dragons guard the riverbank, which is lined by colorful tile mosaics made by schoolchildren. If you go there in the summer, don't forget to take along your swimming gear and enjoy the swimming pool.

## Sun Moon Lake National Scenic Area - Xiangshang Visitor Center

TEL: +886-49-285-5668

Address: No.599, Zhongshan Rd., Yuchi Township, Nantou County 555, Taiwan (R.O.C.)

The Sun Moon Lake, located in the middle of Taiwan, with an elevation of 748 meters above sea level, is the only natural big lake in Taiwan. The southern part of Lalu Island is shaped like a new moon, and the northern part is shaped like a sun; hence the name Sun Moon Lake.

Scenic resources

The most famous sights around Sun Moon Lake are the Itashao, Lalu Island, the Xuanzang Temple, the Ci-en Pagoda, and the Wenwu

Temple and so on. The natural forests bordering these roads are good places for bird watching. There are a lot of birds that live on the mid-elevation, such as the Grey-cheeked Fulvetta, Grap-throated Minivet, Formosan Yuhina, Gray Tree Pie, Bamboo Partridge, Chinese Bulbul, Muller's Barbet, and the Black Bulbul.

Colonies of Black-crowned Night herons and Egretta garzettas , and birds such as the common kingfisher and the Green-winged Teal can be seen at the Dazhuhu water reservation, situated around the water gate. Besides these birds, fish, insects and wild vegetables are flourishing in the region as well. These are all natural resources of the Sun Moon Lake region.

The Shao Clan is the earliest clan that lived in the Sun Moon Lake region. The Harvest Festival, Sowing Festival and their special handicraft fair every year, as well as their articles have helped to preserve the particular culture of the Sun Moon Lake region.

Xiangshang Visitor Center

The Xiangshang Visitor Center is both for tourism and administration use. The uniquely designed building has wood-patterned exteriors and wings that stretch like human arms embracing the earth. In addition, the two giant canopy structures, 34 meters long and 8 meters tall each, allow people to enjoy beautiful views of the Sun Moon Lake from the top.

Xiangshang Cafe

Not only does Xiangshang Café offer lovely views of Sun-Moon Lake, it has a distinctive feature which is the internationally-renowned avant garde building designed by a Japanese architect; the nearby round-the-lake trail is complete and is certain to become a favorite scenic spot for cyclists; adding to its appeal are the building's lights that by night create a totally different and breathtaking scene and style. Interior design was carried out after discussions with Norihiko Ddan and Associates and also with the assistance of Professor Zhang Zi-long of National Taiwan University of the Arts, the aim being to create a simple-but-fashionable café with a modern style, with main color of the building being white to match the building. The main bar combines glass and light elements, creating a pleasant visual effect. The shop area has an open layout and overturns the disorderly impression that shops often give, increasing the feeling of space and having a simple style. The seats are high-class with a pronounced design feel and the clever use of lights adds interest to the indoor space; as for the outdoor seats, the bright colors create a rich and lively visual effect. The "exterior beauty" of the café alone is captivating; getting to know its "inner beauty" is a really good reason to visit Xiangshang Cafe when you visit Sun Moon Lake.

## Dapeng Bay National Scenic Area - Dapeng Bay Visitor Center

TEL: +886-8-833-8100

Address: No.169, Datan Rd., Donggang Township, Pingtung County

Dapeng Bay covers the two designated scenic areas of Dapeng Bay and Little Liuqiu. The northern boundary of Dapeng Bay is the Provincial Highway 17 and the Ping 63 County Road. The eastern and western boundaries are Linbian and Xinggou in Donggang Township respectively. To the south, there is a 600-meter sea area starting from the high tide mark of the coastal line. The main features of Dapeng Bay include the Qingzhou Rest Area. In this region, there is a famous boat festival of the Donglong Temple in Donggang. Tourists can also enjoy the beautiful submarine scenery on Little Liuqiu Island.

Dapeng Bay is the largest inner bay in Taiwan, providing rich resources of sea animals and plants in this region. Redwoods and sea eggplants are growing by the sea; Ipomoea pes-caprae, Excoecaria agallocha, and Clerodendron inerme are all very famous. The animals in the Dapeng Bay National Scenic Area are mainly birds, fish and mollusks. There are about 95 kinds of birds, including migratory birds. Fish include groupers, and other sea animals include a special kind of tide-waving crabs on the wetlands.

Little Liuqiu is the only coral island found among the 14 islands around Taiwan. It is famous for three features: the best location for watching sunsets, the largest variety of corals, and the entire island as a coral reef. The whole island is full of strange rocks and reveals many beautiful ocean landscapes.

There are around 100 temples in Liuqiu and Dapeng Bay. Many temples are located around Donggang Town, and the Linbian and Nanzhou Townships. Among all the temples, the Donglong Temple in Donglong Village, Donggang Township has the longest history. Once every three years, people there will hold a ceremony to "burn the boat" and this is considered the biggest celebration of this kind. Seafood is famous around Taiwan and is inexpensive. Donggang has three treasures: blue fin tuna, cherry shrimp and fat roe. Liuqiu is also famous for its barbecued squid and sausage.

Dapeng Bay Visitor Center

Be sure to catch the smiles of our volunteers as you browse through a variety of tourist information at the Dapeng Bay Be sure to catch the smiles of our volunteers as you browse through a variety of tourist information at the Dapeng Bay Visitor Center, the first place you shall notice upon arrival at the Dapeng Bay National Scenic Area. Here you can learn about which hours in a day are the best for finding fiddler crabs and mudskippers in our wetlands. There is also the bay's map which helps you to find the directions of and distance between each scenic spot.

The center holds rubbing activities for parents and kids, so that they can bring beautiful memory home on paper. Sometimes, by “liking” the center’s Facebook articles, you can get a gift for free. The volunteers here are ready to play games with you and give you more small gifts. Our flyers introduce the bay’s wetlands and many other leisure spots in detail, in Japanese, English and Mandarin. At the center, you shall find all the info you need. Why not pick a book at our book crossing spot to let the book be your travel companion at the bay. If you are Muslim, feel free to use our prayer room and enjoy some quiet spiritual moments.

We always welcome visitors like you and we want you to be happy, with all the things we offer. You are cordially invited to visit the center and be filled with joy!

Multi-media briefing room:

The room has 100 seats. On weekends and holidays, films on the nature and culture of the Dapeng Bay National Scenic Area and the Hengchun Peninsula are screened.

## National Center for Traditional Arts

TEL: +886-3-950-8859

Address: No. 201, Sec. 2, Wubin Rd., Wujie Township, Yilan County

This new 24-hectare facility is located beside beautiful Dong Mountain (Dongshan) River in Yilan. In addition to organized displays and performances of culture and art, it also provides a stage where performing artists can show off their creative works. The emphasis here is on the continuous propagation, innovation, and renewal of traditional arts. You can stroll casually among artistic creations, listen to elegant music, and enjoy exciting opera performances and you can even participate in the process of artistic creation yourself. From the Center, you can take a boat and visit the Dong Mountain (Dongshan) River Water Park.

## Penghu National Scenic Area - Penghu Visitor Center

TEL: +886-6-921-6445

Address: No. 171, Guanghua Township, Magong City, Penghu County

All of the islands in Penghu have a similar terrain, and most of them are flat. Clear seawater, pure beaches and beautiful skies make Penghu a favorite ocean resort area. Both Kuroshio tributary current (during summer) and Mainland China's coastal current (during winter) pass through the Penghu sea territory. Because of this the marine life in this area is very rich, making Penghu an outstanding classroom for marine biology.

During the migration season, all kinds of birds pass through this area. Tourists can often see beautiful views of hunting seagulls, and the 200-plus different bird species here. This makes Penghu an excellent location for bird watching. Tourists can also came to Penghu for fishing and snorkeling; they can take boats and travel around the neighboring islands to enjoy the sea views and savor a wonderful vacation at sea.

Penghu shows its uniqueness in its cultural resources, thanks to the influences of its environment as well as Chinese culture and history. Many religious activities take place in Penghu; among 97 villages and towns in the islands, there are 183 temples. The ones with the longest history include the Tianhou, Wusheng, City God, Bao-an Temples, and the Guanyin Pavilion. There are also many important sites with great historical value. Penghu is famous for seafood such as groupers, abalone, lobsters, clams, and shellfish. Peanuts, sponge gourds, and cantaloupes are the main agricultural products. The best-known mineral is the veined stone, which is found only here and in Italy. The veined stones of Penghu are very famous for their color and quality, which is recognized as being the best in the world. Many arts and crafts stores can be found in the city of Magong, where tourists can find inexpensive and beautiful artworks carved from various kinds of stone.

Penghu Visitor Center

Offer introductions of Penghu's tourism resources, journey consultation, multi media playing, wash up, wireless network.

## Jianshanpi Jiangnan Resort

TEL: +886-6-623-3888

Address: No.60, Xushan Village, Liuying District, Tainan City

Jianshanpi Reservoir is a famous natural ecological scenic area. The dam was established in 1938 and is conveniently located in Xushan Village, Liuying District, only 12 km away from Xinying District. It was originally reserved for the use of the Xinying Plant of Taiwan Sugar Corporation.

However, it was later developed into a scenic resort as its picturesque landscape became known near and far. It is planned to change its name to Jianshanpi Resort and to establish a modern tourist hotel to boost the tourist industry within the area. The measure of the entire area amounts to more than one hundred ha., including the Jianshanpi water area (approximately 76 ha.) and the land area (27 ha.). Apart from the camping area, three different types of accommodation facilities are available here: Moon Balcony, Jiangnan Garden, and Log Cabin. The resort currently owns two traditional-style decorated vessels for visitors to go sightseeing on the reservoir with tour guides to introduce the history, ecology, and landscape of the area. The fifty-percent train at Wu-Shu-Lin Sugar Factory, Nanjing Recreational Selling Exhibition, and Taiwan Sugar Corporation's orchid farms are some of the spots nearby that are worth visiting.

## Tri-Mountain National Scenic Area - Lion' s Head Mountain Visitor Center

TEL: +886-3-580-9296

Address: No.60-8, Liuliao, Qixing Village, Emei Township, Hsinchu County

Lion's Head Mountain was rated as a provincial scenic area in 1993, and its scope includes Lion's Head Mountain, Emei Lake, Wuzhi Mountain, and Beipu Area. Wuzhi Mountain has an attractive forest and several trails. Emei Lake is very beautiful and has a suspension bridge called the "Emei Bridge." The Beipu cold spring has a large water volume and the Suilian Cave is deeply hidden in the mountain area. Lion's Head Mountain has traditional Hakka culture and boisterous festivals. Agricultural and forest specialties include Eastern Beauty Tea, Persimmon Cake, Three Bay Pear, Hakka rice, Lei Tea and trout.

Ever since the late Ching Dynasty, the temples and caves of Lion's Head Mountain and Mt. Wuzhi have been so famous that they were listed among the 12 most enchanting scenes in Taiwan. This scenic area encompasses the townships of Beipu, Emei, and Zhudong in Hsinchu County and the townships of Sanwan and Nanzhuang in Miaoli County. Located between the Provincial Highway No. 3 road system and the Xueba National Park system, this region covers an area of 24,221 hectares and is rich in natural (cold springs, forest and lakes) and ecological resources as well as notable cultural attractions, including temples and historical artifacts of the Hakka people and the aboriginals (the Atayal and Saisiat tribes). Since its establishment in 2001, the Tri-Mountain National Scenic Area Administration has worked to develop a high-quality tourist region focusing on naturism, education, ecology, and sustainability. Some of the promotional events for tourism development to date include lifestyle and historical tours; exploration of the traditional culture of the Hakka people; discovery of the mysteries of the Saisiat Tribe's Sacrifice to the Short Spirits; a river ecology tour; a tour of the natural habitats of insects; and a tour of mining and unique industries.

Lion' s Head Mountain Visitor Center

The Lion's Head Mountain Visitor Center was opened in 2001. It was built over the former Shishan Elementary School and designed to retain the Hakka style. In addition to the facilities, the restaurant, Xixin Tea House is appended to theVisitor Center, offering dining and refreshment services to the public.

## Southwest Coast National Scenic Area - Budai Visitor Center

TEL: +886-5-347-6788

Address: No. 61, Shun'an Rd., Budai Township, Chiayi County

In contrast to the northern and eastern coastlines, which are characterized by steep cliffs and rugged mountains, the western coast of Taiwan is largely flat. The stretch of coast from Taipei in the north to Kaohsiung in the south is heavily industrialized, but there are a number of areas that serve as natural habitats for wildlife including migratory birds and other coastal dwellers. In order to protect these precious habitats and to create a recreational area for visitors at the same time, a new national scenic area was established in the end of 2003, which is administered by the ROC Tourism Bureau. The Southwest Coast National Scenic Area, which includes the coastal areas of Yunlin, Chiayi, and Tainan counties, is known for its sandbanks, marshes, river deltas, and wetlands, which are home to a large number of endemic bird species and serve as a resting place for many migratory birds during the winter. Besides its ecological value, this new scenic area also has a lot of other attractions, such as the traditional production of salt from seawater, the local fishing industry, old temples and other historic sites that make a trip worthwhile.

Ocean Hotel Visitor Center

Standing beside the Budai port, this hotel has a beautiful ocean style. The huge crab decoration and blue painting make you feel like you're living in Greece. There is a visitor center on the first floor which provides tourist guide service. Also, there are shops beside it where you can find souvenirs.

## Baxianshan National Forest Recreation Area

Once one of Taiwan's three major forest reserves, Baxianshan Forest Recreation Area is located at Bo'ai Village, Heping District, Taichung City. The highest peak in the Mt. Baxian group has an elevation at more than 2,000 meters and total area around 2,397 hectares. Standing on the top of highest peak, you have great views of Mt. Jade, Mt. Nenggao and Mt. Qilai. This forest recreation reserve contains a perfectly preserved forest and crystal-clear streams and rivers whose adjoining terraces and tablelands are broad and wide. With its stark and pristine views, this recreation area is an ideal place for mountain climbing, forest baths, and bird-watching.

## Maolin National Scenic Area - Rinari Visitor Center

TEL: +886-8-799-7245

Address: No.63, Sec. 1, Heping Rd., Majia Township, Pingtung County

The Maolin Scenic Area covers the townships of Maolin and Liugui in Kaohsiung City, as well as parts of the administrative areas of Sandimen Township in Pingtung County. The Maolin Scenic Area has many scenic spots, such as the Baolai Hot Spring, Bulao Hot Spring, Duona Hot Spring, Shiba Luohan Mountain (Luohanshan), Meiya Valley Fall, Longtou Mountain, and Maolin Valley. Scenic resources Near the Shiba Luohan Mountain (Luohanshan) Reservation Area and the Meiya Valley, tourists can often see Formosan Macaque, squirrels, Varicorhinus barbatulus, and Taiwan blue magpies. All of them are precious resources in the Maolin Scenic Area. The state-owned forest in this area is another natural feature. The artistic side of the Maolin Scenic Area includes tunnels, temples, suspension bridges and aborigine cultures. Maolin, Wan Mountain (Wanshan), and Duona in Maolin Townships are reserved for aborigines. It is the home of the Rukai Tribe. The Rukai Tribe is famous for its slate houses. At present about 30 slate houses are being preserved in the Duona village of the Maolin Township, making it the largest collection of preserved slate houses in Taiwan. The Liugui Tunnel, consisting of six parts, is the only highway tunnel in southern Taiwan. Because of its views, the Liugui Tunnel has become a famous scenic spot. The Maolin Scenic Area has beautiful scenery and a lot of well-known Buddhist temples, such as the Miaotong and Miaocueng temples. The Maolin Scenic Area has many suspension bridges, the Duona Suspension Bridge being famous for its length.

Rinari Visitor Center

Rinari Visitor Center provides travel information and an introduction of indigenous tribes' culture. You must come to take a look and change into a traditional tribal costume, and experience the beauty of the culture.

On the weekends, there will be a fair in front of the center. You can find some indigenous handicrafts as unforgettable souvenirs.

## Ita Thao

TEL: +886-49-285-5668

Address: Yuchih Township, Nantou County 555, Taiwan

Ita Thao is called Barawbaw in thao language. The Han people call it North Cave. It was named Te Hua village after the restoration of Taiwan, and is under the administration of Yuchi.

Barawbaw is the last residence of the thao people at Sun Moon Lake. On account of the continuous stream of tourists, many Han people moved here to go into trade. Therefore, Ita Thao becomes the most populous area around the Sun Moon Lake. There are stores, restaurants, and hotels in the village. Also the thao people establishes the "thao Cultural Village" for tourists to appreciate the traditional culture, songs, and dancing of the thao tribe.

The harvest ceremony, the most important and splendid ceremony among all the others held during the year, is held every year during August in lunar calendar. If you visit Ita Thao during this month, you will have the chance to appreciate the culture of thao people. Barawbaw(Ita Thao) is the entrance to the Shuishe Mountain.

## Qinbi Village

Qinbi Village is located on Beigan Island of  Matzu, between the Qin Mountain and the Bi Mountain. It features the typical southern Fujian village. The community here began developing since the 13th century and major industry here is fishing industry. During 1951 to 1961, the KMT government sent army here to control the outflow of residents due to its thriving fishing industry. Qinbi Village has the most sophisticated buildings in Matzu. Since the 1970s, people have been moving to Taiwan and thus the buildings present the 1970s architectural style.

Buildings in Qinbi Village are mostly made of granite and marble, featuring beautiful colors. The fish-shaped object on the roof is used to drain water on the roof. In front of the buildings are stone lions, which are used to expel evil spirits. In order to prevent strong wind and bandits, stones are placed on the roof tiles and windows are higher. These characteristics are those of the eastern Fujian style.

Beigan Visitor Center

No.43, Banli Village, Beigan Township, Lienchiang County

Tel: +886-836-56531

## Northeast and Yilan Coast National Scenic Area - Fulong Visitor Center

TEL: +886-2-2499-1210

Address: No. 36, Xinglong St., Fulong Village, Gongliao District, New Taipei City

The Northeast Coast National Scenic Area is located in the northeast corner of Taiwan, stretching 102.5 kilometers from Nanya District in

New Taipei City to the south cape of Neibi Beach in Su'ao Township. It encompasses 17,421 hectares of land and sea.

This scenic area is noted for its numerous capes and bays backed by green mountains. Its attractions include spectacular rock formations, unique sea-eroded landforms, beaches of fine golden sand, a rich diversity of marine life, and an unspoiled cultural heritage. It is a multipurpose tourist destination that serves the dual functions of a fascinating natural classroom and an enchanting coastal playground. The Tourism Bureau established the Northeast Coast National Scenic Area Administration in 1984, charging it with the development and management of the area's tourism resources as well as the preservation of its environment. In addition to developing areas of outstanding scenic beauty as tourist items, the Tourism Bureau has also established nature preserves here, both on land and at sea, in order to sustain forever the ecological vitality of the Northeast Coast.

The Northeast Coast National Scenic Area, which runs from Juifang south to Beigangkou in Yilan County, is noted for its natural beauty: reefs, rivers, terraced rice paddies, rolling green hills, lighthouses, and two of Taiwan's best beaches. Recreational opportunities include camping, rock climbing, hiking along a 200-year-old footpath, and water sports, such as swimming, surfing, wind surfing, jet skiing, boating, snorkeling and scuba diving.

Fulong Visitor Center

The Fulong Visitor Center is right next to the Fulong Beach. It is located within a white-walled, red-tiled building along with the Northeast and Yilan National Scenic Area Administration. You can find information on the Northeast Coast's nature, culture and scenic spots.

The men and women's toilets beside the parking lot are especially equipped with the "occupied" lights so that no doors will be opened by accident when someone's responding to nature's call. In these green toilets, all transom windows are built with wavy cast iron materials that symbolize ocean waves. Winds and sunshine come through, whilst users' privacy is kept. Even rainwater is collected to flush the toilets. In these energy and water-saving toilets, users can even listen to melodious music played through a digital broadcasting system.

1F: There are two briefing rooms, a biking experience zone, a driftwood sculpture display, a Northeast scenic spot hunting map and a service center. The big briefing room can accommodate up to 160 audience members, the 15-minute widescreen "Loving Mountains and Oceans" is screened here regularly. In the small briefing room, the 20-minute "Landscapes of the Turtle Island" and 18-minute "Wise Turtle of the North Coast" are shown. You can ask for travel tips from the service center or preview the area's biking routes at the biking experience zone. Exhibits on the Northeast Coast's oceanic and mountain ecologies can also be found. Don't forget to take a picture at the postcard-photo taking machine.

Driftwood Sculpture Hall: Taiwan was hit by Typhoons Toraji, Nari and Haiyan in a row in 2001. After the disasters, pieces of driftwood were brought to the Northeast Coast. Some were recycled at first, but others were kept because they have come from precious native Taiwanese trees. To raise people's environmental awareness, promote local tourism and cultivate art talents, the Northeast and Yilan Coast National Scenic Area Administration entrusted 22 wood sculptors from Sanyi and the Taiwan Wood-carving Association to make driftwood sculptures themed by the nature and culture of the Northeast Coast. In this way, the driftwood has also been given a new life and artistic values. To better preserve these sculptures, which are mostly made of rare Formosan cypress, camphor and Taiwan incense cedar, the Driftwood Sculpture Hall was built. Today, they symbolize the green spirit of the Northeast Coast and the artisticness of its culture.

2F: Northeast Coast Virtual Experience Zone Fun Kingdom of Sand Sculptures: Introducing the origin and history of the Fulong International Sand Sculpture Festival, how to make sand sculptures, and sand sculpture tools. Previous festival photos and videos are also on display. Story of Fishery Village: Introducing the Maoao stone houses and the lives of fishery village households. Colorful Undersea World: Showcasing the colorful oceanic world of the Northeast Coast.

Railway Stroll: Highliting the Pingxi Line and the history and features of the old Pingxi Train Station. Travel in Northeast Coast: Listing all travel info about the Golden Fulong Route of the Taiwan Tourist Shuttle. Swipe QR Code to learn more!

## Heping Island Park

TEL: +886-6-921-6521

Address: County Hwy 203, Xiyu Township, Penghu County

Heping Island was called Sheliao Island in the past. It is located at the north of Taiwan. Heping Bridge connects the island to Keelung City. In 1626, the Spanish army built castles, churches and fortresses, preparing to do business with China and Japan. The castle on the southwest is called San Salvador, the saint savior. This is the first and currently the only castle in Keelung. During the Spanish occupation, Heping Island had busy trading activities with Southeast Asia. After World War II, the island was renamed Heping Island. Today, it is a famous tourist attraction.

Heping Island is perfect for diving and sea fishing. With years of erosion by the wind and sea, the eroded rocks and coasts have formed special shapes. The Keelung government has made Heping Island a coastal park with swimming pool, tour track, tourism service center and food and beverages.

## Xiyu Western Fort

During the ruling of the Qing Emperor Kuang Hsu, China and France had a war and signed a truce. The Qing government ordered magistrate Liu Ming-Chuan to build 10 fortresses to protect Taiwan from the harassment and attacks of pirates and bandits. Xiyu Western Fort was one of them. It is also the best-preserved and largest ancient fortress in Penghu, 8 hectares in area. The fortress is secure under thick rocks and spacious with a capacity of thousands of soldiers. It is not only a military base, but also has magnificent scenery.

Xiyu Western Fort has two arches in the entrance and the stone board on the out gate was inscribed by Li Hung Chang, a famous Qing official. There are many tunnels inside, leading to different chambers. The fortress has cliffs in the back, ocean in the front, which makes it perfectly secure. It also presents Penghu's peculiar position in history. Visitors to Penghu should never miss Xiyu Western Fort.

## Taiwan Indigenous Culture Park

In order to preserve aboriginal culture and resources, the government established Taiwan Indigenous Culture Park in Pingtung County in 1987. The park is 82.65 hectares in area, presenting each of the aboriginal tribes and their characteristics. The park is next to Fugu Bay, which as a natural and graceful scenery. There are no modern architectures in the vicinity. With the convenient busation, the park is perfect for holiday recreation.

The Taiwan Indigenous Peoples Cultural Park has traditional tribal cabins, which are located according to each tribe's tradition and lifestyle. There are a wax figure room, a multimedia room and an exhibition room in the park, presenting the development and culture of the aboriginal tribes. The handicraft room shows how the aborigines create their unique handcrafts.

## Fugang Geopark（Little Yehliu）

TEL: +886-89-281-136

Address: No. 500, Songjiang Rd., Taitung City, Taitung County (Xiaoyeliu Visitor Center)

Located at the 159-kilometer mark near the southern end of the East Coast National Scenic Area, Fugang Geopark (Little Yehliu) offers a rich variety of fascinating rock formations similar to those found at Yehliu on Taiwan's North Shore. Unlike the rest of the Philippine Plate that determines the geology of this area, the rock of Fugang Geopark is sandstone. This prompts geologists to believe that it originated somewhere else. You should first study the detailed explanations of the geological displays in the Visitor Center before going to the seashore and examining the tofu rock, honeycomb rock, fungus rock, and other strange ormations there. On clear days, you can easily see Green Island from the shore at Fugang Geopark.

Xiaoyeliu Visitor Center

Situated at the main entrance to the Xiaoyeliu Scenic Area, the Xiaoyeliu Visitor Center features a geology exhibition hall with many carefully-designed models and rock samples introducing the geological features of Siaoyeliou and the Coastal Range. This is a good place to get orientated before heading out on tours of this area.

## Tri-Mountain National Scenic Area - Baguashan Ecological Visitor Center

TEL: +886-3-864-1691

Address: No.100, Huantan N. Rd., Chinan Village, Shoufeng Township, Hualien County

Liyu(Carp) Pond is located in Shoufeng Township, just south of Hualian. With an area of approximately 104 hectares, it is the largest lake in this region; its size caries somewhat, however, with the amount of rainfall. The lake is encircled by a four-kilometer road that can be walked in about an hour. Popular activities include camping, picnic, and rowing on the lake. When the weather is favorable paragliders take off from Mt. Liyu just to the east of the lake, adding splashes of color to the green mountain landscape.

The Liyu Pond used to have abundant carps and the area is 104 hectares. It is the largest inland freshwater lake in Hualien. In addition, the Liyu Pond is also famous for its beautiful scenery, attracting many tourists. However, due to the development of out-ring highways, the number of tourists has declined. Therefore, local people have endeavored to conserve the environment and set up resort hotels, hoping to revive tourism around the Liyu Pond.

The Liyu Pond is suitable for camping and picnicking. Surrounded by mountains, the Liyu Pond is tranquil and peaceful. Tourists can sail on boats to appreciate the beauty of nature. The tour track around the lake is 4 kilometers long and tourists can either walk or ride bicycles along the track. In addition, gliders are also available here with the guidance of professional trainers.

## Guanziling Hot Springs

TEL: +886-6-682-2344

Address: Guanziling, Baihe Dist., Tainan City

Guanziling is the peak of Zhentou Mountain, Tainan City. The mountain was the residence of Pingpu Tribe until 1898, when Japanese soldiers found a hot spring and developed the area. Guanziling Hot Spring is a famous hot spring in southern Taiwan. The spring water is dark gray and bitter, emerging from the rocks.

Guanziling Tourist District is famous for the hot spring, Hongye Park, Daxian Temple, Biyun Temple and Xiangong Temple. The hot spring is on the side of the mountain, where hotels, restaurants and spring pools can be found. The natural gas and the spring water exist together in the cave, presenting a peculiar view.

## Longdong South Ocean Park (Longdong Four Seasons Bay)

TEL: +886-2-2499-1210

Address: No.48, Hemei St., Gongliao Dist., New Taipei City

Longdong South Ocean Park is 16 hectares in area, with Longdong Cape in the north and Yacht Port in the south. It is the first outdoor natural educational center which combines a yacht harbor, seawater swimming pool and marine exhibition rooms. Tourists can enjoy sailing and swimming and absorb oceanic knowledge here. Longdong (Dragon Cave) got its name due to the dragon-shaped rock caves stretching in this area. The management bureau has set up a tourist service center and an exhibition room here. The coasts are open year-round.

There are 4 ocean water pools in south Longdong. Tourists of different age groups can swim or enjoy diving here. The best time to enjoy the water is May to October. Every year, divers visit here to appreciate the beautiful fishes and coral reefs. The northeastern coasts are the diver's paradise and Longdong South Ocean Park is the best diving site.

For those who are interested in oceanic knowledge, the natural geography and intertidal zone here are the best classroom.

The ocean park at Longdong Park's south entrance is an outdoor education center that combines seashore fun with learning about the marine ecology. It is an ideal spot for swimming, snorkeling, and observing the marvels of the undersea world. Within the park are three former abalone ponds that have been converted to natural seawater swimming pools. The depth of the water varies with the tide, from knee-deep at low tide to three meters at high tide. Since the pools are connected with the sea, they are inhabited by tropical fish, sea anemones, starfish, shrimp, crabs, and other sea life. The pools are open for swimming from May to October. The Visitor Center here contains an exhibition hall with displays that explain the geology and coastal life to be seen along the Northeast Coast. On the platform below the center, you can observe sea-eroded formations and intertidal organisms in their natural environment.

## Fulong Beach

TEL: +886-2-2499-2381

Address: No. 40, Fulong St., Fulong Village, Gongliao District, New Taipei City

Fulong Beach is located at the mouth of Shuangxi River at Santiaowan, Gongliao District, New Taipei City. The beach stretches as long as 3 kilometers with golden sand. It has always been a summer resort in northern Taiwan. Every summer, a good number of tourists would gather here to swim and enjoy the sun. Fulong Beach was famous during the Japanese occupation of Taiwan. 24 hectares in area, Fulong Beach faces the Pacific Ocean and has special golden sand. It is the most famous beach in northern Taiwan, just as Kenting is the most famous beach in southern Taiwan. In addition, the plants and ecological environment near the Shuangxi River are educational for the visitors.

Fulong Beach has clear seawater and long soft beach. It is perfect for surfing, sliding, and sailing. There is a spacious parking lot, camping area, restaurants and food court. It is best organized bathing beach in northern Taiwan. Every summer, people come here for a swim or to appreciate the beautiful ocean. Besides, it also attracts many fishing lovers. The inner ocean and the outer ocean are connected by an arched bridge. Those who love exciting sea activities can never miss Fulong Beach.

Fulong has long been the most popular swimming beach on the Northeast Coast. In addition to the open beach, the calm and sheltered water of the Shuangxi River, which empties into the ocean here, makes this an ideal spot for wind surfing, canoeing, and other non-powered boating activities. The large sandy beach itself is perfect for swimming, sun-bathing, and other beach recreation. The red-roofed, white-walled headquarters building of the northeast Coast National Scenic Area is located near the entrance to Fulung Beach. Next to the headquarters is a Visitor Center with exhibits, video briefings, and other information on the rich variety of natural and cultural resources on the Northeast Coast. Fulong Beach is currently under the management of the Taiwan Pineapple Co. Various types of equipment are available for rent, including kickboards, inflatable swimming rings, and four-person rubber boats. A variety of other water and beach activities are offered for a fee.

## Sanxiantai

TEL: +886-89-854-097

Address: No. 74, Jihui Rd., Sanxian Village, Chenggong Township, Taitung County

Situated at the 111-kilometer mark on the coastal highway, Sanxiantai consists of a headland facing a small island in the sea. The three huge rocks that make up the island's most prominent feature have given rise to a local legend that three of China's Eight Immortals once landed there; hence the name of the island, which means "terrace of the three immortals." The island was once connected to the headland by a neck of land which has been eroded away; it is now connected by a red, scalloped footbridge, and the island has a network of footpaths for viewing its geological features such as potholes and sea-eroded caves and trenches, as well as rare coastal vegetation. The island is surrounded by coral reefs and a multitude of tropical fish, making this an ideal spot for skin diving.

Sanxiantai Visitor Center
Sanxiantai is one of the most popular scenic spots in East Coast. You can find out more about these natural wonders and ecology of this area before departing on your tour from the Sanxiantai Visitor Center.

## Wushantou Reservoir Scenic Area (Coral Lake)

TEL: +886-6-698-2103

Address: No. 68-2, Jianan Village, Guantian District, Tainan City

Coral Lake is at the border of Guantian and Liujia. The lake is formed with the convergence of over 30 rivers. A reservoir was built here in 1920, which was the largest reservoir construction at that time. There are over 100 isles on the lake. The designer of the reservoir was Japanese, who was sent to Southeast Asia by the army. After World War II, his wife drowned herself in the reservoir. There is a statue of the Japanese engineer by the reservoir.

The reservoir has a special structure and the water flowing out of the reservoir forms a beautiful waterfall. On the left of the waterfall is Kuo Min Hotel, in back of which is a camping site. Beside the lake is Zhongzheng Park, which is on top of a hill. The park overlooks the lake and the mountains beyond. Nearby the lake is temple worshipping Goddess of Mercy and Sakyamuni Buddha.

## Scenic Spots

### Chulu Ranch

TEL: +886-89-571-002, +886-89-571-815

Address: No.1, Muchang Rd., Mingfeng Village, Beinan Township, Taitung County

Chulu Ranch grows on a slightly acidic sandy hillside at an elevation of 200 to 390 meters above sea level and receives about 1,900mm of rainfall annually. The 70-plus hectare ranch has 45 hectares of pasture and grazing land, making it the biggest hillside pasture in Taiwan. The 350 resident Holstein dairy cows produce about 500 metric tons of milk a year. The pasture also buys milk from a cooperative of seven dairies with 1,100 Holsteins and an annual milk production of about 3,000 metric tons. The milk is processed at the ranch into about 3.5 million kilogram boxes of fresh milk.

In addition to the dairy operations, Chulu Ranch is beautifully landscaped and equipped for visitor recreations and educational pursuits. The pasture serves an ecological and cultural preservation role as well, making it an excellent destination for ecotours in a rustic setting. Visitors can also enjoy horseback rides, take a spin in a horse-drawn carriage, and buy a wide range of locally made dairy products at the ranch store.

### Dongyong Lighthouse

Dongyong Lighthouse was built in late 19th century by British engineers. This white lighthouse has been designated as a third grade national ancient site. In late 19th century, the Qing government opened several ports in this area and thus the lighthouse was built to guide ships. The construction was completed in 1902.

Dongyong Lighthouse faces the Taiwan Strait, located on the northeast of Dongyin Island. It is made of bricks and painted white on the outside walls. The lighthouse is 14.3 meters in height and the light flashes 3 times every 20 seconds. The lighthouse, designed by the British engineers, consists of the main body, the lamp and the roof. It is beautifully designed and has become a tourist attraction in recent years.

Dongyin Visitor Center

No.160-1, Lehua Village, Dongyin Township, Lienchiang County

Tel: +886-836-77266

## Songboling Forest Park

TEL: +886-49-273-2116

Address: No. 181, Sec. 2, Minsong Rd., Mingjian Township, Nantou County

Songboling Forest Park has an altitude of 500 meters and is famous for the production of tealeaves and Taoist Shoutian Temple. Shoutian Temple was established in the 18th century and it is an important

Taoist temple in Taiwan. Songboling is famous for its high quality tealeaves and has the highest production in Taiwan. The tea here was named longevity Tea by late president Chiang Ching Kuo.

Near Shoutian Temple, there is a tourism service center, providing tourism information in Songboling. Shoutian Temple has four stories and it overlooks the Qingshui River and Zhuoshui River. One tour track leads to Tianzhong and has two pavilions for visitors to rest. Tea lovers can never miss Songboling Forest Park.

## Tri-Mountain National Scenic Area - Songboling Visitor Center

TEL: +886-49-258-0525

Address: No.181, Sec. 2, Minsong Rd., Mingjian Township, Nantou County

60% of the scenery spots of the Baguashan (Mt. Bagua) range are inside the Changhua County boundary while the rest 40% are within the Nantou County. The whole area has more than ten cities and towns, namely Changhua, Huatan, Tacun, Fenyuen, Yuanlin, Shetao, Tianzhong, Ershui, Nantou, Mingjian, etc. Baguashan (Mt. Bagua) situates on a plateau about 1 kilometer from the eastern side of Changhua (the only plateau land in the Changhua County). Hence the mountain is also called Bagua Plateau. The whole plateau is tilting from north to south and from the mountain top one can see the streets of the whole Changhua City as well as fishing boats in the distant sea.

This unique feature of enable one to have full view of its surroundings had made Baguashan (Mt. Bagua) a very important military guarding point in ancient time. In the 20th years of Emperor Kuang Shu's rule (year 1894), the Sino-Japanese War broke out and as a compensation for the lost of the war, the Treaty of Ma Kwan was signed whereby Taiwan was given by the Qing Government to Japan. Taiwan people did not accept such outcome and they organized their own army to fight the Japanese.

The Japanese army landed from the north-eastern corner of Taiwan at Yen Cheng and marched southwards. They were sternly resisted by the local patriots and out of all the battles; the one in Baguashan (Mt. Bagua) was of the largest scale. Later the Japanese demolished the guard point and after the Second World War, the whole place was replaced with the Baguashan (Mt. Bagua) Giant Buddha. Nowadays, in the Memorial Park there is Memorial Hall built in memory of those who died in the battles against Japanese invasion. Also, the two cannons which were used in the battle are in exhibition there.

Its total area is approximately 22,000 hectares, including the Baguashan (Mt. Bagua) Park, the Chiang Kai Sek Park, the Jiulong Pond, the Giant Buddha of Changhua, the Fushan Rock, the Baozang Temple, the Bi Mountain (Bishan) Rock and the Qingshui Rock, etc.

which are full of cultural heritage. Amongst the above scenery spots, the historical Baguashan (Mt. Bagua) Giant Buddha is the most well known one. The statue measures 72 feet in height from its lotus seat to the top and the whole body is built of steel bars and cement. In front of the statue stand two lion sculptures. Its base occupies a total area of 7 hectares and inside there are altogether 6 separate levels. The lowest level is a small worship hall. The second to the fifth levels are for the exhibits of Buddha's work during his life time. Under the steps platform in the front is the Jiulong Pond; the right is an aquarium and at the back is a piece of woodland. The whole place gives one a sense of quietness and tranquility.

## Tsou Ma Lai Farm

TEL: +886-6-576-0121

Address: No.60, Qiziwa, Danei Dist., Tainan City 742, Taiwan

Over 300 years ago, Tsou Ma Lai was the residence the aboriginal tribe Pingpu. It has become a tourist attraction because it is surrounded by Zengwen Reservoir (Tseng-Wen Reservoir), Wushantou Reservoir, Hutoupi (Hutou pond), Nanhua Reservoir, Yu Mountain (Yushan) National Park and Southern Highway. Tsou Ma Lai has special geography as the rivers cut across the mountains. With the efforts of Tainan County, Tsou Ma Lai has the best recreation and conference facilities. The park is 120 hectares in area, 80 hectares of which is spectacular green grass.

There is an archery field, racetrack, pasture, camping site, barbeque site, and many other recreational facilities. Visitors can come here either on vacation or for a conference. The well-organized facilities and services are well known at home and abroad. The park has just established a mini-golf course, attracting more golf lovers.

## Baxian Cave (Baxiandong)

TEL: +886-89-881-418

Address: No. 1-4, Shuimuding, Sanjian Village, Changbin Township, Taitung County

Baxian Cave (Baxiandong) is located in the north of Hua Tung Mountain by the coast of Changbin Township. "Baxian" (eight deities) are famous Chinese deities. Fogs drift perpetually around the caves and the interior is damp and misty. As the environment resembles that in the folklore when the eight deities cross the ocean, the caves were named Baxian. In the caves, Taiwan's first prehistoric site was discovered. As the earth's crusts elevated, the mountains were constantly eroded by the sea and 16 caves of different sizes were formed along the cliff as high as 100 meters.

Wooden tour tracks and stone tour tracks lead to all the caves, including Lingyan Cave, Chaoyin Cave, Yong-an Cave, Hailei Cave, Chaoyang Cave, Qianyuan Cave, Gongchen Cave and Kunlun Cave. A prehistoric site was discovered in the highest cave. There is an exhibition center showing the objects found in the site, including bone-made objects, stone objects, etc.

## Taipei Zoo

TEL: +886-2-2938-2300

Address: No.30, Sec. 2, Xinguang Rd., Wunshan District, Taipei City

The Taipei Zoo is the largest city zoo in Asia. Upon entering the grounds, you will find an extremely popular panda facility on your left. If you can't find the cute pandas, don't worry; they're probably sunning themselves! Next, take the visitors' tram. Listen to the recorded guide as he takes you along to the bird sanctuary, the Amphibians and Reptile House, the Penguin House and other areas such as the Tropical, African, Australian, Desert Animal Areas. In the Insect House, it is possible to come in contact with insects up close.

On holidays, explanations are given at each site. Free-guided tours are also available upon advanced reservation. And if you love animals, you can consider adopting an animal and becoming its babysitter!

## Buluowan

TEL: +886-3-862-1100~6

Address: Buluowan, Fushi Village, Xiulin Township, Hualien County

Buluowan is a settlement where the Atayal tribe originally lived. Buluowan is surrounded by mountains, and during festive occasions, the powerful singing of the tribes' people resonates among the valleys. Two or three hundred years ago, the Atayal Tribe decided to relocate, and some tribes people left their original homes in upstream Zhuoshui River, and crossed over the Central Mountain Range to settle by Liwu River and Mugua River in Hualien.

Buluowan was the settlement which the aboriginals of Taroko had built near the Liwu River. The settlement was divided into upper and lower Buluowan, and was led by the two ruling clans. It was not until the Taroko Gorge Incident in 1914 and the Wu Sher Incident in 1930, that the Taroko aboriginals were forced by the Japanese to move out of the gorge, into flatland areas, like Fushi Village and Siulin Village in Sioulin Township. Buluowan, which is 370 meters above sea level, has a temperature that remains at an average of 21.5 degreed all year long.

Buluowan is a double layered river steppe, with Mt. Da standing on its south, and Liwu River flowing on its north. It has abundant natural biological resources, which include varieties of tropical monsoon rainforest plants, and many animal species. The place is ideal for conducting natural observation activities.

The Buluowan Administration Station in Taroko National Park's Administration Center spent years cultivating the Formosan Wild Lily; now a sea of wild lilies bloom each year, from March to May. The lily fields near the Buluowan Tourist Center are a beautiful sight, which continually amaze and attract visitors.

Buluowan is divided into upper and lower platform areas, and the most singular sight in the scenic walkway in the upper platform area. When the hanging tendrils of the banyan trees come into contact with the earth, it automatically curls around objects, creating the curious scene of vines embracing stones.

The Atayal Cultural Center is a specially designed tourist area in Buluowan; it has an administration center, an Atayal culture exhibition area, a multimedia presentation center, and a circular theater. In the exhibition area, there are elderly Atayals demonstrating how they weave cloth and rushes in the traditional method. There are also 20 or so bamboo huts built in the Atayal style, where visitors may stay overnight.

## Tianzhong Forest Park

TEL: +886-49-258-0525

Address: Sec. 2, Zhongnan Rd., Tianzhong Township, Changhua County

Tianzhong Forest Park is located in the east of Tianzhong Township. The park enjoys dense forests and the tour track stretches along the mountain, overlooking the Changhua Plain and the Taiwan Strait. The track is 3 kilometers long and it takes about 2 hours to finish the track. With an altitude of 325 meters, the Zaojue Pavilion is on the track, overlooking the Zhuoshui River and the Taiwan Strait.

Besides the forests, it also has tables, chairs, amusement facilities and some sports equipment. The forests are suitable for hiking and have perfect mountainous scenery.

## Shimen Reservoir

TEL: +886-3-471-2000

Address: No.68, Sec. 1,Huanhu Rd., Daxi Dist., Taoyuan City, Daxi Dist., Taoyuan City

Shimen Reservoir is the biggest reservoir among far eastern countries. The scenery of the lake and mountains surrounding it is poetic and spectacular all year round. It is also a good place to go on holidays. Shimen Reservoir is connected to more than ten outside tourist sites. There are bicycles tracks and lake cruises.

The reservoir has many different functions such as generating power, watering agricultural plants, preventing floods, offering drinking water and sightseeing. Shimen reservoir is also a good place to watch the maple leaves. In winter, people are able to see the golden maple leaves everywhere. The plum blossoms are always beautiful as well. The white blossoms always catch people's eyes.

By the time spring comes, the peach blossoms, cherry blossoms and azaleas seem like they are having a beauty contest. Their beauty is appealing. Whenever the rainy season comes, the spectacular view of floodwater being released always attracts many visitors.

## Jibei Island

TEL: +886-6-921-6521

Address: Jibei Island, Baisha Township, Penghu County

Jibei Island lies 5.5 kilometers north of Baisha Island; its size is about 3.05 square kilometers, and it is not only the sixth largest island in the county, but it is also the largest inhabited island among the 28 isle within Baisha village, except for Baisha Island itself. There are two sources for the name of this Island: one is that the hidden reefs growing among the periphery if Jibei Island is shaped like the character (auspicious) in Chinese. The other is that refers to a faraway island where there are many shell (shell is pronounced in mandarin) mounds. According to historical studies, Jibei is part of the orth Sea Fishing Grounds fishermen were active in the islands surrounding sea territories in as early as the Ming Dynasty, and they had also erected a temple here, which is what is called the Wusheng Temple today.

Jibei Island is 3.1 square kilometres in area, with a coastline of 13km; it is the largest island on the North Sea, and one of the most popular tourist spot in Taiwan. The "Sand Beach Beak" at the south end houses a white sand beach extending 1500m, it is a marine deposit landform "Sand Spit" formed by corals and shells that were moved here by the sea; it is a spectacular sight when looked down from the air, a truly world-class natural landscape.

Jibei is heaven for water activities, housing various types of recreational activities, including banana boat, dragged buoy, two-man speedboat, water motorcycle, under-the-sea sightseeing boat, paragliding and snorkeling, you name it, you got it! Those that enjoy water activities will sure have a wonderful time here at Jibei. Another tourism feature of Jibei is the number of "stone weirs" housed here; there are over 80 stone weirs, more than any other places in Penghu, thus winning the name "Home of the Stone Weirs."

## Sun Moon Lake Lalu Island

TEL: +886-49-285-5668

Address: Sun Moon Lake Lalu Island, Yuchi Township, Nantou County

Located in the center of Sun Moon Lake, Lalu Island was called Guanghua Island in the past. Sun Moon Lake is the most famous water reservoir in Taiwan. Lulu Island is known as the island on the water. This area was dwelled by the Shao tribe in the past and the island had been called Lalu until 1946, when the government renamed it Guanghua Island. In the severe earthquake in 1999, Sun Moon Lake reservoir was damaged and a historic site of the Shao tribe was discovered. Thus, in 2000, the island was renamed Lalu again. The Shao tribe considers the island a sacred place and thus tourists cannot visit the island; however, you can still learn about the Shao tribe along the tracks surrounding the lake.

Lalu Island is said to be a sacred place for the Shao tribe. Witch candidates of the tribe would have to come to the island to seek approval of the ancestors' spirits. The witches are in charge of incantation and rituals. The Japanese also left a stone monument, remembering the development of Sun Moon Lake during Japanese occupation.

## Taroko National Park - Taroko Visitor Center

TEL: +886-3-862-1100~6

Address: No.291, Fushi, Fushi Village, Xiulin Township, Hualien County

Taroko became a national park in 1986, including Hualien County, Nantou County and Taichung City. Taroko is famous for its spectacular mountains and marble canyons. Cliffs and canyons stretch along Liwu River. Four million years ago, the island of Taiwan was formed by the collision of plates. After millions of years of wind erosion, the marble rocks were exposed and cut by Liwu River, creating impressive grand canyons. From Qingshui to Nanhu Peak, the drop height is 3,742 meters. Such special geography has also bred special flora and fauna in this area.

The waterfalls characterized Taroko National Park and the most famous ones are Baiyang Waterfall, Yindai Waterfall, Changchun Waterfall, and Lushui Waterfall. Swallow Grotto (Yanzikou) and Tunnel of Nine Turns (Jiuqudong) are the most impressive natural scenes in Taroko and the canyons here are the narrowest. Tourists can appreciate the natural beauty along the tour track. Swallows nest on the cliff, chirping and flying back forth. The Taroko monumental is designed in Chinese style and Changchun Temple is to remember those who sacrificed their lives for building the central highway.

Tianxiang

This is the site of an old Atayal village at the confluence of the Liwu and Dasha Rivers. Its name commemorates Wen Tianxiang, who lived in the 13th century and was the last prime minister of the Song Dynasty.

Scenic spots at Tianxiang include Xiangde Temple, Tianfeng Pagoda, a suspension bridge, the Wen Tian-siang Memorial Garden, the Plum Garden, and Tianxiang Church. In winter each year the Plum Garden blooms forth, forming a sea of white blossoms stretching from the highway to Xiangde Temple. Shanyue Village at Bulowan, another old tribal settlement in the gorge, offers a new and unique type of accommodation for the area.

## New Era Art Resort & Spa

TEL: +886-49-291-2248

Address: No. 1, Sec. 4, Zhongshan Rd., Puli Township, Nantou County

The New Era Art Resort & Spa in Puli was established in 1987 to display the work of renowned Taiwanese sculptor Lin Yuan. In addition to its original function as a sculpture park, the 6.6-hectare sculpture park has evolved over the years into a resort area with vacation cabins, conference facilities, a spa and restaurant specializing in healthy cuisine. The tung blossoms are another major attraction at this resort and center of art.

## Beihai Tunnel

Beihai Tunnel is located between Ren-ai Village and Meishi Village. In 1970, the military excavated a tunnel here for the ships to avoid bad weather and attacks. The tunnel could harbor several naval vessels, but after a severe typhoon, it was damaged. As the cross-strait relations grow friendlier, the tunnel has become a tourist attraction. With a total length of 700 meters, the tunnel is also called as the nderground dock featuring Matzu military importance in the past.

Beihai Tunnel goes deep into the granite mountain. The waterway is 18 meters in height, 10 meters in width and 640 meters in length, capable of harboring 120 small vessels. It took 820 days to complete the establishment of the tunnel. The construction was very difficult at that time, and some soldiers even sacrificed their lives during the construction.

Matzu National Scenic Area Administration

No.95-1, Ren-ai Village, Nangan Township, Lienchiang County

Tel: +886-836-25630

## Beiguan Tidal Park

TEL: +886-3-978-0727

Address: Sec. 4, Binhai Rd., Toucheng Township, Yilan County

Beiguan Park, also known as Lancheng Park, is a coastal park located in the northeast of Taiwan, Toucheng Township. With Nanguan in the south, it is the entrance to Lanyang Plain. During the Qing Dynasty, Beiguan is a military outpost and the Qing government encamped soldiers here. There are 2 ancient cannons of the Qing Dynasty in the park. After millions of years of erosion, there are many natural scenes in the park, especially the rocks. The park also has a great view of the ocean and the surging waves.

Guanhai Pavilion overlooks the Guishan Island, Wai-ao and Beiguan. The Guanhai Pavilion is a perfect place to appreciate the sunrise and the raging waves. The best time to visit Beiguan is when the tide rises or when the sun sets. The waves surge over the rocks with very loud sound. The 2 ancient cannons are over 160 years old, adding to the antique atmosphere of Beiguan.

During the Qing dynasty, Beigang ("northern pass") was a military outpost guarding the Yilan area to the south; today, only an old cannon battery remains to remind visitors of that early mission. The most notable geological features of this area are cuesta formations and tofu rock. Beiguan Tidal Park is situated on the top of the largest of the cuestas; just follow the footpath, and you can see interesting rock formations as you enjoy the pounding of waves against the rocky shore. Food stands in the neighborhood offer a mouth-watering array of snacks and seafood.

## Taichung Metropolitan Park

TEL: +886-4-2461-2483

Address: No. 30-3, Xiping S. Lane, Xitun District, Taichung City

Taichung Metropolitan Park is designed to conserve nature, to educate citizens and to provide a leisure space. Citizens can spend the leisure hours here to expose themselves to the nature and to learn more about the ecologic system. The main purpose of the park is to provide a leisure space, purify the air, reduce air pollution, conserve water and soil, regulate temperature and reduce noise.

Besides the educational function, people can take a walk in the park and enjoy the starry skies. Situated in the suburban area, the park has a clear sky and a beautiful view of stars. Visitors can enjoy the night view of Taichung City on the right and Shalu on the left.

## Wufengqi Scenic Area

TEL: +886-3-988-0940

Address: Wufeng Rd., Jiao River (Jioxi) Township, Yilan County

The Wufengqi Falls are one of the eight great scenic spots of the Lanyang Plains, belonging to Jiao River (Jioxi) Township in Yilan County. The Wufengqi Falls are named for the five sharp peaks which stand in a row behind the falls, that look like the five triangular banners that usually hang down the back of the war generals costume in Chinese Opera.

Fog and mist drift gracefully around the mountaintop year-long, and torrents of mountain springs continuously flow down its slopes, forming the three layers of cascades that are now the Wufengqi Falls. There are three layers to the Falls, and they measure 100 meters from top to bottom. The entrance to the scenic viewpoint is situated near the bottom layer of the Falls, and there is also a barbecue area, and a play area for children to splash in the pools. A viewing pavilion is constructed at the mid-layer of the Falls; there is a vast expanse of vision at this point, and tourists may enjoy viewing the lush mountains, and the cascades shooting out from the precipices.

The scene in the eight famous scenic views of Lanyang that is poetically named, mists draping the western peaks refers to the Wufengqi Falls. The Falls are situated in an enclosed valley, which enhances the mystic beauty of the peaks. At dawn, as the sky slowly begins to brighten, musical birdsong can be heard resonating throughout the valley; the unique tranquility in the atmosphere is indescribable.

The Ancient Horse Route: Starting from Jiao River (Jioxi) and going upwards along the foot of the Wufeongqi peaks, there is an ancient route, called the ncient Horse Route by the locals. Before the Taipei-Yilan Highway was constructed, this route was the only means of reaching Taipei from Jiao River (Jioxi). Now, orange and kumquat orchards dot both sides of the route, creating lush scenery and a rustic atmosphere.

## Renyi Lake Reservoir

TEL: +886-5-276-9625

Address: No.30-2, Hongmaopi, Fanlu Township, Chiayi County

Located in Fanlu, Renyi Lake is a natural lake with beautiful scenery. Rising mists and clear water pose a contrast to the green mountains. However, with the rapid development of cities and growth of population, the government turned Renyi Lake to be a reservoir in 1987. The reservoir not only supplies drinking water to Chiayi County, but it is also a tourist attraction.

Around the Renyi Lake, there are pavilions and beautiful plants. Visitors often play kites or walk carefree by the lake. There is also a tour track beside the lake. Visitors can enjoy the fresh air, the starry skies and the beautiful nature here at the Renyi Lake.

## Xiao Wulai (Little Wulai) Scenic Area

TEL: +886-3-382-1235

Address: No.4-6, Xiayunei, Fuxing District, Taoyuan City

In the mother language of the Atayal tribe, Wulai represent the meaning of the hot springs. The names of hot springs in the old Atayal language are all called Wulai. Xiao Wulai (Little Wulai) with many gorges locates in the region of the Fuxing District. The famous inner scenery is the Xiao Wulai (Little Wulai)Waterfall, Long waterfall, and the Wind Stone. Yunei Stream locates in the village of Fuxing District in Taoyuan. The stream is the upper branch of the Xiao Wulai (Little Wulai) Waterfall. Therefore the flows of the water are strong because of the plentiful rain. The Xiao Wulai (Little Wulai) Waterfall is not affected by the dry season in winter.

Xiao Wulai (Little Wulai) Waterfall broke out into three sections. The middle section is the most impressive. It belongs to fault hanging valley type waterfall. The apex of the stream is narrow as the little street, and then meets the downfallen formation cape. The stream falls straight 50 meters down to the deep pond from the leftward notch. The water split out like the fog and the mist. This is the special view of wonderland.

There is a four-floor observatory at the side of the highway, and this is a good observe point. The seasons of watching the birds are May to June and November to the next February every year. You can enjoy the forest shower here, and also watching the waterfall and the birds. During the deep autumn, Yunei stream is the upper branch of Xiao Wulai (Little Wulai); the red maple leaves will cover the road besides the stream or flow in the stream. The stream with the flown maple leaves and the waterfall make the beautiful scenery. There are the three sections of the Xiao Wulai (Little Wulai) Waterfall from top to down near the observatory besides the main road. The drop height of the upper section is only about 3 meters. You can see it from the observatory. The drop height of the middle section is about 50 meters. It is the special waterfall with the high drop height in the northern part. The flow is vigorous, the sound is like thunder, and the water bloom splashes, these are condign grandeur. There is a small lake on the upper part of the middle section of the waterfall. The water on the upper section of the waterfall runs into the small lake, it is quite grandeur.

## Taipei 228 Peace Park

TEL: +886-2-2389-7228

Address: 103, Huaining Road, Zhongzheng District, Taipei

Taipei 228 Peace Park was called Taipei Park at first and then changed to New Park in the past. The park was established in the Qing Dynasty and is the oldest park in Taipei. After World War II, the KMT government took over Taiwan. However, economic monopoly and corruption of the government led to civil resistance. On February 27,

1947, people gathered in front of the police department but were shot by the soldiers. The next day, people gathered in the Taipei Park and broadcast the movement at the radio station. The KMT government used military force to restrain the protesters and arrested alleged participants afterward. In order to relieve this historic pain, the park was renamed to 228 Peace Park in 1996.

In order to remember the innocent people sacrificed in the event, a monument was set up in the park. Creator of the monument, Cgeng Cai Zi (Cheng Tze-Tsai), also suffered during the movement. He had studied in the USA in 1962 and learned the importance of democracy and freedom. Thus, when he came back to Taiwan, he decided to improve Taiwan human rights and independence. Cheng even tried to assassinate President Chiang Ching-Kuo when he visited the USA. Cheng became an exile for over 20 years ever since. The monument has detailed description of the 228 event in 1947, hoping that people can learn from this painful lesson.

## Zhongzheng (Jhongjheng) Park

TEL: +886-2-2428-7664 (Keelung City Visitor Information

Address: Shoushan Rd., Zhongzheng Dist., Keelung City

Zhongzheng (Jhongjheng) Park is situated on the side of Dashawan Mountain, which is at the east of Keelung City. There is a white statue of Goddess of Mercy in the park. This 25-meter high statue has become one of the characteristics of Keelung.

The park overlooks Keelung City and the harbor. There are three levels in the park. On the first level is a historic canon fort. On the second level is a Buddhist library, Martyrs' Shrine and Zhuputan Temple. The temple attracts many worshipers on July 15. On the third level is Guanhai Pavilion. Sitting in the pavilion, visitors can see the entire Keelung and the ocean.

The statue of Goddess of Mercy is the landmark of Zhongzheng (Jhongjheng) Park. It is the biggest Goddess statue in Southeast Asia. Inside the statue is a stairway leading to the top. Zhuputan is where worshipers gather on Zhongyuan Festival. The first immigrants to Taiwan used to fight with each other for land. In order to stop the disputes, they set up a temple for yearly worship. The temple was in Gaosha Park during the Japanese occupation and moved to Zhongzheng (Jhongjheng) Park.

## Little Liuqiu

TEL: +886-8-861-4615

Address: No.20-1, Minzu Rd., Liuqiu Township, Pingtung County 929, Taiwan (R.O.C.)

Little Liuqiu is originally named Samagi. Its history can be traced back to 1775 AD (Qian-long year 20, Qing Dynasty), when Mr. Lee Yue reached the island from his hometown at today's Kaohsiung Port (of Fu-jian province, Mainland China then). The first time ancestor Lee stepped on the land was to take shelter from the storms.

After scrupulous adventure, however, he found the place inhabitable for its copious catch of fish and nice weather. Taking advantage of its natural resources, Lee called about 20 Lee families to migrate overseas here and started their living by fishery. For being separated from the motherland Taiwan, this island to the Lees was just like a ball drifting on the sea, from which Liuqiu (drifting ball) was named. To tell Liouciou from Okinawa, Japan, which pronunciation is the same as Liuqiu in Chinese, people here is used to calling it Liitle Liuqiu.

Little Liuqiu is the general name of Liuqiu Island. It is only 6.8 square kilometers large, with a 12km coastline. The only offshore coral reef island of Taiwan, it is 14km southwest of Donggang Township, Pingtung County. Little Liuqiu is blessed with many tourist resources. Because is not influenced by northeastern monsoons in winter, this island can be visited all year round. Especially on chilly days, it is still suitable for travel.For its unique geological formations, Little Liuqiu has a diverse natural ecology and plenty of beautiful coastal views. The amazing rocks in different sizes and shapes make its scenery even more charming. People are simple and honest here. Temples are everywhere, and graceful old houses abound. A leisurely fishery village it is. There are no traffic lights at all on this island. Pace of life is slow and free. No big budget is needed to enjoy this island of diverse ecology, authentic culture, and LOHAS life. It is pretty convenient to get to the island, too.

## North Coast & Guanyinshan National Scenic Area - Baisha Bay Visitor Center

TEL: +886-2-8635-5100

Address: No.33-6, Xiayuankeng, Shimen District, New Taipei City

Rocky and unforgiving in several places, Taiwan's North Coast also boasts fine sandy beaches and stunning vistas. Inland, typically it is rugged and precipitously steep, but there are also hot springs, rushing rivers, and several waterfalls. Unfriendly to farmers and often hazardous to seafarers, this landscape is certainly dramatic - and, for that reason, very attractive to tourists.

The North Coast & Guanyinshan National Scenic Area encompasses two separate sections of North Taiwan's New Taipei City. The larger part consists of the seashore, part of the ocean, and a strip of land either side of Fugui Cape, Taiwan's northernmost point. The smaller part of the Scenic Area is centered on the 616-meter-high mountain called Guanyinshan. Waimushan, Lovers Lake and Heping Island in Keelung City are important coastal tourist attractions in northern Taiwan. It was thus announced on December 15, 2014, that these sites would be made part of the North Coast and Guanyinshan National Scenic Area.

Whether you're seeking a bleak, deserted strip of shore, the sun beating down on a sandy beach, or history, culture and good food, you'll find it in the North Coast & Guanyinshan National Scenic Area.

## Yingge

TEL: +886-2-2678-0202, 0800-271-181

Address: Yingge District, New Taipei City

Yingge is a pottery town, known as the "Jingde Township of Taiwan." The town has several hundred pottery plants, and equal numbers of pottery shops that sell their products. Jianshanpu Road is the origin of the local ceramics industry, and even today it has an old square coal-fired kiln chimney that serves as its landmark. Every October the town holds the Yingge Ceramics Festival; and, if you want to learn about the development of ceramics in Taiwan, the place to go is the Yingge Ceramics Museum.

Yingge was called Geshi in the past, because there was a bird-shaped stone near the town. After World War II, the government named this place. The so-called Ge Old Street is Jianshanpu Rd. After reconstruction, the old street has become a modern street, along which are pottery and porcelain shops. Though the old street no longer has its antique looks, some ancient buildings can still be found in Yingge Town. The new street is paved with beautiful rocks. Visitors can not only appreciate the pottery and porcelain works, but they can also enjoy the street performance and coffee on the street.

There are over 100 stores on the street. The products were pretty much the same in the past, but now the shops have their own workshops and artists. Each shop has its own characteristics and the pottery works are exquisite and refined. Some of the restaurants will give diners the cups or plates they use for free. Even the ice cream stand has lovely mugs and cups for customers to choose from. Besides purchasing the pottery and porcelain products, you can even learn how to make your own pottery works.

## Guan Mountain (Guanshan) Water Park

TEL: +886-89-551-637

Address: No. 1, Longsheng Rd., Guan Mountain (Guanshan) Township, Taitung County

Guan Mountain (Guanshan) is a green mountain famous for its beautiful scenery. Guan Mountain (Guanshan) Township is not only surrounded by mountains but also a river on the east. Ever since the Qing Dynasty, Guan Mountain (Guanshan) has been the administrative city for the East Rift Valley. In recent years, Guan Mountain (Guanshan) is famous for its cycling tracks. In 1999, Guan Mountain (Guanshan) won the first place in an image contest of resort cities.

Cycling around Guan Mountain (Guanshan) Township, you will see tranquil rice paddies. At the end of the cycling track is a river park next to the mountain. There is even an over-water track leading cyclists back to the start. Guan Mountain (Guanshan) is also famous for its high quality rice and sweet oranges.

## Wushe

TEL: +886-49-280-2534

Address: Wushe, Ren-ai Township, Nantou County

Wushe is located in Ren-ai Township in Nantou. The geographic position is in the middle of the Taiwan Island. It is the way you must past when heading to the middle cordillera. It was named because of the mountain overlap, and the mountain mists form mirage.

The cenotaph is standing among the cherry blossom for people to evoke. Since 1960, the center horizontal is opened, the south branch collect the beauty of the veldt and the valley in Wushe parkland. The climate is cool the whole year in Wushe.

There are cherry blossom bloomy within the precinct. It is named as the same level as the red cherry tree in Ali. Besides the cherry trees, there are peaches, plums, and Li flowers. When coming to the cherry blossom bloomy in January and February every year, the precinct is the best place for watching the beautiful flowers and the famous place for summer time.

## Tiezhen Mountain Scenic Area

TEL: +886-4-2687-4543

Address: No.87, Chenggong Rd., Dajia District, Taichung City

The Tiezhen is named because the looking is similar to iron anvil. There is an old well, Jian Well, located on the top of the mountain. Traditional tale about the well told that this was the place where Cheng Cheng Kung dug with his sword for the water. During the early years, Cheng Cheng Kung led the soldiers passing this place when they left no food and water. And because the weather was torrid, the soldiers and the horses died of no water to drink. Cheng Cheng Kung felt hopeless and a great feeling of the God, he kneeled down on the ground with his sword into the ground praying for the water. Suddenly, the ground dehisced, and the sword really sank into the ground.

Then the spirit water came out for all the people to drink, and saving the lives. Hereafter, people commemorated this great miracle; they called this well the Jian Well or the Guoxing Well. The people in Dajia District set a curve board of Guoxing Well in memory of the miracle that Cheng Cheng Kung inserted his sword into the ground in Tiezhen Mountain. The ancient well was rebuilt in 1953. The protections were set around the well. The ex-supervision administrator, Yu Yu Jen, named "Jian Well (Sword Well)" two words. It becomes the most famous tourism view today.

Zhongzheng Park: It can supply the tourists for photo taking. There are the theme stone sculptures, the windmill, simple physical activity facilities, and small playground path.

## Taichung Folklore Park

TEL: +886-4-2245-1310

Address: No.73, Sec. 2, Lushun Rd., Beitun District, Taichung City

To enable the general public to understand more about the life style of their ancestors so that the younger generations can pay tribute to their past heritage, the Taichung City Council had built the Folklore Park at Lushun Road in Taichung City in July 1984. This is the first Folklore Park built in Taiwan. The whole park which occupies a total area of 1.6 hectare was officially opened in March 1990 and is full of folk heritage of the people living in the coastal Fujian area at the end Qing Dynasty and early post-Qing period.

In the park, the main features are the Folklore Hall, the Folklore and Cultural Heritage Hall and the Folk Arts Hall. They are further enhanced by the Folk Arts Square and the Folklore Square. In addition, in the garden therein are seasonal flowers, artificial scenery and visitors can enjoy the views of the lotus ponds or appreciate the traditional Chinese-style buildings in the pavilions, steps, huts and houses. The basement of the Folklore Hall, an ancient style construction, is for exhibition purpose.

All the exhibits there have their unique historical backgrounds, showing the explorative spirit and the daily life of the early Taiwan inhabitants. In the Folk Arts Hall, during folk festivals, there are cerebration activities, conferences on folklore, tutorial and study meetings as well as performance on local arts and skills take place. This is the spot which provides visitors, apart from enjoying the scenery, an opportunity to recall and reminiscent the works of their past generations. The Folklore Hall is a traditional 4-house combined construction. It is a true representation of the life style in that era. The basement of the hall is the show room. There one can find various farming tools, daily utensils and the costumes of different aboriginal tribesmen.

In the middle room of the Folklore Hall there exhibit the Worship Table, Chairs, Octagon table, Chinese calligraphy and paintings as well as worshipping items. By the two sides are bed rooms and rest rooms. There one can find the bed made of red wood, the make-up table and mahogany chairs. The study room is at the east wing and on its walls hangs a lot of Chinese calligraphy and paintings, indeed making the whole place very scholastic. The west wing is the dwelling place of the younger generations and their families.

Apart from these, in the kitchen there exhibits wooden tables, wooden cabinets, ancient fire stoves, rain clothes, all of which demonstrate the different phases of daily farming life.. Inside the hall there is a tea house whereby on its upper floor visitors can taste the aromatic Chinese tea. With a cup of tea in hand and surrounded by sweet melody, one can easily forget the hustle of modern city life. Apart from the retail shops in the surrounding 8 houses selling traditional folk handicraft and art works, there is also a live shows performing stage. Traditional ancient wedding ceremony, folk drum and flutes music shows are being held in this place from time to time.

The Folk Hall in the Taichung Folk Park was built in the southern Fukien-style of a traditional U-shaped compound. The plaza is used for various cultural and folk performances. Artists- in-residence give displays of dough figure-making, paper-cutting, bamboo weaving, and other traditional skills. On festivals and holidays, the park comes alive with Chinese acrobatic displays, dragon and lion dances, top-spinning, and other activities. Visitors are advised to leave the Sun Yat-sen Freeway at the Daya Chung ching interchange and take Wenxin Road to the park.

## Guishan Island (Turtle Island)

TEL: +886-2-2499-1115

Address: 10 km east of Toucheng Township Coastline, Yilan County

Guishan Island is 10 kilometers east of Toucheng Town and it is the largest island of Yilan County. Guishan Island is also the only active volcano in Taiwan and is the only island with residents in Yilan. Not only is the landmark of Yilan, Guishan Island also an emblem of Yilan spirit. Guishan Island, as known as Guishan Yu, got its name because its shape resembles a turtle. In 1999, the government abolished the martial laws and Yilan government began to petition for making Guishan Island a tourist attraction. In 1999, the government designated Guishan Island to be part the Northeastern Coastal Tourist District. In order to preserve the natural environment, the number of tourists is controlled. With the growing popularity of whale watching, Guishan Island has become the hottest tourist attraction.

Gui Lake, as known as Guiwei Lake, was a freshwater lake. However, the islanders tried to draw seawater to the lake but failed. Thus, currently, the lake is half fresh and half salt water. There is a statue of Goddess of Mercy overlooking Guiwei Lake and the local residents. There is an underwater world in Guishan Island. Despite large amounts of sulfur and acid in the area, it is amazing that crabs still thrive here. The magnificent coastal views are worth visiting.

If you want to visit Guishan Island, you must apply in advance.

## Lala Mountain

TEL: +886-3-391-2761

Address: Tao-116 County Road, Fuxing District, Taoyuan City

The original name of Daguan Mountain was Lala Mountain. Its location is at the border between Fuxing District in Taoyuan and Wulai District in Taipei. The Cultural University professor, Chou Yen Hui, discovered a big chump of giant tree in this reservation region in 1973. Therefore this place became the new redoubt that people gather for leisure time. Also because of its condign abundant forests, it has the biggest area of juniper forest in Taiwan. It formed into the Daguan Mountain Natural Landscape Reservation in 1986.

Some people said that this is the place with the most air in north part of Taiwan. The ambit of the reservation included the mountain region near the north of Balin. The word Daguan in Atayal clan language means beauty. There are lots of abundant forests in the reservation, such as the green Chinese maple, the red maple, the beech, and other trees that the leaves are discolored. Every year to autumn, the green leaves turn red and then turn yellow, this is such a wonderful view in the poem.

Visitors can enjoy these trees with the age in 500 - 3000 years old. The plentiful characteristic of the giant juniper alive likes the magic fairy tale. Among these giant woods, the number five giant juniper is the oldest of all. It has the history of 2800 years. The 18 giant junipers have the trunk peripheral measurement of 188 foot long. The number 18 giant juniper has appearance of white bole, like dying tree, but at the treetop sprout out fresh green leaves. This special view has attracted many visitors to visit.

The worthiness to mention is the howl flat leafed giant juniper of number nine. It is the rare juniper kind at the sea level at about 1500~1600 meter high in Taiwan. It is the kind of evergreen conifer that is worthiness both to use and to watch. The leaves shape like a bud scale, and they grow abundant on the branches. The tree also grows small roundness cones. The cones are tiny and cute. Besides the giant junipers, all kinds of rare birds also color the reservation region.

## Lotus Lake

TEL: +886-7-799-5678

Address: No. 1435, Cuihua Rd., Zuoying Dist., Kaohsiung City

Lotus Lake

This famous scenic area on the northern outskirts of Kaohsiung City is noted for its profusion of temples, with the Confucius Temple at its northern edge and, in the south, the Dragon and Tiger Pagodas and the Spring and Autumn Pavilions. The lake is most beautiful in the late afternoon, when the setting sun is reflected in the water. Nearby are the ruins of the Fengshan County walls and gates, which have been designated a first-grade historic.

Spring and Autumn Pavilions

Two massive pavilions dedicated to Kuan Kung, the God of War, the Spring and Autumn Pavilions were completed in 1951. In front of the pavilions is a statue of Guanyin(Kuanyin), the Goddess of Mercy, riding a dragon. According to legend, Guanyin(Kuanyin) appeared above the clouds riding on a dragon, signifying that believers must erect an image depicting this event between pavilions of summer and autumn: The present-day structures are a result of this vision.

Dragon and Tiger Pagodas

About 700 meters to the south of the Spring and Autumn Pavilions are the Dragon and Tiger Pagodas. The dragon's throat is the entrance and the tiger's mouth is the exit. Entering a dragon's throat and coming out a tiger's mouth symbolizes turning bad luck to good fortune. Inside, paintings depict China's 24 most obedient sons as well as scenes of heaven and hell to inspire people to do good deeds during their lifetime, and to provide threatening examples of retribution for wrongdoing.

## Teresa Teng Memorial Park (Yun Garden)

TEL: +886-2-2498-5900

Address: No. 18, Xishihu, Xihu Village, Jin Mountain (Jinshan) District, New Taipei City

Beautiful Flowers do not blossom all the year round; things are not always as rosy as they sound. These are the verses of the famous Mandarin pop song then Will You Come Back Again that had made its singer a singing legend in every Chinese speaking country. Once you entered Jinbao Mountain, besides being besotted by the surrounding scenery, the memory of Teresa Teng, sometimes intimately called little Teng may overwhelm your emotion because it is here that lies the tomb of this patriotic singer who was the forever darling of the army.

On May 8, 1995 the Chinese speaking community was shocked by the tragic news of the death of their singing idol. Teresa was found dead of asthma while holidaying in Ching Mai, Thailand. At that time she was only 42 years old. Because of her popularity, a lot of people wished to pay tribute to Teresa. To satisfy the wishes of these fans, the Teng family members had chosen the picturesque Jinbao Mountain and built a tomb for Teresa, naming it after her maiden name as Yun Garden so that her fans could come to pay tribute in reminiscence of their idol at will.

A giant keyboard installed in the ground by high-tech design, releasing tunes of melody once being stepped on. In a small flower-bed, scrubs are being cut and arranged in the form of musical notes. A white statue representing Teresa Teng stood in the middle showing her love of music. Automatic Music Box is containing 10 of Teresa's famous pop songs such as "When Will You Come Back Again," "Story of a Small Town" etc. for fans to renew their memory of the sweet voice of Teresa when they pay tribute to their idol.

## Fushoushan Farm

TEL: +886-4-2598-9202

Address: No. 29, Fushou Rd., Lishan Village, Heping District, Taichung City

In 1950, the government appointed retired soldiers to cultivate a new farm in Fushoushan, which can grow apples, peaches, pears and vegetables. The farm is 6 kilometers away from Lishan, 1,800~2,500 meters in altitude. Total area is about 900 hectares. Besides fruits, Fushoushan also grows tea and flowers. The beautiful flowers and the fruitful orchards are the achievements of those retired soldiers.

Lishan Culture Museum on the farm presents documents of the development of Central Highway, Lishan and aboriginal artifacts. The farm consists of vegetable gardens, flower gardens, tea gardens and orchards. Coreopsis can be seen everywhere in the farm. Sung Lu, resort villa of Chiang Kai-Shek, is also located inside the farm. Pine trees surround the villa, which has been open to accommodate civil tourists.

To explore an entirely different part of Mt. Hehuan, it is worthwhile to visit its north section. To get there it is first necessary to go to Lishan, the town lying at the midpoint of the Central Cross-Island Highway on the way to Taichung.

Behind the town is Mt. Fushou, one of the largest fruit and vegetable growing areas in Taiwan. It has a pleasant pastoral air of green fields, small farms, and pine trees. About half way along the road through the area, at the highest point of the plateau, is a lodge once favored by late President Chiang Kai-shek. Further on, the road drops steeply through some attractive aborigine villages and spectacular wooded hills before it comes out on the Mt. Hehuan branch of the Cross-Island Highway just above Wushe. Unfortunately there is no path through to the summit area of Mt. Hehuan from here, but taking the road allows an interesting circuit of the mountains by car or bicycle.

## Lovers' Gorge

TEL: +886-7-688-1001

Address: Rural Route No.132, Maolin District, Kaohsiung City

Lovers' Gorge and Duona Hot Spring are located in Maolin. In 1957, the government renamed the place. The major aboriginal tribe here is Rukai. Lovers' Gorge lies on the south of Zhoukou River and is famous for canyons and rivers. The most famous scene in Lovers' Gorge is Lovers' Waterfall, which has 5 levels. A suspension bridge leads to the first level. Continue climbing for about 10 minutes and you will find the second level. It is very cool and comfortable around the waterfall, which makes it a perfect summer resort.

## Tri-Mountain National Scenic Area - Lishan Visitor Center

TEL: +886-4-2598-1331

Address: No.91-2, Zhongzheng Rd., Lishan Village, Heping District, Taichung City

Located in Heping, Taichung City, Lishan was called Shalamao in the past. It has an altitude of 2000 meters and is a famous summer resort. Lishan is noted for its production of pears, apples and peaches. Surrounded by Fushou Mountain, Wuling Park, and Guguan, Lishan has beautiful mountainous scenery. Lishan is also famous for its flowers, vegetables, and waterfalls.

Lishan Culture Museum is 1 km away from the entrance of Fushou Mountain. The museum presents the history of developing Lishan, Atayal Tribe and the construction of central highway. Lishan Hotel is the first tourist hotel in Lishan. The hotel is of traditional Chinese architectural style. Transportation around Lishan is very convenient. Taroko National Park is on the left, Taichung on the west, Wushe on the south and Yilan on the north.

Located on the upper reaches of the Dajia River, Lishan sits in the middle of the Central Cross-Island Highway. It neighbors the Shei-Pa and Taroko National Parks. Transportation links provide access to Taichung in the west (although this part of the cross-island highway is currently cut off), Yilan in the north, and Hualien in the east. To the south, via Dayuling and Mt. Hehuan, lie Wushe and Nantou. In short, Lishan is a hub connecting the east and west, north and south in central Taiwan. Within the area are spectacular views of the miracles of nature: highlands, steep cliffs, deep canyons, rivers, and forests. This scenic area also offers hot springs, alpine fruits and vegetables, other local products, and Atayal aborigine culture waiting to be discovered.

## Qingjing Farm

TEL: +886-49-280-2774

Address: No. 170, Renhe Rd., Datong Village, Ren-ai Township, Nantou County

Qingjing Farm was established on February 20th, 1961. The farm is for agricultural development, it located in Nantou County, the place of Central Cross-Island Highway's center horizontal road first line #14 near the north end place of 08 kilometer. It is the place you will pass when you are heading to Hohuan Mountain, the center horizontal highroad's organized body branch.

Nowadays the Qingjing Farm follow the herbage rebirth of the seasonal changes in March, the garden turns green, the procreation of the cows and sheep. You will feel the luxuriant of the peach blossom, the pear bloom, and the apple bloom during the spring season in Qingjing Farm. April is the month for picking the spring tea. The digitalis bloomy with purple bright-red flowers is in the bucolic area. May is the season for the chrysanthemum in the bucolic area and the rhododendron bloom in the Hehuan Mountain.

Besides the different views in spring and summer, the scenery during autumn and winter has other kinds of view in Qingjing Farm. You can watch maple in October in Qingjing Farm. The sounds of the stepping on the fallen maples are romantic. Another part, the local agrarian afford different kinds of peach in different seasons, such as the 20-century pear, the California plum, the kiwi, and the high-temperature greenstuffs. The high-temperature greenstuffs mean the vegetable that grew in the higher sea level area with the adaptable temperature between 13~24 degrees Celsius and the bearable cold season greenstuffs for long distance, such as green cabbage, sweet chili, and the peas in local.

Chingjing High-altitude Scenic Trail

The 1.2km-long Chingjing High-altitude Scenic Trail is located at 1,700-2,000 meters above the sea level. It is the longest and highest-altitude trail in Taiwan. Along the path are scenic platforms which provide visitors with birds-eye views of the Central Mountain Ridge, Qilai Mountain and more. Taking a stroll among the crown layer of the trees, visitors can also expect to look at the beautiful Qingjing area panoramically. The trail's accessible designs allow baby trolleys and wheelchairs to move freely, making it suitable for family visitors.

## Shei-Pa National Park - Wuling Visitor Center

TEL: +886-4-2590-1350

Address: No.4, Wuling Rd., Heping Dist., Taichung City

Shei-Pa National Park was established in 1992, located at the border of Hsinchu, Miaoli and Taichung. It faces Guyan Mountain and Leshan in the north, Dajia River in the east, Beikeng Mountain and Xiaoxueshan in the west and Yuluowei Mountain and Dajia River in the south. Total area of the park is 76,850 hectares. Shei-Pa National Park is the fifth national park of Taiwan.

The mountainous scenery is spectacular as there are several mountains in the park. The mountains are of different heights and the drop height reaches 3000 meters. The highest mountain is the Xueshan, 3,886 meters in height and it is the second highest mountain in Taiwan. The Xueshan, Yushan, Nanhuda Mountain, Xiuguluan Mountain and Beidawu Mountain are the five highest mountains in Taiwan. Dabajian Mountain is 3,492 meters in height. Dabajian Mountain, Zhongyangjian Mountain and Dafenjian Mountain are called the three Peak Mountains in Taiwan.

Shei-Pa National Park is noted for its rough geography and natural scenery. Mountains in the park are origins of major rivers in northern and central Taiwan. Erosion by the rivers has formed special scenes in the park. As for climate, the park has both sub-frigid and temperate climates and thus breeds various plants and animals. Wildlife here includes salmon, black bears, etc.

## Huisun Forest Area

TEL: +886-49-294-2001

Address: No.1, Shanlin Lane, Xinsheng Village, Ren-ai Township, Nantou County

Huisun Forest was called Nenggao Forest. It is the largest of the four forests of National Chung Hsing University. "Huisun" is the name of the late university president Tang Hui Sun. In memory of president Tang, the university renamed the forest Huisun. In addition to the dense forest, there are canyons and waterfalls in the forest. The mountain has an altitude of 450~2420 and thus the flora varies in different places. You can find subtropical and temperate plants in this mountain.

## Cihu

TEL: +886-3-388-4437

Address: No.1097, Sec. 1, Fuxing Rd., Daxi District, Taoyuan City

Cihu Presidential Burial Place

Cihu was known in earlier times as Biwei, and today it also has the nickname of Dongkou or "Tunnel Mouth," due to its location at the exit of the Baiji Tunnel. Cihu also reminded Chiang Kai-shek of his hometown in mainland China. The Cihu Villa was built here in 1959 for Chiang's use, and in 1962 the former ROC president had this area renamed as Cihu, or "Loving Mother Lake," in memory of his mother Wang Tsai-yu.

After Chiang's death in 1975, Cihu Villa was renamed as the Cihu Presidential Burial Place. The brick mausoleum faces south to the water is built in the style of a southern Fujianese four-sided compound, with a tile roof and circular entryways on the left and right side of the front leading to the ancillary courtyards. There is even an air-raid shelter in the hillside behind the building.

Apart from the mausoleum, the biggest visitor attraction here is the changing of the honor guard ceremony. On weekends and holidays the cameras are flashing almost non-stop as for this popular ceremony.

Cihu Visitor Center

The Cihu Visitor Center is located in a single-story brick building on the side of the parking lot. The displays inside include numerous photographs of Chiang Kai-shek, as well as original and reproduction calligraphy works by the former president. The visitor center store sells a wide selection of souvenir items featuring President and Madame Chiang. Soft figurines of the presidential couple as well as Madame Chiang's beloved honey plum cake are among the most popular items at the store.

Baiji Trail

Situated behind Cihu, Baiji Trail was originally part of the Cihu military area but was opened to the public in 1998. The trail is covered by a thick canopy of trees with plenty of scenic views and rich butterfly ecology to enjoy along the way. The path slopes gently and the entire trail can easily be walked in about an hour, making it a good choice for the whole family. From the highest point on the trail one can also enjoy a panoramic view of Da River (Daxi).

The forest here is composed mainly of secondary forest, old-growth, and bamboo forests. Commonly sighted birds in this area include the mountain Scops-owl, Chinese bamboo-partridge, yellow-throated minivet, crested serpent eagle, Formosan blue magpie, and various members of the Paridae and Turdidae families. Winter is the best time for bird watching. The trail also branches along the way, with routes leading to Xizhou Park, Xishi Pavilion, and the Dajiugong Trail, which offers some of the most picturesque views of Da River (Daxi).

Houci Lake

Discovering Houci Lake

Shaped like a crescent moon, Houci Lake is fed by small streams on Baishi Mountain (Baishishan). Originally known as Longguomaipi, it currently serves as an irrigation pool of the Taoyuan Irrigation Association, with a water area of 41,076 hectares, and water volume of 177,500cubic meters or enough to irrigate an area of 117,29 hectares, mainly in the Da River (Daxi) and Sanceng areas.

In the 1950s, Chiang Kai-shek discovered Cihu when his car was forced to stop at the mouth of the Baiji Tunnel and he had to make a detour by sedan chair. The scenery reminded him of his hometown of Xikou Township in Fenghua County, Zhejiang Province. In 1955, The Banqiao family headed by Lin Pen-yuan provided 19 hectares of land in Cihu for the construction of a villa. The "Dongkou Villa," as it was then known, was completed on June 13, 1959, and renamed as the "Cihu Villa" in October 1962.

As part of an evacuation plan for the Office of the President in 1962, Chiang Kai-shek instructed the government to purchase land in Cihu for the construction of an air-raid shelter and wartime command center. Quarters were also constructed here for the secretary-general, chief aid-de-camp, and deputy secretary-general to the president. After Chiang's death on April 5, 1975, this site was renamed as the Cihu Presidential Burial Place. The Cihu Presidential Burial Place Administration was also built here to handle reception and management affairs. The five office buildings at Houci Lake were also transferred to the administration, which came under the management of the Taoyuan City government in November 2007 after the Houci Lake area lost its restricted military status. Since then, the county government has been renovating facilities on the site and making other arrangements for opening the area to the public.

As a restricted area, Houci Lake was long protected from outside interference. This isolation has helped to keep the forest and natural ecology in their pristine state, making this an ideal escape for public recreation.

Chiang Kai Shek Memorial Sculpture Park in Cihu

Chiang Kai Shek Memorial Sculpture Park is the only memorial park in the world dedicated to statues of a single person. The park was opened in Cihu by the Da River (Daxi) Township Government in 1997. On February 29, 2000, a ceremony was held for the installment of the park's first bronze statue of Chiang Kai-shek (donated by Kaohsiung County). The park was closed for renovation by the Taoyuan City and Da River (Daxi)Township governments and reopened to the public on April 5, 2008.

A total 152 statues of the former president, including both full statues and busts and even equestrian works, can be found at the park today, each with its unique artistic value. Most were donated by schools and government agencies, including the biggest one, which was donated by Kaohsiung City. The sculptures are linked by a network of paths throughout the park. A landscaped courtyard, small bridge and running stream further add to the park's elegant charm.

## Taipei Botanical Garden

TEL: +886-2-2303-9978

Address: No.53, Nanhai Rd., Zhongzheng District, Taipei City

The Botanical Garden was established in 1921. It has been part of the memory of Taipei citizens. Many people come here to appreciate the lotus in summer and falling leaves in winter. The Botanical Garden was established on January 22, 1921. In 1930, there were 1129 species in the garden, serving greatly to academic research and natural science. However, the garden was deserted during World War II. After the war, the garden was rearranged and new plants were introduced. Currently, the garden is well maintained and has over 100 species of plants.

There are 17 districts in the garden, exhibiting various plants. The 9 ponds are also designed to grow different plants. As green land is far and scarce in urban area, the garden has become a popular leisure space for Taipei citizens. The garden is next to National History Museum, Science Museum and Art Museum.

## Yangmingshan National Park

TEL: +886-2-2861-3601

Address: No.1-20, Zhuzihu Rd., Beitou District, Taipei City (Yangmingshan)

Yangmingshan National Park is located in the north of Beitou. Yangmingshan was called Caoshan (Grass Mountain) during Japanese occupation of Taiwan, because it was covered with grass and seldom visited. After World War II, the KMT government renamed the mountain Yangmingshan and built a park here. Yangmingshan National Park is the only park in Taiwan that has volcanic geography and hot springs. It is next to Shamao Mountain and Qixing Mountain with

Datun Mountain on the right and Guanyin Mountain in front. The magnificent mountainous scenery and comfortable weather have made Yangmingshan National Park a perfect summer resort. Total area of the park is 125 hectares, designed in traditional Chinese style. The natural beauty of the part has won it the reputation as urban forest and the Taipei garden.

The park is characterized by a large clock made of flowers with a diameter of 22 feet. Water runs around the flower clock and music is played every hour. The clock is the characteristic of Yangming Park. Opposite the clock is a statue of late president Chiang Kai-Shek; on both sides of the statue are the cypresses planted by president Chiang himself. The Xinhai Guangfu Building was completed in 1971, right in the center of the park. In addition, there is a statue of Wang Yang Ming, the famous Chinese scholar in the 17th century.

## Yangming House

TEL: +886-2-2861-1444

Address: No.12, Zhongxing Rd., Beitou District, Taipei City

Yangming House was a hot-spring villa during Japanese occupation of Taiwan. Late president Chiang Kai-Shek loved the beautiful scenery here and built Zhongxing Hotel to accommodate foreign guests and to spend summer; the hotel was later reconstructed as Yangming House. As Yangming Villa and Zhongshan Building were constructed nearby, important government officials often gathered here, making Yangming Mountain (Yangmingshan) the decision center for the government. After the death of Chiang in 1975, historical KMT documents were moved from Li Yuan in Caotun, Nantou to Yangming Mountain (Yangmingshan) for exhibition in memory of Dr. Sun Yat-Sen and late president Chiang Kai-Shek. As late president Chiang had respected and admired Mr. Wang Yang Ming, the building was named Yang Ming In 1996; KMT donated the Academy to the Ministry of Interior, providing a recreational and educational space for Taipei citizens.

Yangming House is a 2-story, traditional Chinese building. The theater, VIP rooms, offices, and restaurant are on the first floor. The second floor was used by Mr. and Mrs. Chiang and their paintings and some personal belongings can still be found here. On the wall of Chiang bedroom, there is a wedding photo taken in Shanghai on December 1, 1927. In addition, there are other photos of the couple visiting different places.

## Caoling

TEL: +886-5-552-3181

Address: County Hwy 149A, Gukeng Township, Yunlin County

The 10 scenic spots of Caoling famous all over Taiwan are Penglai Falls, Broken Hill, Rocky Cliff, Water Shaded Cave, Frog Rock, Marvelous Cave, Dead Man Valley, Tongxin Fall, Beaded Pond, Brook Paradise. All the grand rocks, marvelous stone, falls or streams are not artificially carved or decorated but made by God and formed splendid natural landscape.

After 921 Earthquake, many of the natural landscape were changed. Looking up from the sand bars of Caoling Lake, the natural ecology is presenting with different scene and made itself a demonstrating place for geology and ecology education.

Traditional crafts Gukeng is famous with bamboo and rock, and it seems that most of the residents in Gukeng can make bamboo arts and stone sculpture. Examples are bamboo cylinder, bamboo rack, bamboo serial bead, stone mortar, stone table, stone stool, and stone wall. They all display the skillful crafts of tradition of Caoling.

## Caoling Historic Trail

TEL: +886-2-2499-1115

Address: Gongliao Dist., New Taipei City

The Caoling Historic Trail cuts across Sandiaojiao, starting at Yuanwangkeng, just inland from Fulung, and ending at Dali on the coast. It is the only remaining section (rebuilt by the Tourism Bureau) of the old Qing dynasty trail that was constructed 130 years ago to provide the only land link down the Northeast Coast from Tamsui to Yilan. The present trail is approximately 10 kilometers long and offers a pleasant hike of two to three hours.

Two large boulders along the trail bear Qing dynasty inscriptions and are listed as third-class historic sites. One of the inscriptions has four Chinese characters meaning "Bravely Suppress the Wild Mists" and the other bears the single character "Tiger" (the tiger is believed to control the winds). Both were ordered by the regional commander of imperial forces in Taiwan, and were meant to ward off the baleful influences of nature in this once-remote area.

To hike the Caoling Historic Trail, you can take the train from the Fulong or Gongliao station, and walk (about 40 minutes) from there to the head of the trail in Yuanwangkeng. From the other end of the trail, you can take the return train from the Dali station. If you are driving, you can consider leaving your car at Tiangong Temple in Dali and hiking the trail both ways.

## Matzu National Scenic Area

TEL: +886-836-25631

Address: No.95-1, Ren-ai Village, Nangan Township, Lienchiang County

Matzu is named after the Goddess of Sea, who carried the body of her drowned fisherman father back to shore. The casket of the Goddess is still preserved in a local temple. Matzu consists of more than 10 islets with a total area of 28.8 square km. Due to its sensitive position, Matzu used to be a military fortress like Kinmen. With the cross-strait relations growing friendlier, Matzu is now developing its tourism. In 1999, Matzu was designated as a national tourist district and began attracting tourists.

Scenery in Matzu differs with the four seasons. The spring is the blossom season and the summer is perfect for sea watching. The autumn is particularly comfortable and the winter is suitable for fishing. Islets in the vicinity often attract photographers and painters. Many tourists come here to appreciate the starry skies at night and to enjoy local food.

Matzu National Scenic Area Administration

No.95-1, Ren-ai Village, Nangan Township, Lienchiang County

Tel: +886-836-25630

Dongyin Visitor Center

No.160-1, Lehua Village, Dongyin Township, Lienchiang County

Tel: +886-836-77266

Beigan Visitor Center

No.43, Banli Village, Beigan Township, Lienchiang County

Tel: +886-836-56531

Juguang Visitor Center

No.1, Neighborhood 1, Fuzheng Village, Juguang Township, Lienchiang County

Tel: +886-836-89388

## Chenggong Fishing Harbor

TEL: +886-89-841-520

Address: Chenggong Fishing Harbor, Chenggong Township, Taitung County

With a population of 20,000 the town of Chenggong is the largest community between Hualien and Taitung cities and is also the location of the largest fish market in this area. Every day between three and four o' clock in the afternoon, to Chenggong harbor after spending the previous day at sea. The day's catch in unloaded, after which and auction takes place. The hustle and bustle, color and noise generated by the fishermen and their buyers make an exciting and memorable sight and one which the visitor should make every effort to experience.

The town abounds with seafood restaurants selling the freshest fish you are likely to try anywhere and there is ample hotel accommodation available for those who wish to spend more time exploring the town and the surrounding area.

## Shiba Luohan Mountain (Luohanshan)

TEL: +886-7-688-1001

Address: At Prov. Hwy No. 27A, Liugui Dist., Kaohsiung City

Shiba Luohan Mountain (Luohanshan) (Eighteen Arhats Mountain) lies next to Laonong River, Kaohsiung. Shiba Luohan Mountain

(Luohanshan) consists of more than 40 mountains. Years of erosion have resulted in its rough geography. Legend says that the eighteen arhats will safeguard local people and their wealth, but the people will be punished if they spend the money elsewhere.

Shiba Luohan Mountain (Luohanshan )has very special geography and geology. The best positions to appreciate the mountains are the outlook point on Linpan track and the other one next to the 185 Highway. With Laonong River running by, the mountains present spectacular scenery. There are macaques in the mountains as well.

## Flying Cow Ranch

TEL： +886-37-782-999

Address： No. 166, Nanhe Village, Tongxiao Township, Miaoli County

The ample Bao'an woodlands inner Hulin Pan was locate in Nanhe neighborhood in Tongxiao with 110 hectares in 1980. Afterward the ample Bao'an woodlands were reclaimed to be Taiwan Youth Dairy Village which is now the predecessor of Flying Cow Range. In this topography, against Fire Hill, you can overlook Taiwan Strait from the ascent of the hill. And there is a historical denotation of Salt Ku path behind the mountain; this Salt Ku path was established by cobbles. In 1985, Taiwan Youth Dairy Village has turned to be the leisure range type. Howbeit the process of turning types the ideals of the design was combining the advantage of the Japanese hacienda and the American view designing company.

With ten years of layout time makes the vision today. The primary natural biome resources in the range are milk cows and butterflies. The sign of the flying Cow were designed according to these. Also with the colors of the sky, veldt, and the milk layout the peculiar sign of Flying Cow Range. In June the year of 1995 year, the range become dairy plant demonstrates area, and is opening to the outside world. Under the guidance of the council of agriculture, Flying Cow Range is developing to become Leisure range with the community type of hacienda providing the commonwealth a place with the natural country wild.

Because of raising cattle, Flying Cow Range has a great amount of manure resources. The range uses these excretions of the cattle to amend the soil, making it organic change for planting organic greenstuffs. In three-hectare organic garden area with the condition of no water and air pollutions, the range planting general family uses of greenstuffs, supplying the uses of the restaurant in the range. And the range is heading toward to develop organic farming. The professional management on raising cattle presents multiple sight view with educational and knowledgeable.

The finished layouts in the range are: the butterfly garden, veldt activity area, organic plantation area, children area, and the hacienda area; And the wedding piazza, playing park, restaurant, camping area, musical piazza, blockhouse and climber footway are planning now. In here, you can have the experience of dairy lives and understand the biome of the bovine. The demonstration of the cow house is also shown here, you can see the daily life of the milk cow and experience the cow galactic production line.

## Shifen Scenic Area

TEL: +886-2-2495-8409

Address: Pingxi Township, New Taipei City

Shifen Special Scenic Area is located in Shifenliao between Shiding, Ruifang and Shuangxi in northeastern Taiwan. Administratively part of Pingxi District, New Taipei City, the terrain here has been carved by a tributary of the Keelung River, northern Taiwan's largest and longest river, into a ravine with a dissected topography. The faults and rock formations have given birth to numerous waterfalls along the river extending north from Houtong to Sandiaoling and onwards to Shifenliao and Pingxi. Among the biggest and best known of these falls, and a popular visitor attraction, is Shifen Waterfall.

Shifen Waterfall

Shifen Waterfall lies between Dahua Station and Shifen Station on the Pingxi Railway Line in Pingxi District, New Taipei City. Torrents of water thunder down this curtain-type fall like a white satin sheet. As the water plunges into the large, deep pool beneath, it raises mists that often enshroud the falls. On sunny days, the mists paint dazzling rainbows in the blue skies: a sight that has earned the waterfall pool the nickname of "Rainbow Pond." Because its bedrock slopes in the opposite direction of the water flow, Shifen Waterfall is a cascade-type waterfall similar to North America's Niagara Falls, earning it the nickname of "Taiwan's Niagara Falls."

Shifen Station

The Pingxi Branch Rail Line extends 12.9 kilometers through Keelung River Valley from Sandiaoling to Jingtong stations. The line was built in 1918 to transport coal; and in 1992 it was repurposed as a tourism route. Shifen is one of the stops along the line. The station is located in a scenic area that greets visitors with beautiful waterfalls and streams. Shifenliao is home to a broad river terrace and is also traversed by the Pingxi Line. Homes hug closely to the tracks, adding to a nostalgic ambiance that has made the area a popular site for filming ads. Jing'an Suspension Bridge, a 128-meter-long span connecting the villages of Shifen and Nanshan, is one of only a few well-preserved pedestrian suspension bridges in Taiwan. The romantic beauty of the landscape has made this area a popular visitor attraction.

Shifen Visitor Center

The Shifen Visitor Center is located in the Ruifang Special Scenic Area. The scenic area covers an area of 56.89 hectares starting from the upper reaches of the Keelung River and embracing Shifen, Xinliao and Nanshan. This scenic paradise has been generously endowed with beautiful mountains, mighty waterfalls, and the intriguing river potholes in Dahua. The visitor center can be reached by a 15-minute walk from Shifen Station along the Old Street. The center presents free scheduled video showings daily; and group showings can be arranged by phone reservation. The center also offers classes on making sky lantern.

## Jinshan (Jin Mountain)

TEL: +886-2-2498-8980

Address: Jinshan District, New Taipei City

Jinshan (Jin Mountain) hot springs, located in Jinshan (Jin Mountain) and Wanli Townships of Taipei County, produce carbonic acid water at temperatures of 45 to 86 degrees Celsius.

These hot springs arise in the Datun geothermal zone, like those of Yangmingshan (Yangming Mountain), and are the northernmost hot springs in Taiwan. While other hot-spring areas are lucky to have two types of water, Jinshan (Jin Mountain) provides four: oceanic sandy, sulfuric, carbonic acid, and iron. Hot-spring hotels have sprung up in the Jinshan (Jin Mountain) area in rapid succession in recent years, making it haven for vacationers who enjoy the variety of water types available.

## Shanhou Folk Cultural Village

TEL: +886-82-313100

Address: Shanhou, Jinsha Township, Kinmen County

Shanhou Folk Cultural Village is located in Shanhou Village. The village was built in Ching Kuang Hsu year 26 (1900). With an area of 1230 pings, the village has eighteen buildings and houses of traditional Fujian style. The buildings were built by the Chinese Japanese Wang Kuo Chen and Wang Ching Hsiang for their relatives and materials were shipped from Changzhou, Chuanzhou and Jiangxi Province. It took 20 years to finish the construction. The eighteen buildings and houses were damaged after years of wind erosion. The Kinmen government redecorated the buildings and claimed it a cultural village.

The buildings here are carefully-designed and well-decorated in traditional Chinese style, presenting the characteristics of Chinese architecture. The structure, paintings and sculptures are refined. In 1979, the Kinmen government reconstructed the ancient buildings and set up museums and exhibition rooms, presenting the best characteristics of Kinmen.

## Kinmen National Park

TEL: +886-82-313100

Address: No. 460, Sec. 2, Boyu Rd., Jinning Township, Kinmen County

Kinmen National Park was established in 1995, 3,780 hectares in area. It is the sixth national park of Taiwan. The island of Kinmen was constantly harassed by Japanese pirates in the 16th century; thus, the government equipped the island with defense works and arms. During the war between KMT and the Chinese communists, there were several memorable battles in Kinmen. In addition, there are traditional southern Fujian buildings and shell mounds in Kinmen. The park is to preserve history and culture and to remember previous wars.

"Kinmen also has unique cultural attractions that belie its small size and population of only 50,000.

The government has taken steps to preserve the island's cultural sites and practices so that visitors today can observe its vibrant, living culture. Residences in Kinmen are mostly of the three-winged Fuchien-style architecture. The island's history can be traced also through the colorful traditional residences that are scattered throughout the landscape. While the island's people live simple lives closely linked to the sea, their religious convictions are strong. Folk spirits are venerated along with such Buddhist and Taoist deities as Chenghuang (the city God), Mazu (Goddess of the sea), and Guanyin (Goddess of

Mercy). A special cultural/religious feature of Kinmen is the Wind Lion, a local deity originating in the worship of the forces of nature.

The massive construction of ships by the late-Ming patriot Cheng-kung (Koxinga), who fought against the Manchu court of the succeeding Qing Dynasty, denuded the previously fertile soil of Kinmen of trees and transformed it into wasteland. With the very soil and rocks eroding away, the people were losing their means of livelihood; in desperation they turned for help to the Wind Lion, who, they believed could control the winds. They still have faith in this spirit, whose carved image can be seen at strategic locations all over Kinmen. The images are full of local flavor and manifest a combination of the god's animistic and anthropomorphic characteristics.

## Kenting (Kending) Rangeland

TEL: +886-8-886-1358

Address: No.1, Muchang Rd., Kenting Village, Hengchun Township, Pingtung County

Kenting (Kending) Rangeland covers an area of 1,149 hectares of pasture and research facilities. It is managed by the Taiwan Livestock Research Institute's Hengchun Station. The entrance to the farm is through the research facility, which is located on the outskirts of the town of Kenting (Kending), at the 33-kilometer mark along the Pingtung-Eluanbi Highway.

The farm was first established in 1904 during the period of the Japanese occupation. Since the land in the area is too dry and too windy for crop farming, it was earmarked for pasture. In the wide expanse of grassland, cattle graze freely under the imposing presence of Mt. Dajian Rock . The research station is involved in the testing and promotion of meat products, and also in disease prevention among livestock. Visitors to the station can sample freshly pasteurized cow's and goat's milk at the visitors center and also wander around the expansive and idyllic pasture where cattle graze.

## The Lin Family Mansion and Garden

TEL: +886-2-2965-3061~3

Address: No.9, Ximen St., Banqiao District, New Taipei City

The best garden in northern Taiwan, Lin Family Gardens, used to be called "Lin Ben Yuan's Garden" or "Banqiao Resort." Lin Ben Yuan is not a person's name. It represents the meaning of "remembering one's origin" when 2nd generation ancestor, Lin Pingho distributed property among his five sons. Among the five sons, only the 2nd and the 5th sons are Lin Pingho's blood descendents. Thus, the words of "Ben" and "Yuan" are used for commemoration.

The Garden was built during 1888 to 1893 and it is the only classic garden as historical site. It is also the well-kept model building representing gardens and residences of Qing Dynasty. Its garden scenes are inspired by Chinese traditional gardens as well as the style of south of Yangtze. It is admired as "the best garden in Taipei." Part of the construction materials and technicians came from Changzhou of China.

The scale of construction was huge. Other than the garden and the architecture, a "three-section mansion" for 150 years old has been restored and presented to the public. The outer walls are covered with brick ornaments. There is delicate carving on the door, within the halls and on the poles supporting roof covers above front porch. There are unique windows of different styles. They are rare items in Taiwan and they fully reflect the beauty of Chinese traditional architecture.

## Shin Kong Chao Feng Ranch & Resort

TEL: +886-3-877-2666

Address: No.20, Yongfu St., Fenglin Township, Hualien County

Located in the Fenglin Township, Hualien County, Shin Kong Chao Feng Ranch & Resort covers an area of 726 hectares. It makes use of the alluvial deposits of Shoufeng Stream to grow such crops as guavas, avocados, star fruit, lemons, oranges, and peaches all the four seasons of the year. Another part of the farm is devoted to educational plantings of medicinal herbs and flower beds. In the dairy area and petting zoo area, visitors can get close to cows and other animals.

Other facilities include a landscaping area, camping and barbecue area, a creek stocked with loaches to catch, and a visitor center.

## Fushan Botanical Garden

TEL: +886-3-922-8900

Address: Fushan No. 1, Shuangpi Rd., Yuanshan Township, Yilan County

This 410-hectare branch of the Taiwan Forestry Research Institute is the largest botanical park in Taiwan. It is located on the boundary between Yilan County's Yuanshan Township and New Taipei City's Wulai District. The area includes 20 kilometers of self-guided trails, with interpretive plaques for visitors to use. The park was established to preserve the characteristic forest ecology of northern Taiwan; most of its plant cover consists of natural temperate-zone broadleaf forests, and there is a complex mix of local vegetation as well as numerous species of wildlife in the area. Prior application is required to visit the park, and the number of visitors is currently limited to approximately 300 per day. The purpose of this is to protect the natural ecology and allow the environment to continue relatively undisturbed.

## Xitou Nature Education Area

TEL: +886-49-261-2111

Address: No.9, Senlin Lane, Lugu Township, Nantou County

Xitou is located in the Phoenix hill of Lugu village, and is embraced by mountains from three sides. Its name is derived from the Chinese meaning: the origin of the river (Beishi River). Xitou has plenty of rains, and is cool and moist all the year round. Therefore, it is one of the most famous resort spots in summer and the most romantic place for new couples to spend their honeymoons. Xitou is part of the experimental forest belonging to the National Taiwan University, and here grows cedars, Chamaecyparis obtuse, red spruces, Phyllostachys edulis, and many other different kinds of trees.

Except for a small well-preserved natural broad-leaves forest, most parts of this area have been developed and cultivated purposely. Generally speaking, the feature of the forest here is beautiful and tidy. Here you can visit the unique pure ginkgo forest, the rare plant of redwood, the divine tree 46 meter high and 16 meter broad and with an age approaching 3,000, Youth's Activity Center, birds observing footpath, hotels, restaurants, camping area and so on.

The University Pond, one of the representative sightseeing spots in Xitou, with an area of 0.5 chings and a depth of 10 meters, has limpid water and is a good place for taking pictures. There are over 70 varies of birds available in Xitou, which makes this place a good one for birds observing. River Blacks, White-ears Thrush, Redhead Warblers, Shao-Yen Thrush are representatives of low and middle elevation in Taiwan.

Buildings in Xitou are made of wood and have a smell of natural harmony.

## Wulu Gorge and Wulu Hot Springs

TEL: +886-89-551-637

Address: Wulu, Haiduan Township, Taitung County

Wulu Gorge is located between the South Cross-Island Highway and Lidao, and is a large S-shaped gorge cut by the Wulu River. It is about 4 kilometers in length. Due to the fact that the Guan Mountain (Guanshan) Mountain peak in the Central Mountain Range forms broken ridges at this point, and also due to the long-term erosion caused by the flow of the high mountain rivers, the Wulu Gorge is made up of steep precipices, resulting in a very majestic landscape.

In Wulu Gorge, the Tianlong Suspension Bridge crosses over the Wulu Stream. It is about 110 meters long and less than 1.5 meters wide. It connects the precipices on each side of the gorge. Looking down at the landscape from the suspension bridge, one can see the surging, rushing waters of the Wulu River, 80 meters below.

In addition to the gorge with its suspension bridge, another unique natural resource in this area is the Wulu Hot Springs. The spring water of the Wulu Hot Springs is of a low alkaline, carbonate, hydrogen-sodium quality. The water contains fluoride, and is crystal clear, colorless, and odorless, with a heat ranging from 70°C to 80°C. The most unique feature of the Wulu Hot Springs is that the water does not emit from underground, but gushes out from the narrow crevices in the mountain cliffs located in the Wulu Gorge.

## Lushui Trail

TEL: +886-3-862-1100~6

Address: Lushui Trail, Xiulin Township, Hualien County

Lushui Trail was part of the Old Cross-Hehuan Mountain Road. The width of the path is about 2 meters which is about the same as during the Japanese Era. (1895-1945) The trail has a gentle slope and is easy to walk. It is a sight-seeing path that is suitable for all ages. There is a 30 meter tunnel along the trail, so please bring a flash light.

Dense forest, cliff terrain, plants growing on the rock and historical monuments are the characteristics of the Lushui Trail. You can view the historical monuments of Tailuge (Taroko) National Park and observe the special botanical ecosystem. Walking on this historic path you follow in the footprints of earlier people.

Standing on the cliff, you overlook the Liwu River valley and the Lushui terrace. There are plants growing on the rocks that symbolize vitality. Among those plants, the Tailuge (Taroko) oak is a rare species in Taiwan.

## Presidential Office Building

TEL: +886-2-2311-3731

Address: No.122, Sec. 1, Chongqing S. Rd., Zhongzheng District, Taipei City

The Presidential Office Building is located on Chongqing S. Road and facing Ketagalan Boulevard. On the back it is Bo'ai Road, on the left it is Baoqing Road, and on the right it is Guiyang Street. The Presidential Building is close to Taipei Main Station and Ximending. The building was built during Japanese colonization period. It was the governor's mansion at that time. During the ending period of World War II, the building was seriously damaged due to bombing. After Taiwan was reclaimed by R.O.C., the building was re-constructed in 1946. The building was re-named as "Jieshou Building" in celebration of the 60th birthday of former president Mr. Chiang Kai-shek. The building has been used as the presidential mansion after the central government of R.O.C. was re-instated in Taiwan.

The main body of the Presidential Office Building is a five-floor structure and the central tower is eleven-floor high. The area is 6,930 square meters. The outer portion is covered with steel concrete. Gravel is used as decoration horizontally. A sense of grandeur and vigorousness is presented via the red-white composition. The Presidential Building was announced by the President as "national historical site" in 1998 and was open for public tour since then. The general public will be able to see in person the location where the president works. The distance between the President and his people will be shortened.

After touring the Presidential Office Building, one can further visit the following interesting nearby sites: Taiwan Bank, NTU Hospital, Taipei Guest House and February 28 Peace Park.

## Suao-Hualien Highway

TEL: +886-3-862-1100~6

Address: Suao-Hualien Highway, Xiulin Township, Hualien County

In addition to the Central Cross-Island Highway, another road that offers considerable attractions for the tourist is the old Suao-Hualien Highway. First opened to traffic in 1932, this 118-kilometer-long road was the first government-built road in the area, but its origins go back to 1874, when a road was first cut between Su-ao and Hualien under order of the imperial Chinese government.

North along the road from Hualien is the Chongde Control. In the early stages of its development, the road could carry traffic in only one direction at a time, and vehicles had to wait at the control station for convoys going the opposite direction to pass. It rapidly developed into a spot where travelers would stop to enjoy the scenery, have a snack, and buy souvenirs.

At the northern mouth of Chongde Tunnel, 182.5 kilometers along the Suao-Hualien Highway, is the Shiahai Trail. This is a perfect spot to view the Pacific Ocean. A walk of 10 minutes down the trail brings visitors to a shingle beach featuring limestone formations and a variety of rock-growing plants.

The 20-kilometer stretch of highway between Chongde and Heping is the most tortuous and spectacular section of the Suao-Hualien Highway. Cliffs of gneiss and marble from sheer drops of more than a thousand meters, and the road winds its way precariously between the cliffs on one side and the ocean on the other. After this stretch, the road runs through to Heping and Guanyin, funnily reaching Nan-ao and Dong-ao. In the vicinity of Nan-ao, the Wushr Promontory protrudes majestically into the Pacific Ocean, dividing the Suao-Hualien coastline into the Nan-ao and Dong-ao bays. Dung-ao is a major producer of lilies; moreover, the Japan Current brings this coastal area a rich annual harvest of fish.

## Baiyang Trail

TEL: +886-3-869-1162

Address: Baiyang Trail, Xiulin Township, Hualien County

The entrance of the Baiyang Trail is located about 300 meters from Tianxiang on the Central Cross-Island Highway. Near Wen Mountain (Wenshan), hikers will come upon the tunnel that is the beginning of the Baiyang Trail. Along the trail there are six tunnels of different lengths that provide a certain frisson as groups feel their way through the semi-darkness. The longer tunnels have solar-powered lights.

This trail is particularly popular with locals, for it has an atmosphere of mystery and romance. A turn in the trail at the end of the third tunnel offers an excellent view of Tacijili River, and at the end of the sixth tunnel the truly spectacular goal of the trail, Baiyang Waterfall, comes into view. The water roars as it plunges into the deep pool that it has worn in the rock. The Baiyang Suspension Bridge offers spectacular views of the waterfall and the river valley. A seventh tunnel leads to a cave behind the falls; because of the danger of falling rocks, this area is closed to the public. Although this trail is not physically challenging, additional clothing may be necessary to ward off chilly air in the vicinity of the Baiyang Waterfall and back takes approximately 1.5 hours.

## Tamsui

TEL: +886-2-2622-1020

Address: Tamsui District, New Taipei City

Tamsui used to be called Huwei. It is a derivation from the ancient tongue "Hoba." It means the river outlet. Tamsui is located in northwest of Taipei basin. Tamsui is surrounded by mountains and rivers and the scenery is beautiful. Hongmao Castle is a historical site in Tamsui with historical meaning. It was built by the Spaniards in 1626 and restored by the Dutch. The castle was called Anthony Castle. Because Taiwan people called the Dutch people Hongmao (people with red hair), the castle thus was called Hongmao Castle. It was also called Huwei Castle.

The castle was once taken by the English and it was returned to our country in 1980. The castle is more than 300 years old and is designated as 1st class historical site. The building is red brick construction. The original furniture is reserved for indoor decoration. There are exhibition showrooms for historical data and pictures related to early Taiwan years. Across the lawn and garden, there is another red brick building facing the castle. It used to be the dormitory of British Consulate. When one ascends to the overlook platform, one can view one of the eight great scenes of Tamsui, the sunset at Shutai.

Nearby there are Old Oxford School, Residence of Dr. Mackay and Tamsui College. These old buildings are mostly well preserved. When one walks among these buildings, he (she) would feel that times have turned back. One can enjoy the old streets, the cool breeze, the flower/trees planted by residents and the sense of relaxation. Walking on the old streets along the riverbank, visitors may view the old buildings and may try the tasty local dishes, such as fish dumplings, Ah Gei (Oily Bean Curd) and hard eggs, etc. The dock is a good place for marvelous sunset viewing. Visitors can also take the boat ride between Tamsui and Bali. Anyone would love to watch the flying cranes and listen to the river flowing. At Bali, they have this famous dish from peacock clams. Tamsui is such a wonderful place and be sure to visit it.

## Wuling Farm

TEL: +886-4-2590-1259

Address: No.3-1, Wuling Rd., Heping District, Taichung City

"For those interested in high mountain farm life there are several farms in these mountainous regions that welcome visitors and offer an insight in local rural life. One of the most prominent farms, which can be easily reached from Mt. Hehuan, is Wuling Farm, located about 29 kilometers from Lishan on the Yilan branch of the Central Cross-Island Highway. This farm was established in 1963 to provide employment for retired servicemen. On the more than 700 hectares of land, at an altitude of 1,740-2,100 meters, high-mountain fruits (pears, peaches, apples, etc.) and vegetables (cabbage, spinach, etc.) as well as tea (Qingxin Oolong) are grown.

The spectacular scenery of the surrounding mountains, with nice walks to scenic spots like the 50-meter Taoshan Waterfall, creates an oasis of tranquillity. It is hard to tell the best time to visit Wuling Farm, as nearly all year round you will be delighted either by blossoming fruit orchards (spring and early summer ) or the abundance of harvest (summer and autumn). Formosan Salmon, also known as the "Cherry Blossom Hook Salmon", which is unusual in this part of the world, is a very rare variety of fish on the verge of extinction. Wuling Farm is the home of this land-locked salmon and you can find it in the Qijiawan Creek Ecological Protection Area."

## Qimei Island

TEL: +886-6-921-6521

Address: Qimei Township, Penghu County

Qimei is the southernmost island in the Penghu archipelago. There is a moving story behind the name of the island, which means Seven Beauties. According to the legend, seven maidens were doing their laundry beside a well long ago when they were attacked by Japanese pirates; unwilling to submit to insult at the hands of the scoundrels, they all killed themselves by leaping into the well. The local residents filled in the well and left it as a tomb, from which, later on, sprouted seven trees. It is still there: the Tomb of the Seven Beauties. In earlier times the island was known as Widow's Island, and there is a story behind this name too.

Even today, on the shore below the Nan Lake (Nanhu) Lighthouse, there is a stone formation known as Watching for Husband Rock. The stone is in the form of a reclining woman, who is said to have turned to stone there waiting for the return of her fisherman husband. There is a road all around the island, which makes travel convenient. Nan Lake (Nanhu) Fishing Harbor has more activity than any other place on Qimei, and its lighthouse is the southernmost one in the Penghu islands. In the vicinity of Yueli Harbor there is a Stone Lion formation which, along with much of the terrain here, is formed of columnar basalt left from the volcanoes that produced the islands.

## Hot Springs

### Su'ao Cold Springs

TEL: +886-3-996-0645

Address: No. 6-4, Lengquan Rd., Su-ao Township, Yilan County

The Su'ao cold springs have a temperature of less than 22°C and the water from these springs are clear, colorless and emit no smell. This rare type of cold springs is only found at a few places around the world, among which Italy, and is suitable for bathing and consumption. The cold spring area of Su'ao can be found at the northern side of Su'ao village, some 300 meters from the Su'ao train station around Zhongyuan road and Lengquan road. As the water temperature of the cold springs is lower than our body temperature, you will first feel cold when immersing into the water, however, after having soaked for some 5 minutes, your body will start to warm up. As the water of these cold springs contains high levels of carbon dioxide, it can also be used for food and beverages, such as goat-meat stew and glass-bead soda. The latter is not produced anymore, but goat-meat stew is still a specialty of the Su'ao area.

Su'ao is situated at the southern end of Yilan County, where it occupies a long, narrow strip of land backed by mountains and facing the sea. The fine natural harbor here was expanded and upgraded into an international harbor in 1974. In addition to its harbor, which is one of the five largest in Taiwan, Su'ao is also known for its rare cold mineral springs and its lively Nanfang'ao Fishing Harbor.

The water from Su'ao's mineral springs emerges from the ground at a temperature of about 22 degrees Celsius. This cool, clear, odorless, naturally carbonated water can be used for drinking and bathing as well.

To get to the springs, walk about 300 meters from the Su'ao Railway Station to Lengquan (Cold Spring) Road. When you first lower you body into one of the pools you will feel exhilarated by the shock of coolness, but after five minutes or so you will feel warm all over. Besides bathing and drinking, this water is also used in the production of Su'ao's famous jelly cake; in earlier times, it was used to produce naturally carbonated soda as well.

## Jiaoxi Hot Springs

TEL: +886-3-987-2403

Address: No.16, Gongyuan Rd., Jiaoxi Township, Yilan County

The special ground or crust stratum in Yilan County had made this area well known for its numerous hot springs, which are the result of air warmed by some source underground, and rising upward blended with under-layer water. Among them you would see the most historic "Jiaoxi Hot Spring," which is quite rare in Taiwan for its occurrence on a flatland. "Tangwei Hot Spring," meanwhile, has been famous since Qing Dynasty and placed on the list of "Eight Scenes of Lanyang Area."

The Jiaoxi Hot Spring originates at the foot of a hill behind Fuchung Temple at Deyang Village, Jiaoxi Township. While streaming along the ditches and highways, running through the railroads, the welling hot waters gather into a brook, serving local people as natural baths at the string of boiling ditches in ancient times.

However, there are only two public bathhouses left for those who want to try an absolutely different bath. As an alkaline fountain, Jiaoxi Hot Spring is crystal-clear, odorless, yet contains a considerable amount of minerals like Potassium chloride, Sodium sulphide, Potassium hydrogen carbonate, Technical Granular, Floating Acids as well as rich organisms.

Being honored as "The Hot Spring among Hot Springs," you would find your skin smooth and fine without the slightest stickiness after a bath at Jiaoxi.

All these years the Farmer's Association of Jiaoxi has been developing hot spring vegetables, hot spring drinking water, and hot spring breeding. They devote themselves to give full play to the possible usage of hot spring, so as to gain financial ground for agricultural economy and tour industry in Jiaoxi.

## Xinbeitou Hot Springs

TEL: +886-2-2720-8889

Address: Zhongshan Rd., Guangming Rd., Beitou Dist., Taipei City 112, Taiwan (R.O.C.)

Broadly speaking, the Beitou hot springs region refers to an area covering the Hell Valley, Longfeng, Fenghuang, Hushan Village and Xingyi Road. In a narrow sense, the region mainly refers to an area consisting of Zhongshan Road, Guangming Road, Xinmin Road and Quanyuan Road surrounding the Beitou Hot Springs Waterside Park. The hot springs hotels in this area are larger both in scale and number, and the natural and humanities resources are also the most plentiful here.

## Ruisui Hot Springs

TEL: +886-3-887-5306

Address: Ruisui Township, Hualien County

This is one of the three top hot spring spas in the valley, the other two being Hongye and Antong. Ruisui was first developed in 1919, with a public bathing area and Japanese-style hotel; and it is still in operation, with an open-air pool where visitors can enjoy a soothing soak and enjoy the fresh air at the same time.

The spring water emerges from the ground at 48 degrees Celsius and is rich in iron; the iron oxidizes upon contact with the air and gives the water a yellowish tint, causing some first-time visitors to mistakenly think that it is unclean. The water has a slightly salty (indeed, salt crystals float on its surface), rusty taste; it is the only carbonate hot spring in Taiwan.

## Sichongxi Hot Spring Area

Sichongxi Hot Spring Area is located at Checheng Township in Pingtung County. The water here is carbonated, excellent quality mineral water. The Sizhong River Hot Spring Area is considered one of the four major hot-spring areas among Taiwan, along with Yangming Mountsain (Yangmingshan) , Beitou, and Guanziling. At Sichongxi you may have the pleasure of enjoying a hot spring bath. The carbonated water here is clear and transparent, and the volume of water is extremely abundant and flowing all year long. The water ingredients include many kinds of minerals which are excellent for promoting circulation and relieving stiff muscles.

## Wulai Hot Springs

Wulai hot springs, in Wulai District of New Taipei City, produce weakly alkaline carbonic acid water at temperatures of 55 to 80 degrees Celsius.

The hot springs of Wulai produce mineral water in abundance and were developed long ago; the very name Wulai, in fact, is said to have come from the Atayal aborigine word for "hot springs." The water is clear, colorless, and odorless; it is said that bathing in it keeps the skin moist. Wulai boasts the largest free-of-charge hot-spring area in Taiwan. It is especially popular in early spring, when red cherry blossoms fill the mountainsides so that visitors can enjoy the beautiful scenery as they soak in the hot springs and bask in the romance of the Atayal aborigines.

## Jinshan (Jin Mountain) Hot Springs

TEL: +886-2-2498-8980

Address: Jinshan District, New Taipei City

Jinshan (Jin Mountain) hot springs, located in Jinshan (Jin Mountain)and Wanli Districts of New Taipei City, produce carbonic acid water at temperatures of 45 to 86 degrees Celsius.

These hot springs arise in the Datun geothermal zone, like those of Yangmingshan, and are the northernmost hot springs in Taiwan. While other hot-spring areas are lucky to have two types of water, Jinshan (Jin Mountain) provides four: oceanic sandy, sulfuric, carbonic acid, and iron. Hot-spring hotels have sprung up in the Jinshan (Jin Mountain) area in rapid succession in recent years, making it haven for vacationers who enjoy the variety of water types available.

## Zhaori Saltwater Hot Springs

TEL: +886-89-671-133

Address: No. 167, Wenquan, Ludao Township, Taitung County

The Zhaori Saltwater Hot Springs has been well known since the late 18th century for their clean, transparent water and ideal temperature, which fluctuates between 60 and 70 degrees centigrade. The springs are fed by seawater and underground water heated by the volcanic lava of Green Island. This is one of only three saltwater hot springs in the world along with the springs on Kyushu Island of Japan and Sicily in Italy. Zhaori has three open-air pools and a spa pool where visitors can listen to the sound of the surf, enjoy the sunrise, or watch the stars as they soak away the stress.

## Antong Hot Springs

TEL: +886-3-887-5306

Address: Antong Hot Springs, Yuli Township, Hualien County

The Antong Hot Springs is located on the bank of Antong Stream southeast of Yuli Town. The crystal-clear water of this alkaline spring is clear but has the unpleasant odor of hydrogen sulfide. It emerges from the ground in copious quantities at a temperature of 66 degrees

Celsius. It is said to cure wounds, skin ailments, and gastric complaints, among other things. Visitors here can choose between a Japanese hot-spring hotel and a modern-style hostelry.

## Jinping Hot Spring

TEL: +886-3-584-1001

Address: Jinping Village, Jianshi Township, Hsinchu County

Located in Jinping Village in Jianshi Township, Hsinchu County, it is a newly emerged spa area preserving the quiet natural landscapes. The water of the hot springs there is natural and clear, being carbonate salt springs suitable for spa and relaxation.

Nearby attractions include the Lidongshan Ancient Castle and Xiakaluo Historic Trail. These spots have gorgeous scenery in "aboriginal" flavors; therefore, they are recommended to visitors. Besides tasting sweet persimmons and understanding the culture of the Atayal Tribe and the rich ecology of the area, visitors can relax by enjoying the carbonate salt spa for a happy weekend or holiday.

Jinping Bridge

The bridge is located at the entrance to the Jinping Tribal Area where there are cliffs and steep rocks. To promote tourism, the tribesmen built a bright tunnel in the cliff and erected a totem statue of an Atayal hero there. This hero has an aboriginal face, holds a long spear in hand, and is ready to hunt, marking out the style of aborigines. As it stands at a high point, its grand posture is very splendid and eye-catching.

Water quality: Carbonate salt spa

PH value: 7

Water temperature: 30-43.2

## Zhiben (Jhihben) Hot Springs

TEL: +886-89-357-131

Address: Beinan Township, Taitung County

Zhiben (Jhihben) Hot Springs have the reputation of being "the greatest scene in eastern Taiwan." In the early years, hot springs emerged from riverbeds. There are carbonic acid springs (with the nature of base). There are colorless, odorless and their temperature reaches more than 100 degrees (Celsius). The springs are of high quality.

Zhiben (Jhihben) is divided into the inner hot spring area and the outer hot spring area by the Zhiben (Jhihben) Creek. Inner hot spring area was developed late. However, due to presence of five-star resorts, the area has become the largest business district. It attracts many foreign tourists who demand services of higher quality.

The "Zhiben (Jhihben) Hot Springs" generally known by the public is located in outer hot spring area. There are many middle-size and small hot spring inns. It is convenient to get accommodation or enjoy hot spring spa. Now the inner hot spring area and the outer hot spring area have expanded and joined together. However, the inner hot spring area is close to Zhiben (Jhihben) Forestry Park and its scenery is even better.

Zhiben (Jhihben) Hot Springs are the gathering place of aboriginal people. It provides the delicious dishes of aboriginal people and country dishes. Other than stores of country dishes, there are venders selling fruits like Shijia, pineapple and Luoshenhua. It has the flavor of eastern Taiwan.

## Jiaoxi Hot Springs Park

TEL: +886-3-9872998

Address: No.16, Gongyuan Rd., Jiaoxi Township, Yilan County 262

Located about 500 meters north of Jiaoxi Railway Station, Jiaoxi Hot Springs Park is a leisure destination with tree-lined paths and the namesake springs for which Jiaoxi Township is known. The sodium bicarbonate springs, among only a few springs in the flatland areas of Taiwan, are rich in sodium, magnesium, calcium, potassium, and carbonate ions. Soaking in the springs or drinking the (treated) mineral-rich water is said to be good for health. The Japanese-style soaking pools here can accommodate about 200 bathers. The visitor information center at the park provides Yilan travel information and assistance, helping visitors to enjoy a hot spring escape at any time of the year.

## Yangmingshan Hot Springs

TEL: +886-2-28613601

Address: No.1-20, Zhuzihu Rd., Beitou Dist., Taipei City 112

The Yangmingshan Hot Springs are located in the Datun Volcano Group. The geothermal heat from the volcanic activity here has given birth to a number of hot springs: mainly of the white sulfur variety, followed by green sulfur springs. Yangmingshan joins Beitou, Guanziling, and Sichongxi as one of Taiwan four major hot spring areas. The springs are divided into the Qianshan and Houshan areas. There are several spring resorts in the area. The park's rich natural ecology, geological landscapes, and mountain cuisine further make this a good place to vacation in northern Taiwan.

## Tai'an Hot Springs

TEL: +886-37-941-025

Address: No. 18, Jinshui Village, Tai'an Township, Miaoli County

Tai-an Hot Spring was called Takeshima Hot Spring during Japanese occupation and Hu Mountain (Hushan) Hot Spring after World War II. In 1978, late president Chiang Ching-Kuo visited the hot spring and renamed it as Tai-an. Besides Tai-an Hot Spring, Hu Mountain (Hushan) Hot Spring and Tenglong Hot Spring are also located nearby.

The spring water is abundant and the cherry blossoms are graceful during the blossom season.

Tai-an Hot Spring is colorless and odorless. It is the best hot spring in Taiwan. The magnificent scenery in the area makes the hot spring even more attractive. Besides the hot spring, visitors can also play with water or fish in the rivers nearby. In autumn and winter, there are grand mountainous views in Hu Mountain (Hushan) and Henglong Mountain (Henglongshan) (altitude 1,500 meters). The hot springs here include Hu Mountain (Hushan) and Tai-an, and they have the same origin.

## Qingquan Hot Springs

TEL: +886-3-585-1001

Address: Qingshi Road, Wufeng District, Hsinchu County

Qingquan Hot Spring lies in Hsinchu County. It was called Inoue Hot Spring in the past. Due to geologic changes, the hot spring had disappeared for several years until September 21, 1999, when a severe earthquake caused the hot spring to emerge again.

Qingquan Hot Spring is colorless and odorless with a temperature of 48°C. Besides the hot spring, the beautiful mountains and graceful peach blossoms also attract many tourists. Visitors can walk along the tour tracks and enjoy the hot springs after the walk.

### Dongpu Hot Springs

TEL: +886-49-279-2106

Address: Dongpu Village, Xinyi Township, Nantou County

Dongpu is one of the entrances to Yushan National Park and there are beautiful mountains and rivers in the vicinity. The most famous tourist attraction here is the hot spring. There are 12 hot spring hotels in Dongpu and each has its own characteristics. Some of them have open-air hot spring pools, spas, sauna, etc. Tourists can enjoy the hot spring and the mountainous scenery at the same time.

Besides the hot spring, Dongpu is also famous for its plums. The plums are used in food and wine. Other special foods include persimmon, tea, spring coffee, sweet potato, etc. Visitors can visit Dongpu Cliff, Batongguan Ancient Trail and Rainbow Waterfall in early morning.

## Museums

### Lin An-Tai Historical House & Museum

TEL: +886-2-2599-6026

Address: No.5, Binjiang St., Zhongshan District, Taipei City

Lin An-Tai Historical House & Museum is located in Binjiang Park. The house is a traditional Chinese courtyard house with elegant decorations and is one of the few traditional houses preserved in northern Taiwan. The Lin family came to Taiwan in the 18th century and engaged in trade in northern Taiwan. With the money they made, they built a house and named it. Today, the house is over 160 years old. It is the best-preserved and maintained ancient house in Taipei City.

Lin An-Tai Historical House & Museum is famous for its delicate carvings; one of the examples is the creative dragon carving on the front door. There are six dragons, representing the six sons in the family. The carvings of vases and bats carry the meanings of good luck, wealth and safety. Some of the tiles and bricks of this ancient building have been restored due to its long history, but the stones and woods have remained intact over the long years. The crescent shaped pond in front of the building was used for defense, raising fish, prevent fire, water supply and keep a moderate temperature.

## Chi Mei Museum

TEL: +886-6-266-0808

Address: Sec. 2, Wenhua Rd., Rende Dist., Tainan City

Chi Mei Museum is funded by Chi Mei Corp., a petrochemical company. Chairman Hsu Wen Lung set up Ching Mei Culture Foundation in 1977 and decided to improve public culture. Thus, he established the museum for art exhibition as well as art education. Currently, most paintings in the museum are classical and impressionist. The museum also loans its violins to excellent musicians. Established in 1990, the museum is open to the public and has several exhibition areas, including art, natural history, historic weapons, musical instruments, ancient objects and industrial techniques.

The museum has a collection of European paintings in the 18th and 19th century, presenting the development of western art. The historic weapon exhibition presents weapons from prehistoric time, the Bronze Age, the Iron Age to modern times. The two canons in front of the museum were designed and built in 1689. They were taken away by foreigners in the 19th century until Chi Mei Culture Foundation purchased them in 1994. The museum also collects valuable violins, including 5 Antonio Stradivaris, 2 Guarneri del Gesu, Nicolo Amati, Jacob Stainer, Amati, Rogeri, Joseph Guarneri Filius Andrea, Seraphin, Gagliano and Guadagnini.

## Pinglin Tea Museum

TEL: +886-2-2665-6035

Address: No.19-1, Shuisongqikeng, Shuide Village, Pinglin District, New Taipei City

Located beside the Beishi River in Pinglin, New Taipei City, Pinglin Tea Museum presents the Chinese tea culture and is worth visiting for tea lovers. Pinglin Tea Museum has an abundant collection of materials on tea culture. Within the museum are theme exhibition areas and seasonal theme exhibitions. The exhibitions include physical aspects and cultural aspects, presenting all information concerning tea drinking in Taiwan. The museum is made up of the Exhibition Hall, Theme Hall, Multimedia Hall, Tea Art Hall and the Promotion Center. The Exhibition Hall has 3 exhibition areas: tea history, tea making and tea leaves, introducing how tea culture has developed in the Chinese history, rituals of tea making and commercial development of tea. We believe the visitors will have a better understanding of tea history after visiting the museum.

The Exhibition Hall has 3 exhibition areas: tea history, tea making and tea leaves. Tea History Area introduces how tea has developed in the Chinese history, tea making, rituals of drinking tea, tea culture and commercial development of tea. On the east side of the museum is a well-designed garden of Southern Chinese style. Inside the garden, there are 2 traditional Chinese buildings, corridors, rockery, pavilion and bamboos.

## Yingge Ceramics Museum

TEL: +886-2-8677-2727

Address: No.200, Wenhua Rd., Yingge District, New Taipei City

The Yingge Ceramics Museum is the first professional pottery museum in Taiwan. First planned by Magistrate Yu Ching, the museum was finally completed after 12 years of construction with efforts of 3 magistrates. The museum opened on November 26, 2000. The museum is made up with modern constructing materials and transparent glass, presenting a limitless sense of space and the beauty of simplicity. The special structure also enhances the exhibition. The Yingge Ceramics Museum presents 200 years of ceramic techniques and folk culture in Taiwan.

At the same time, the museum also has educational function with its modern technology, making it an ideal place for families to visit at leisure. This museum is not for Yingge citizens alone; it also shows how the Taiwanese have endeavored to achieve what we are today. It is a historic and cultural emblem; moreover, it is also place for the peace of mind.

Traditional Ceramics Hall presents traditional ceramic techniques and tools. On the 2nd floor, pottery history and features are exhibited and Taiwanese pottery works are introduced. Features and functions of the works are presented, showing how pottery interacts with life. Children Experiencing Room is an experimental pottery area is designed for children aged from 4 to 8. The children can experience and play freely with the clay in this area. In addition, there is a pottery workshop for ceramic artists and experts to exchange experiences and thoughts. Ceramic works are widely used in today's world, from artificial teeth, computers, telephones, cell phones, to cylinders. Here in the Future World, you can see how pottery develops into elements and materials for modern technology and how it will be utilized in the future.

## Juming Museum

TEL: +886-2-2498-9940

Address: No. 2, Xishi Lake, Jin Mountain (Jinshan) District, New Taipei City

Born in Tongxiao, Miaoli in 1938, Juming a.k.a. Chu Chuan Taiis an art master in Taiwan. Juming Museum is surrounded by lush forests, ample space and infinite view. Next to Jin Mountain (Jinshan), Juming Museum is the largest outdoor art museum in Taiwan. The spacious museum presents Juming's creative works from 1987 to 1999. Master Juming himself participated in locating, designing and constructing this museum. After being exhibited in Tokyo, Hong Kong, Paris and Luxembourg, Juming's works have been shipped back to Taiwan and are presented in this outdoor museum. With 50 years of extensive experience from at home and abroad, art master Juming places his creations in Juming Museum, which is a place worth visiting for art lovers.

Painting exhibits include oil paintings, Chinese ink paintings, multimedia works, etc. Sculptures and pottery works are also exhibited in the galleries. Taiji Square is with 3 lawns, Taiji Square is bright in green, with more than 30 pieces of Taiji works exhibited on the lawns. This is actually why the square is named Taij.

Living Presented on the Living World Square, of course, are the Living World art works made mainly of bronze and stone.

## Taipei Fine Arts Museum

TEL: +886-2-2595-7656

Address: No.181, Sec. 3, Zhongshan N. Rd., Zhongshan District, Taipei City

Taipei Fine Arts Museum opened on December 24, 1983. Located in Yuan Mountain (Yanshan), it is the first museum of modern art in Taiwan. The main tasks of the museum are to organize exhibitions and to collect valuable works at home and abroad. The museum also makes efforts to exchange art views and works with international art museums. The museum has special designs and the scenery near the museum is also very beautiful.

The art museum holds regular exhibitions and works with schools to introduce art works to the students. The virtual reality art museum provides a 3D interactive environment for museum-goers. The MOD system provides a digital random system by which visitors can choose DVD and tapes to watch.

## National Taiwan Arts Education Center

TEL: +886-2-2311-0574

Address: No. 47, Nanhai Rd., Zhongzheng District, Taipei City

In order to promote art education and culture, the government established Taiwan Art Education Institute in Nanhai Campus. The main purpose of the institute is to stimulate the interaction of people and art. The institute has promoted research on art education and cooperated with Taiwan art education reform. Through the promotion of general art education, social art education and professional art education, the institute hopes to enhance and improve people's knowledge and application of art.

The National Taiwan Arts Education Center has three major facilities, that is, a concert hall, Nanhai Art Gallery and Zhongzheng Art Gallery. The concert hall and the galleries are within the same building. The concert hall is 479 square meters in area with 530 seats on the first floor and 127 on the second. The gallery is 240 square meters in area, providing advanced equipment and space for artists and exhibitions. In addition, the outdoor gallery and the performance square are 1,004 square meters in area. The center has made great contribution to Taiwan art education.

## Taipei Astronomical Museum

TEL: +886-2-2831-4551

Address: No.363, Jihe Rd., Shilin District, Taipei City

The Taipei Astronomical Museum took over the responsibilities of its predecessor, the Taipei City Observatory. The dome is made up of geometrically identical pieces joined together and an avant-garde cover that takes advantage of natural lighting. Together with an altazimuth and solarium, it embodies the Taipei Astronomical Museum's design concept - a symbol of the immensity and profundity of space.

The IMAX Theater is a spherical building 35 meters in diameter topped by a gold-covered aluminum dome. It not only shows the entire sky, but also employs sound, light, electric and other instruments to give visitors a feeling of being at the scene. If you would like to take a relaxing visit to the sea of stars and appreciate the beauty of space at the same time, make a visit to the Taipei Astronomical Museum - it can impart to you a sense of space that you've never experienced before.

## Kaohsiung Museum of History

TEL: +886-7-531-2560

Address: No. 272, Zhongzheng 4th Rd., Yancheng District, Kaohsiung City

Kaohsiung Museum of History is located next to Love River, Kaohsiung City. The museum was reopened in 1998. The building itself was built in 1938, which means it is over 60 years old. After World War II, the building was used as Kaohsiung City Hall. As the building is significant as a landmark and in Kaohsiung's history, the building was rebuilt as a history museum. Beside the museum are the Industrial Exhibition Center and the Concert Hall.

Kaohsiung Museum of History is a professional museum, collecting and filing historical documents and objects in Kaohsiung. Besides the categorizing of historic sites, the museum will enhance its research ability and combine local resources so as to preserve the diverse development of Kaohsiung.

## National Museum of History

TEL: +886-2-2361-0270

Address: No.49, Nanhai Rd., Zhongzheng District, Taipei City

The National Historical Museum was founded in the year 1955. Here collections are primarily the historical materials from the middle of China districts and also few from the other local areas. Majority of them are from the take-over from the Ho Nan Museum when it moved to Taiwan in the 1956 - 1957 periods and from the hand - over by the Japanese after the Second World War. Among these historical materials are: copper utensils unearthed in the Sancheng, Fuiyuan and Anyang areas in the Henan Province, Mainland China; the string - pattern pottery of the Qing Dynasty dig - ups from the Loyang areas; the Green-Paint Pottery of the Han Dynasty, the Music and Dance

Statues of the Six Dynasties, the art - craft of the Tang Dynasty, etc. With the allocation of fund by the government and the donations from more than 400 private collectors, the content of the Museum has been very much enriched.

Besides, as a result of years' hard work of Mr. Bao Jun Peng, the first head of the Museum, and his successors, it has now been developed into an establishment with a very solid foundation. The Historical Museum is a place which presents the re-occurrence of past events and the development progress of human beings. Owing to the limited space of the Museum, an enlargement plan is now under review. The authority intends to divide the Museum into three main parts in conjunction with the development of the Nanhai Scholastic Park Project After completion, the three separate museums, namely, the Middle China Hall, the Local Hall and the Overseas Hall, will comprehensively exhibit the historical progress of our cultural heritage. It is hope that through this, we will appreciate more on our culture and that our quality of life will advance. Also with such common interest, the whole human cultural development will move a step further.

The National Historical Museum is inside the Nanhai Scholastic Park, Taipei City. At its eastern side are the Taiwan Institute of Art Education and the Taiwan Institute of Science Education. Its western neighbor is the Taiwan Province Forest Test Laboratory. In the front of the

Museum, separated by a street, is the Jianguo High School and at its back are the botanical garden and the lotus pond. The place picturesque surroundings attract sight - seeing visitors coming here all the year round.

## Aug 23rd Artillery Battle Museum

TEL: +886-82-313-100

Address: Sec. 3, Taihu Rd., Jinhu Township, Kinmen County

Located in Zhongzheng Park, this museum was built in 1988 as a memorial to the long weeks of the artillery war. Its displays are designed to give a sense of the valorous events of that period.

On either side of the main entrance to the museum are carved the names of the 587 soldiers who lost their lives in the bombardment. On the left side are displayed the man air fighter used by the Nationalist forces at that time- the F-86 Saber and the main artillery piece, the 155mm cannon. On the right side is one of the amphibious landing craft - an LTV-that played such a vital role in transporting troops and materials during the battle. These displays help observers imagine what the joint operations of the three service branches must have been like.

Inside the museum are historical artifacts in 12 display areas for charts, photographs, documents, relics, and models. Together, these comprise a complete history of the artillery war. A visit to the museum gives observers a strong feeling of how the military and the civilians of Kinmen drew together to resist the aggressor when artillery shells were falling on the island in a dense downpour.

Memorial tablets commemorating the victory in the August 23 Artillery War have been erected at Magpie Mountain and on Little Kinmen to remind visitors of the sheer determination and resolute will which allow life to go on, even in the most trying circumstances.

## Guningtou Battle Museum

TEL: +886-82-313-100

Address: S. Hill, Jinning Township, Kinmen County

This was the scene of the 56-hour bloodbath that began when Communist troops landed on the shore and ended in victory for the Nationalist forces. A memorial tablet on the coast commemorates the battle, and the battlefield's entrance, built in the form of a Chinese city gate, is topped by a bronze statue of a heroic soldier.

This steel-reinforced cement building on the site of the Guningtou Battlefield is designed to resemble a fortress. It was built in 1984 as a memorial to the heroic actions of Kinmen's defenders, who at great cost drove off the Communist invaders and won a great victory for the Nationalist forces.

The sides and entrance of the museum are adorned with large relief sculptures portraying the spirit of the soldiers who fought in this notable battle. On grassy areas to either side are displayed "Kinmen Bears" -the M5 Al tanks which played a decisive role in the fighting. In a circle at the front of the building is a sculpture of three heroic fighters.

Inside the museum are 12 oil paintings by prominent artists depicting the battle, along with displays of other materials, documents, and photographs relating to the fighting and the victory that followed. The aim of the museum is to portray the spirit of sacrifice manifested by the soldiers who fought so hard and gave so much for their country.

## Fo Guang Shan Buddha Museum

TEL: +886-7-656-3033#4002

Address: No.1, Tongling Rd., Dashu Dist., Kaohsiung City 840

Completed in 2011, this popular religious culture attraction covers an area of more than 100 hectares in Kaohsiung. The Fo Guang Big Buddha behind the Main Hall towers 108 meters high, making it the tallest sitting bronze Buddha statue in the world. Other attractions here include the Three Acts of Goodness Children's Gallery, Cultural Square at the Four Givings Pagoda, House of Joy and Celebration at the Five Harmonies Pagoda, and sutra transcriptions, prayer service, and Tea Chan at the Twin Pavilions.

The Main Hall is dedicated mainly to the holy relics of the Sakyamuni Buddha. In addition to the Main Hall, there is a permanent museum and exhibition hall. The 2,000-person capacity Great Enlightenment Auditorium regularly hosts performances and international seminars. The museum is especially busy during the period from the Lunar New Year holiday to the Lantern Festival. At that time, the hillside is covered with lanterns, creating a festive mood.

## Lanyang Museum

TEL: +886-3-977-9700

Address: No. 750, Sec. 3, Qingyun Rd., Toucheng Township, Yilan County

Yilan itself is a museum

Rich in both natural and cultural resources, the Lanyang Plains are characterized by ecological and ethnic diversity, warm and friendly people, and a vibrant culture. It is said that Yilan itself is a museum and we believe the Lanyang Museum serves as a sort of window to those wishing to learn more about Yilan. The Lanyang Museum's mission is to bring together Yilan's local resources through books and displays as well as tourism and recreation to promote activities of museums throughout the county to ensure the sustained development of "the museum that is Yilan."

At Yilan's cultural and historical epicenter

The Lanyang Museum is located on the site of Wushi (Literally, "black rock") Port which during the Qing Dynasty bristled with the masts of the vessels coming and going. The harbor was not only an artery for the physical materials needed by the people of Yilan, it was an important hub of cultural exchange with the outside world. The Lanyang Museum was erected on this site to symbolize the fact that culture in Yilan is breaking new ground and reaching new heights and milestones.

One with the land

You might be curious as to why our building looks so different. The architecture of the Lanyang Museum was inspired by natural elements found locally. Architect Kris Yao incorporated the cuesta, a gently tilting stone escarpment common to Taiwan's northeast coast, into the building's design, allowing structure to blend into the natural environment. From a distance, it resembles a huge black rock; up close, you discover a place of unique beauty that coexists in harmony with the land.

Permanent displays

Upon entering the Lanyang Plains, you note the blending of mountain and sea. In the museum's exhibition area, therefore, we have set up displays reminiscent of the geographical and spatial characteristics of Yilan. They hint at the local mountains, plains, and ocean and convey the idea of interacting with the environment.

The permanent displays, which take advantage of the building's special characteristics, include the Introductory Exhibition as well as the Mountain Level, Plain Level, Ocean Level, and Time Corridor Exhibitions spread over the building's four floors and suggesting Yilan's overall geographical and cultural context.

## National Theater & Concert Hall

TEL: +886-2-3393-9888

Address: No. 21-1, Zhongshan S. Rd., Zhongzheng District, Taipei City

Built in 1987, the National Chiang Kai-Shek Cultural Center at Chiang Kai-Shek Memorial Hall is the first national-level cultural venues in Taiwan. In addition to hosting major performances, the two major buildings of the center the National Theater & Concert Hall are major Taipei landmarks. The two buildings are designed in a traditional Chinese palace style, with distinctive yellow tiled roofs and red pillars adding to their stately elegance.

In addition to enjoying world-class musical, dance and theater performances, center visitors can also tour the cultural gallery and performing arts library. The center also offers regular guided tours for a more in-depth look at the world of performance arts in Taipei.

## National Chiang Kai-Shek Memorial Hall

TEL: +886-2-2343-1100

Address: No.21, Zhongshan S. Rd., Zhongzheng District, Taipei City

National Chiang Kai-Shek Memorial Hall is located in the heart of Taipei City. The area is 250,000 square meters and it is the attraction most visited by foreign tourists. Outside the gate of Chiang Kai-Shek Memorial Hall, there are poles carrying the sign of true rightness. The architecture of Chiang Kai-Shek Memorial Hall is inspired by Tiantan in Beijing. The four sides of the structure are similar to those of the pyramids in Egypt. The material is white marble. The roofs are decorated with deep-blue glass as part of the reflection of blue sky and bright sun. It adds a touch of grandeur. The garden is planted with red flowers. As a whole, the colors of blue, white and red express the National Flag and the spirit of freedom, equality and brotherhood.

The great building has become a landmark of Taipei City. There are also places for international art performances. They are National Theater and National Concert Hall. World famous musicians (such as the great cello performer Yo Yo Ma and the great violinist Shao Lian Lin) and renowned playgroups have conducted performance here. The garden with beautiful flowers, miniature hills and plants, ponds, ornamental bridge and waterfalls as well as green grass presents scenery beauty. The walls surrounding the area are with nostalgic design. The place is enriched with the beauty of traditional Chinese gardens. There are various activities taking place in the square. There are the concert of the world renowned three tenors, school band performances, cheerleader performances and fairs. One can pay respect to the historical great leader, as well as participate in the relaxation activities of local residents. The place provides a precious plain view among the tall buildings of Taipei.

## National Dr. Sun Yat-sen Memorial Hall

TEL: +886-2-2758-8008

Address: No.505, Sec. 4, Ren'ai Rd., Xinyi Dist., Taipei City 110, Taiwan (R.O.C.)

National Dr. Sun Yat-sen Memorial Hall was built in 1972. It is located in east side of Taipei and is close to Taipei City Government. The memorial hall was built to commemorate the great founding father of R.O.C., Dr. Sun Yat-sen and was built on the 100th birthday of Dr. Sun. The building is inspired by structure of Chinese palace. It is grand and beautiful. There is a statue of founding father in the building for the public to pay their respect.

There are exhibitions of historical items related to creation of R.O.C. The memorial hall has a concert hall that can accommodate more than 3,000 people. It is equipped with excellent facilities and hardware items and has become an important place for performance. The lecture room in Sun Yat-sen Memorial Hall frequently hosts academic and other lectures. The main building is surrounded by a long, winding porch. Four great exhibition rooms frequently host works of famous artists and various exhibitions.

Outside the main building there is great space. You can usually see people flying kites here. The colorful, high-flying kites add touch of vigor to the serene hall. There are many roller skaters gathering here to practice their techniques. It is a good place for the public for sports and recreation. The willow trees along the lake in Zhongshan Park, the garden with lush flowers, and the beauty of Chinese garden attract many visitors. There is a library in the main building housing 400 seats and 140,000 books. Sun Yat-sen Memorial Hall is a place of commemoration and also a park for outdoor, recreational and art activities.

## 921 Earthquake Museum of Taiwan

TEL: +886-4-2339-0906

Address: No.192, Xinsheng Rd., Kengkou Vil., Wufeng Dist., Taichung City

At 1:47 AM on September 21, 1999, Taiwan experienced one of its worst natural disasters of the past century - a 7.3-magnitude earthquake that devastated the central part of the island. The 921 earthquake museum of Taiwan located in Wu-Feng County conserved the damage caused by Ji-Ji earthquake such as collapsed school buildings, fault rupture and elevation of riverbank. And thus the museum is a precious teaching material for natural science. All the construction of the museum was done by September 2007, and it included Chelungpu Fault Gallery, Earthquake Engineering Hall, Image

Gallery, Disaster Prevention Hall, and Reconstruction Records Hall. The museum& rsquo;s exhibit features its phenomenal architecture in addition to site conservation, natural science, humanity and historical records.

The Chelongpu Fault cut across the campus and destroyed almost all of the school buildings. To make the ruined landscape and damaged structures stand out, the architect surround the geological changes with the five exhibition halls. The Chelongpu Fault Gallery also includes an art piece symbolizing needle and thread used to sew up Taiwan's wounds the surface rupture brought by fault. Following the visiting route, one can see how the fault passed though and study how the land was deformed. The fault line actually connected the five separated exhibition halls all together by the story line of Jiji earthquake.

Chelongpu Fault Preservation Hall:

The Chelongpu Fault Preservation Hall holds many images of scenes involving the fault line of the Jiji Earthquake, linking pictures of its current look with how it looked in the past. This is a very personal way to witness and learn about the power of nature and earthquakes for the public.

Earthquake Engineering Education Hall:

The exhibition area was planned and developed by the National Center for Research on Earthquake Engineering and features houses that are safe in design and construction, how modern buildings minimize the effects of earthquakes, and earthquake safety in public areas.

The Earthquake Engineering Education Hall will help visitors understand the relation between earthquakes and how a building is constructed. It will introduce visitors to some of the principles involved in putting up a building that can withstand some of the effects of an earthquake so that visitors will come away better educated on how earthquakes happen and the importance of building to minimize their effects.

Image Gallery:

The Image Gallery was originally the Student Activity Center of Kuangfu Junior High School. Rebuilt after the quake, it displays photographs and audiovisual materials featuring the Chi-Chi Earthquake, and presents the memories of the earthquake from the angles of the humanities, society, and historical records. The Image Gallery has three large theaters; the Ture Feeling Theater, the Bird's eye view Theater and the Earthquake Experience Theater. Each of the three theaters has its own main points and its own lessons for the visitors. Watching and listening to these images and accounts of what happened during the earthquake and its aftermath will give the visitors a good idea of what the people here experienced on that night and how strong the will was to rebuild their home.

Disaster Prevent Hall:

Prevent the possible disaster and getting ready for it far outweighs the value of repair afterward. It is the objective of Disaster Prevention Hall. The goal of the gallery is to give knowledge of refuge and rescue, and related information to the audiences, to establish the correct concept of the disaster prevention.

Reconstruction Record Hall:

The Reconstruction Record Hall documents the reconstruction efforts that have been done after the Jiji Earthquake. These display the tremendous achievements of the disaster relief and reconstruction work done by the government and the people. The design of the Reconstruction Record Hall intended to bring new life to the running track. The outdoor track keeps extending interior, representing the idea of keeping running no matter how hard life is. And the mobile cabinets displaying reconstructive records along the indoor track indicate the long laborious reconstruction process which was like a relay race involving many dedicated individuals.

## Image Museum

Built in 1933, the Yule Theater was the first air-conditioned theater in Taiwan. The 500-person capacity theater joined both ancient Roman and Arabian motifs to present a vision of grandeur intended to display the national power of the then occupying Japanese government.

The second floor of the theater was heavily damaged by aerial bombing in 1944. Two years later, the theater was brought under government administration and renamed the Guomin Theater. It subsequently attracted huge crowds as a movie house. It also was used for concerts and army recruitment drives. In the 1980s, the theater became involved in a property dispute between the Hsinchu county and city governments. It also suffered from declining attendance with the rise of rental videos, forcing the theater to close its doors in 1991.

The theater was reopened in 1996 to serve as the Hsinchu City venue for cultural events organized as part of a national arts festival. The reopening sparked renewed interest among locally prominent persons and movie buffs in restoring the theater. The Chinese Taipei Film Archive was commissioned to draft a plan for the establishment of an Image Museum at the theater. In 1998, the Council for Cultural Affairs provided funding for the yearlong restoration project culminating in the museum's opening on May 21, 2000.

The mission of the museum is to preserve the cultural experience of the Guomin Theater and to serve as a shared image space for city residents. In addition to promoting and showing alternative and older movies, the museum archives, displays, and researches cinema-related items and promotes cinema education.

## National Taiwan Museum

TEL: +886-2-2382-2699

Address: No. 2, Xiangyang Rd., Zhongzheng District, Taipei City

The National Taiwan Museum, formerly known as "Bureau of Productive Industries Museum, Taiwan Sōtokufu Museum" during the Japanese colonial rule period, was established in celebration of the completion of the Main Line Railway in Taiwan. The current building, located in the 228 Peace Park, was completed in 1915 and designed by Japanese architect Nomura Ichiro in a Renaissance style. The magnificent structure and the exquisite architectural artifacts has made it an important treasure in modern Taiwan.

For a century, the Museum has been standing in front of the Taipei Railway Station, on the north-south and east-west pivotal crossroads of old Taipei. Its elegant architecture, abundant and diverse collections and unique geographical location have made the Museum an important landmark in Taipei City. Containing more than 100 years of objects on anthropology, geology, zoology and botany, it is the oldest natural history museum in the country. Through the Museum, you will see the tracks of development and the different faces of Taiwan.

Taiwan Land Bank Exhibition Hall of National Taiwan Museum

The Taiwan Land Bank Exhibition Hall was previously the site of the Taipei Branch of Japan Kangyo Bank, and designated by the Ministry of the Interior as a Level III Historic Site (now a "Taipei Municipal Historical Site") in 1991. When it was transformed into a museum in 2010, not only did the building rekindle its past glory, but also a physical embodiment of Taiwan's financial, economic, architectural, craft, and museum histories.

The major permanent exhibition of the Land Bank Exhibition Hall is the Gallery of Evolution. The Gallery exhibits large natural historical artefacts, such as Tarbosaurus, Velociraptor, Tricerotops and Huanghetitan, and therefore the Museum is also nicknamed "the Dinosaur Museum" and loved by young visitors. The Gallery tells the story of the earth from Cambrian trilobites, Devonian fishes, Mesozoic reptiles to Cenozoic mammals, uncovering the secrets of biological evolution and offering visitors a perfect venue for learning prehistoric biota and the current Taiwan endemic fauna. After the dinosaur tour, visitors can have a taste of the peculiar "Dino Geological Cake" in the 2F Dino Café.

In addition to the Gallery, the Museum also displays the past of the Land Bank, including precious historic relics and manuals, land measuring instruments, land reform historical records, land bonds, public land sale manuals, and financial business machines.

Tel.: +886-2-2314-2699

Add.: No. 25, Xiangyang Rd., Taipei City 10046, Taiwan (R.O.C.)

Nanmen Park of National Taiwan Museum

The park was once the Taipei Nanmen Factory and the only official camphor refinery in Taiwan during the Japanese colonial period. In 1998, it was designated as a national heritage site. After 8 years of restoration, if officially opened in 2013, allowing visitors a chance to step back in time.

There are many onsite displays in the park allowing visitors to recollect of the past glories of the old camphor factory. Meanwhile, the content of the Nanmen exhibition on restoration introduces the architectural features of each building in the park, the archeological discoveries during the restoration, and the contribution of the crafts men.

Inside the Park, the beautiful garden displays various kinds of Taiwan endemic plants and temperate plant specimens. The Children's Corner in the Depository features the story of "the Kingdom of Camphor Trees," allowing parents and kids aged 3 to 10 to read and learn about urban ecology together. What's more, the second floor special exhibition in the Red House, "A-Nong's Fantastic Adventure" and the numerous non-scheduled featured mini exhibitions of plant and animal specimens are all very suitable for families with kids.

Tel.: +886-2-2397-3666

Add.: No. 1, Sec. 1, Nanchang Rd., Zhongzheng Dist., Taipei City 10074, Taiwan (R.O.C.)

# Night markets & old streets

## Shilin Night Market

TEL: +886-2-2882-0340

Address: In the neighborhood of Dadong Rd., Danan Rd., Wenlin Rd. and Jihe Rd., Shilin Dist., Taipei City 111, Taiwan (R.O.C.)

Shilin Night Market is the one of the largest night markets in Taipei. The market is centered on Yangming Theater and Cicheng Temple. The night market is formed by many prosperous shops on Wenlin Road, Dadong Road and Danan Road, etc. Among them, Shilin Market was built as early as in 1899 and the market is famous for various snacks and eatery. Many visitors have come to Shilin Night Market to enjoy the delicious foods, such as large pancake enfolding small pancake, hot pot on stone or Shilin sausage. Shilin Night Market has become a renowned place for great foods.

Because the night market is close to many schools, students are the main customer group. Goods are sold at less expensive prices as compared to regular stores. There are special areas for furniture, clothing, photo shops or pet shops. The finery shops and cold dessert shops in "lover's lane" attract most student customers.

Shilin Night Market covers a large area. When one walks in the turning lanes and alleys, he (she) would often find something unexpected. The night market is packed with many people during holidays. We can often see families carrying many things from shopping and enjoying good meals. Their satisfaction is fully shown from their happy expressions.

## Sanxia Old Street

TEL: +886-2-2671-1017

Address: Minquan St., Sanxia Dist., New Taipei City

Sanxia is a traditional district located in northern Taiwan, easily accessible from Taipei. It has become known in recent years mainly because of its Qingshui Zushi (Qingshui Master) Temple, which is unique among all the Chinese temples of the world for the painstaking and time-consuming dedication to classical temple arts that is manifested in its modern reconstruction work.

The town, originally named Sanjiaoyong after its location at the confluence of three rivers, was given its present name of Sanxia (Three Gorges, also the name of its main river) in 1920. Nestled where fertile plains meet mountain foothills, and blessed with convenient inland river transport, Sanxia offered excellent conditions for development in the early years of Taiwan's settlement by the Chinese. It quickly became an important goods distribution center and a base for the production of camphor, the growing of tea, and especially the dyeing of cloth. As transport shifted elsewhere and the use of river transportation declined, however, Sanxia gradually lost its importance as a commercial center.

Even as the town lost its economic importance, though, its cultural value remained undiminished, mainly because of Qingshui Zushi Temple. With its unparalleled combination of religion and art, this temple is the epitome of exquisite carving and complex structure as well as dynamic center of Chinese religious worship. These features have also made it a powerful attraction for tourists from all over Taiwan and the world.

Sanxia Old Street refers to the south section of Minquan Street in New Taipei City. Its length is about two hundred meters, and its architecture dates back to the early days when the Republic of China was newly established. Walking along Sanxia Old Street is like walking into a time tunnel; the arched red brick hallways, the traditional architecture, the beams, columns, ancient wooden plaques, the squat maidens walls and the figure carvings upon the buildings are all very unique. Walking along this ancient street brings a feeling of nostalgia for the good old days, and makes visitors want to linger.

Sanxia Old Street is best preserved the along the Minquan Street, Heping Street, Ren'ai Street and Zhongshan Road. Minquan Street was the commercial center in the past, and the commercial stores and alleys that date back to the time of Japanese Occupation are still in good condition. Both the town and its street underwent modification during the Japanese Occupation; streets were expanded, rooftops, walkways, and drainage systems were also re-organized, and it was transformed into a stately, modernized street. During the time of Sanxia's heyday, the street was lined with shops that sold dyes, manufacturing materials, and tea, and western-style houses were also being built quickly. Nowadays, only the red brick buildings with arched hallways and Baroque styled architecture remain to tell of their past glory.

The characters carved upon the ancient buildings in the street show the first and last names of the occupants, or their occupations, or the names of the store. The character is most frequently seen here, showing that there were many dye shops; the plaques hanging above the entrance of shops also had the shop's name, as well as the proprietors names carved into them. This was a much-used method of propaganda in those days. A section that jutted out from the wall of a building, and had different shapes carved upon it, was termed a mountain wall or a building these sections were usually higher in the middle, and flatter on either sides.

The ornate figures upon the mountain walls had significance attached to them as well; a vase symbolized safety and an octagon was used to ward off evil. Red brick was the main material used for the side of the buildings facing the street; pebbles were less used, and cement was not used until recently, for renovations, was used for the interior walls of the buildings. Because the merchants who lived along the Street in those days were all well-to-do folks, the architectural style and the building materials used were the cream of the crop; many materials were imported, and some of the residents employed architects from as far as England. The protruding sections on the roof of the buildings and the carved patterns under the windowsills on the second floor of the buildings enhance the beauty of these constructions. The patterns are widely varied and extremely interesting to study.

## Huaxi Street Tourist Night Market

TEL: +886-2-2388-1818

Address: Huaxi St., Wanhua District, Taipei City

Huaxi Street Tourist Night Market is located nearby Longshan Temple. The night market, together with night markets on Guangzhou Street, Wuzhou Street and Xichang Street, has formed a large unique market. Various commodities are sold here and it is one of the favored sites of tourists. In the early years, Huaxi Street is famous for congregated porno shops. After prostitution is banned by Taipei City Government, the sightseeing quality is greatly uplifted and the place becomes safer.

A Chinese traditional post stands at the entrance of Huaxi Street Tourist Night Market. Chinese traditional lamps are hung along the street. There are old, historical shops along the street that provide great dishes. For example, the Danzai noodle restaurant, the favorite of Japanese tourists, started its business here. Other great dishes like meat soup and squid soup attract many people. In the summer, chopped ice plates and fresh juice are in great demand. In the winter, dishes with Chinese medicine attract many visitors.

## Liuhe Tourist Night Market

TEL: +886-7-7995678

Address: Liuhe 2nd Rd. & Zhongshan 1st Rd. intersection, Xinxing District, Kaohsiung City

You will not be considered to visit Kaohsiung if you miss out Liuhe Night Market. As early as in 1950, more and more stalls stationed in Dagangpu of Xinxing District in Kaohsiung, finally forming the well-known "Dagangpu Night Market." The night market is developed into large-scale, known as Liuhe Night Market. The Night Market is not far away if you walk from Kaohsiung Railway Station along the Zhongshan Road straightforward, which takes only ten minutes more, and then turn right to Liuhe Road. In daytime, the market is a straight road, and turns into prosperous market area in nighttime.

There are 138 stalls in Liuhe Night Market, most of them serve snacks and provide entertainment and games for recreation, the garments/apparels and groceries are rarely seen in the market. In particular, the dozens of steak houses boom around the market offering beef steak at reasonable price or family-size package meal. No matter what you like to have, a variety of delicious food, specialties, cold drinks, ices and seafood here are offered for your choice. Just remind you, don't miss the opportunity to taste the papaya milk and steamed salty shrimps in Kaohsiung.

## Keelung Miaokou Snacks

TEL: +886-2-2428-7664 (Keelung City Visitor Information

Address: Ren 3rd Rd., Ren'ai Dist., Keelung City

Keelung Miaokou surrounds Dianji Temple on Ren 2nd Road in Keelung. It is located on Ren 3rd Road between Ai 2nd Road and Ai 3rd Road. There are many kinds of eatery here and more than 200 food stands gather in the area of 400 meters. When walking in the food market, one would wish that he (she) had an unlimited appetite to taste all of the delicious foods here. The owner of each food stand strives to create delicacy.

Good materials are used for the dishes and prices are modest. The market attracts huge crowd each day. The famous dishes include soup mix, fried fish pastry, meat soup, fried oysters and meat on rice, etc. There are seafood, fried chicken, cold desserts, and more. Visiting the food market will give you a chance to taste all of the famous dishes in Taiwan. Other than local residents, many tourists visit the place for a good bite. Please do visit the food market in Keelung for Taiwan's delicacy.

The food market in Keelung is open until late at night, about 2:00 am or 3:00am. You can see many food stands spreading smell of tasty foods at this hour. Nearby there are also stands for clothes and daily items. One can go for some shopping after a good meal.

## Wufenpu Garment Wholesale Area

TEL: +886-2-2720-8889

Address: Zhongpo N. Rd., Songshan District ,Taipei City

Here's a premium shopping trip for you: know that in Taipei "value for money" in clothing and accessories means the Wufenpu Garment Wholesale Area . Located in the eastern part of Taipei City, here your tourist dollar travels far.

The literal translation of "Wufenpu" is "five parcels of open land," indicating that in pioneering days the first Chinese settlers bought up a large plot here in modern Taipei's Songshan District in a group of five. To today's Taipei residents, however, the place name is synonymous with a renowned wholesalers' district stuffed to the brim with quality inexpensive clothing and related adornments and stuffed with happy bargain-hunters most every day. It is now rightfully gaining recognition on the tourist map as well.

Some people release the stress accumulated in the workaday world by climbing mountains (read this issue's article on hiking). Some find release by sitting quietly and reveling in the appreciation of the more delicate beauties created by Mother Earth (see our article on bird-watching). And some "many" seems more appropriate find blissful release by going out for a day of ardent purchasing of material goods, taking possession of items they may or may not have known in advance that their little heart desired.

Wufenpu officially called Wufenpu Garment Wholesale Area is just the antidote, then, for those in the last category seeking pure joy, and just the thing for those in all categories in need of clothing necessities or gifts for those waiting back home.

## Guanghua Market-Consumer Electronics

TEL: +886-2-2341-2202

Address: No.8, Sec.3, Civic Blvd., Zhongzheng Dist., Taipei City

Guanghua Market opened in 1973 under Guanghua Bridge between Bade Road and Civic Boulevard in Taipei. It was originally occupied by used book shops relocated from Guling Street and unlicensed shops moved from Bade Road. Business at the market took a while to pick up due to the limited choice of items on sale. This began to change with the arrival of antique, jade and electronic supply shops in 1979; and in the 1990s the market consolidated its reputation as the go-to place in Taipei for computer equipment and other electronic gadgets, with over a hundred shops selling these high-tech items.

On January 18, 2006, Guanghua Market was relocated to a new facility at 77 Jinshan North Road. In addition to computers and other electronic peripherals, the new market sells branded sportswear and athletic gear, DVDs and CDs, posters, PC and console games, books, stereo equipment, mobile phones and more. The market is known for its wide variety, low prices and convenient comparison shopping, making it a magnet for budget-minded student shoppers.

## Bopiliao Old Street

TEL: +886-2-2336-1704

Address: Ln. 173, Kangding Rd., Wanhua Dist., Taipei City

Bopiliao Old Street is located long Lane 173, Kangding Road south of Laosong Elementary School in Taipei's Wanhua District. The street extends north to the school and south to Guangzhou Street. Laosong Elementary School was built in 1896, earning the school's northern building designation as a city historic site. The east and west buildings are also historically significant. The Heritage and Culture Education Center of Taipei is also located next to the school.

At the Bopiliao Historic District, visitors can see well-preserved streets and traditional shop homes from the Qing period, as well as buildings from the Japanese occupation and early post-war periods. These buildings have witnessed the development of the Mengjia area (Wanhua District) over the years and form an important part of Taipei's historic urban landscape. Among the historic buildings here are the Taipei home of the eminent scholar Chang Tai-yan (at No. 123 Guangzhou Street), Yongxing Tingchuantou Store, Song Xie-Xing Rice

Store, residence of Dr. Lu A-chang, Rixiang Travel Agency, Taiyo Bindery, Xiuying Teashop, Changshou Teashop, Weiling (Taoist) Shrine, and Public Bath. Longshan (lungshan) Temple and shops selling spirit money, Chinese medicine, herbs and Buddhist implements further add to the historical and cultural charms of this area.

## Qigu Seafood Street

TEL: +886-6-786-1000

Address: Qigu District, Tainan City

On the sides the County Road 176 of Dacheng Village, Qigu District, there are restaurants everywhere with seafood sighs. The road has become local-known seafood street. Tourists can have local special food of the fresh Milk fish, salt water tilapia, meritrix, fresh shrimps, fresh oysters and a variety of fish. The more famous restaurants in seafood street includes Ange seafood store (the first store in seafood street), Fishing village fresh seafood, Fengxing seafood store, Youyuan seafood store, A-tang seafood store, the Red Windmill, Tongyi seafood store, Tongda seafood store etc. The price of the restaurants is accepted by the mass population. That is why they are always crowded in holidays. The Seafood Street is located along County Road No. 176 and starts business from 10 a.m. to 9:00p.m.

## Jingming 1st Street

TEL: +886-4-2228-9111

Address: Jingming 1st St., West District, Taichung City

Jingming 1st Street is the official pedestrian-only street in Taichung. Along the street are boutique shops, coffee shops, restaurants and galleries. There are outdoor concerts or exhibition on holidays. The street combines the functions of shopping, recreation and art. No vehicles are allowed to enter the street and coffee shops provide many outdoor seats. The street was elected the model street in 1995 and it has become a tourist attraction in Taichung.

In the hectic daily life, Jingming 1st Street provides an artistic and recreational space for city dwellers. Sit on an outdoor seat and enjoy a nice cup of coffee. The street presents an atmosphere just like the Champs Elysee in Paris.

Jingming 1st Street is a 100-meter-long pedestrian full of shops and cafes, also known as the "Taichung Commercial Center Pedestrian Area." The street is known for its boutiques, tea and coffee shops, European-style restaurants, and art galleries Taichung residents can relax here over a cup of coffee at outdoor cafe tables. The street also hosts outdoor music and arts performances on weekends and holiday.

## Historic Sites

### Koxinga Shrine

TEL: +886-6-213-5518

Address: No. 152, Kaishan Rd., West Central District, Tainan City

The Guoxingye's Shrine (Yanping Junwang Temple), located by Kaishan Road surrounded by trees, is the only Fujianese style shrine in Taiwan. This is the shrine built in memory of the work and achievement of Cheng Cheng Kung, the pioneer of Taiwan. Cheng Cheng Kung was originally called Cheng Sun, a native in County Fujian. His father, Cheng Chi Lung, was a wanderer in his early days. He has been a merchant as well as a pirate. His mother was a Japanese lady called Tagawa.

Cheng was born with great intelligence. Not only was he diligent in his studies, he also has a huge ambitious to achieve something big, i.e. to become someone who are good in both academic work and in the military field. By the time he was 21 years old, Wu San Kwei led the Qing army into China and the Ming dynasty thus came to an end. As a result of his father surrendered to the Qing Dynasty and his mother committed suicide, Cheng Cheng Kung suffered a lot of pain and decided that he should turn against the Qing Dynasty to rejuvenate the Ming Dynasty in order to get rid of the shame caused by his father's traitor behavior.

In April, 15th year of Emperor Yung Li (1661 A.D.), he led his army crossing the Taiwan Strait and after 9 months' battle, had finally retrieved Taiwan from the hands of the Dutch. Taiwan thus was no more a colony of the Netherlands. After gaining access to Taiwan, Cheng quickly built up the whole place by setting up governing offices, regulations, education system as well as developing more farm lands to improve the living standards of the local people. He also actively trained people in military tactics, preparing them to fight the Qing army.

However, just half year after he had retrieved Taiwan, Cheng died of illness on May 8, the 16th year of Emperor Yung Li of Ming Dynasty. His aim of rejuvenating the Ming Dynasty was unfulfilled which was the biggest regret of his whole life. In the 13th year of Emperor Tong Chi of the Qing Dynasty (1874 A.D.), emperor's special envoy Shen Bao Chen requested for the enlargement of the then existing Kai Shan Wang' shrine which was in memory of the work of Cheng Cheng Kung. It was approved by the regime and the new shrine was officially called "Guoxingye 's Shrine" and for people to pay tribute to this folk hero.

In side the Guoxingye's Shrine, there is the Tainan Folk Cultural Hall where exhibits various historical culture of Tainan. The first floor is for pre-historic preserves and dig-ups. Apart from illustrating the geographic connection between Taiwan and the Mainland, these things also describe the evolution of life from the past to the present. Most of the exhibits in the second floor are the historical materials of Tainan.

These include the materials and things related to the concerned ancestors, such as the portraits of Cheng Cheng Kung and Shen Bao Chen, and also their works. In addition, daily items of Tainan city of the old like the street signs, bedding equipment, land deeds, money bills are on exhibition so that the public can understand the daily life of the past generations. It is a cultural spot very worth visiting.

## Oxford College

TEL: +886-2-2621-2121

Address: (Aletheia university) No.32, Zhenli St., Tamsui District, New Taipei City

During 1872 to 1880, Dr. Mackay had been preaching to the Taiwanese people outdoors until he felt the need to build a school. Therefore, when he returned to Canada in 1880, he raised money for the school. Construction of Oxford College completed in 1882. In honor of the Canadian contributors, he named the school after his hometown, Oxford. Oxford College has the characteristics of traditional Chinese architecture with a symmetrical structure. There are 8 little Buddhist towers on the roof instead of crucifixes. The school engaged in training missionaries, medial workers and teachers.

Oxford College is considered to have provided an educational foundation for Aletheia University and Dankang Senior High School. The building was designed by Dr. Mackay with traditional Chinese architectural style. Construction materials, such as bricks and roof tiles, were imported from Hsia Men. The bricks were coated with paint to prevent weather damage, while sticky rice mixed with lime and sugar was the major material for the walls.

## Dali Tiangong Temple

TEL: +886-3-978-1075

Address: No. 33, Sec. 7, Binhai Rd., Toucheng Township, Yilan County

The origin name of Dali Tiangong Temple is Qingyun Temple. It locates at the side of the sea highroad in the village of Dali Township in Yilan. The main God is the God of jade emperor (Sky God) worshiped from the Fuzhou. Because the people in the village wanted a spirit center for carry on the soul during 1836 (the Tao Year of sixteenth), then they had a mind of building the temple. The time when it's just built, the temple was simple and small.

After many re-building, until the Kung Year of thirtieth, the temple was built as you seen today with the history of one hundred ninety-five years. The outside castle and the inner part of the Temple are brilliant crocket beam drawn. The place is full of public worship tripod at usual. Not only the main belief center for the people in Dali Town, and also the people who come to worship the God during the Chinese Year time. The inner part of the Temple is brilliant, and the outside part of the Temple outside is beam drawn.

The low front part of the temple has the board of chi Yang the first scenery written by the general Ho Ying Chin. The Northeast coast from Dali forms the single side mountain and the rock landform. The Sky God is faced against the rough wave of the Pacific Ocean. The view is very wide, and you can also enjoy the scenery of the sunrise in Gui Mountain (Turtle Mountain) Island. The scenery is very special and beautiful. Many tourists come to pick the shell at the coast. There is a pathway near the temple forwarding to the back of the mountain. The back of the temple is the exit of the Caoling Historic Trail.

The back of Dali Tiangong Temple is leaning to the Caoling Mountain. It faces toward the blue wide Pacific Ocean. The geographic environment of Dali Tiangong Temple is beautiful and shining. During the January 9th of the Chinese New Year's celebration, many believers came to worship the Sky God from everywhere. Dali used to be one of the eight sceneries of Lanzhou. After worship Sky God, you can overlook the whole Gui Mountain (Turtle Mountain) Island from the story of Dali Tiangong Temple. You can overlook the fine blue sea gather with the bright sky at sunny day, and when it rains, you can see how smoke and fog overflow among the story of the Temple. When the northeast monsoon comes to visit, the waves along the coast are very roughing, magnificent, and vigorous.

## Chung Tai Chan Monastery

TEL: +886-49-293-0215

Address: No. 2, Zhongtai Rd., Puli Township, Nantou County

Chung Tai Chan Monastery locates in Puli of Nantou. Chung Tai Chan Monastery's designation of the construction started since 1990 through out a decade. The accomplishment ended in 2001. The construction of the building combined both Chinese and Western styles. The famous architect, Li Tsu Yuan, designed it. It became the belief center of many Buddhism. The visitors or the crowd of believers come to visit because of its fame. Architect Li Tsu Yuan charged the layout of Chung Tai Chan Monastery. Its adoption was the different law which means the great scale to reach exceptive sight affect.

And the temple was built with perpendicularity development instead of Chinese traditional temple's horizontal extension mode. The main structure of the bodybuilding was stone. It represented the firmness of seminar and the eternal changeless. Looking at the bodybuilding from the side is like a saint seating in the green woods. The main side of the bodybuilding is like the due out of the jet plane. It represents realize suddenly from heart, straight become Buddha of the supremacy heart law. The design contains the new create of generation and extension of the ancient Zen. Chung Tai Chan Monastery's main abbot who started the temple was the old monk, Shang Wei Hsia Chueh.

The old monk was Szuchuan camp mountain county people. When he was 30 years old, he became a monk, cloister, and tonsure in Shih Fang Temple in Keelung. He became the disciple of the old monk, Shu Yun. He has been closed to border through the Auspice temple in Yulan, the Yuan Ming Temple in Hsinchu, the big island mountain in

Hong Kong, and so on. He came back to Taiwan from Hong Kong during the end of 1971.

He lived in the small and simple thatched cottage, which were bought by the people in Shih Ting in Taipei. He then continued his studying of the Zen. During 1985 and 1986, the inner prosperous road built by the Yangming Mountain(Yangmingshan) National Park. More and more passengers knew this. Later on, more and more visitors become the disciples. And throughout the disciples to the people, the old monk's celebrity is passing each day. Until now the disciples have reach to more than one hundred thousands.

Nantou is always famous for its mountain sight, especially Puli, which located in the center of Taiwan's geography. It is the main center of many types of scenery. Chung Tai Chan Monastery's bodybuilding contains Wu Hua changes, Gather lives, education, art learning, art, science. The building of the temple, the statue of Buddha, the fresco, the color paints, the carving structure, the calligraphy and etc, all of these form the content of the art. They show the real truth, the real nice and the real beauty of the spirit of Buddha. All of these are the art and the unimposing. Making a trip of Chung Tai Chan Monastery, you will feel the relaxation. It is just like a heart spirit bathing. You can also gain the peace in your heart.

## Sun Moon Lake Ci-en Pagoda

Ci-en Pagoda is located on Sha Ba Lan Mountain near Sun Moon Lake. It was built by Chiang Kai-Shek in memory of his mother in 1971. The construction was very difficult because the materials had to be shipped over the lake and moved up the mountain. The Ci-en Pagoda is 46 meters in height and has become the famous landmark of Sun Moon Lake. Surrounding the tower are beautiful plants and trees and there are stone tables and chairs for visitors to take a rest. The Ci-en Pagoda overlooks Lalu Island and Sun Moon Lake.

Ci-en Pagoda is an octagonal building; the 3 stories at the base are painted in white, while the 9 stories of the main body are painted in golden red. Tourists can appreciate the magnificent scenery of Sun Moon Lake from the Ci-en Pagoda. The tourists track as long as 700 meters lead to the Ci-en Pagoda. Alongside the track are beautiful trees and flowers, which make the track easy and comfortable to walk along.

## Sanxia Qingshui Zushi (Divine Ancestor) Temple

TEL: +886-2-2671-1031

Address: No.1, Changfu St., Sanxia District, New Taipei City

Qingshui Zushi (Qingshui Master) Temple was built in 1769. The temple was destroyed by an earthquake in 1833 and was rebuilt in 1867. However, during 1895, it was burned down by the Japanese army. After World War II, the restoration was led by the renowned artist Li Mei Shu. The restored temple presents refined carvings and sculptures and it is the work of Taiwanese artists. Qingshui Master is also known as Machang Master or Penglai Master. He was an expert in medicine and a wizard. In memory of Qingshui Master, local people built a temple to worship him. The temple is a third grade historic site and is one of the three major temples in Taipei.

There are five gates in front of Qingshui Master Temple, which symbolizes its honorable and prestigious status. The stone sculptures and carvings in the temple are the works of experienced sculptors. The stone lions at the front gate are so lively and refined. The lions are designed by Mr. Li himself, featuring a more energetic and dynamic style.

## Lukang Tianhou Temple

TEL: +886-4-777-9899

Address: No.430, Zhongshan Rd., Lukang Township, Changhua County

Lukang Tianhou Temple is the one of the three major historic sites in Lukang. It lies on Zhongshan Road, Lukang. In the Ching Dynasty, General Shi Lang built the first temple of Goddess of Sea in Taiwan. The statue in the alter was imported from Meizhou, China. There are over 1 million worshipers coming here every year. With the smoke of the incense, the statues face has turned black, so the Goddess is also called black-faced Goddess.

Lugang Tianhou Temple is sublime and solemn and has elegant murals and paintings. In front of the temple is the dragon pond in a small garden. In the back of the temple, there is a culture museum of Goddess of Sea, introducing the history the Goddess and the role of the Goddess in the society. The historic materials preserved here are valuable, such as the board inscribed by a Ching emperor and officials, photos of the Meizhou Temple, and so forth.

One of the oldest temples in Taiwan to Mazu, the temple you see today is the result of a renovation in 1936, a Taoist divinity venerated as Goddess of the Sea and Empress of Heaven, is situated at Lugang. Mazu's birthday is March 23rd of the lunar year.

## Madou Daitian Temple

TEL: +886-6-572-2133

Address: No.60, Guandi Temple, Nanshi Village, Madou District, Tainan City

Madou Daitian Temple is the Wangye Temple that has the biggest group of worshippers. The temple worships Li, Chi, Wu, Chu and Fan Chien Suis; thus, it is also called Wu Wang Temple (Five Gods' Temple). The temple was built in the 17th century, when a temple ship floated to the shore and local people built a temple called Baoning Temple.

Due to the earthquake, Baoning Temple was moved to another place and renamed Bao-an Temple. In 1955, the temple was rebuilt and renamed Madou Daitian Temple. Part of the building still maintains traditional Quanzhou style.

Madou Daitian Temple has delicate sculptures and paintings. The ridge of the roof is of Quanzhou style and the roof is covered with colorful glazed tiles. In the back garden, there is a giant sculpture of a Chinese dragon, 76 meters long, 7 meters high, and it was built in 1979. Inside the dragon, tourists can find the settings of paradise, inferno, and underwater world. The altar of Goddess of Mercy here is in a round building, which is very different from other temples. It is said that the 108-layer Kuang Ming Lamp here is the highest in the world.

## Baozang Temple

TEL: +886-49-252-2836

Address: No.100, Ln. 135, Sec. 3, Zhangnan Rd., Fenyuan Township, Changhua County

Baozang Temple was built in the Ching Dynasty in Fenyuan. The temple was rebuilt in 1971. It is one of the 2 most famous temples in Central Taiwan. The other temple is Longshan Temple in Lugang. There are several historic objects still preserved in the temple and there are nearly 100 statues of gods. The painting on the walls is very delicate and there is a magnificent view from the temple.

After several reconstructions, today the temple presents refined sculptures and traditional Chinese architectural style. However, the new stone sculptures from China have spoiled the antique atmosphere in the temple. One of the most important historic objects is the board hanging above the main chamber. In 1995, the temple built a parking lot, a tour track and public washrooms, enabling the temple to attract more visitors and to provide better tourist service.

## Dajia Jenn Lann Temple

TEL: +886-4-2676-3522

Address: No.158, Shuntian Rd., Dajia District, Taichung City

People saying that Zhenlan Temple of Dajia was brought in to Taiwan by the Fukien province Tien islander, surname Lin, from Meizhou in 1730. Later on because the public worship tripod, in Yu Year of tenth, the little temple was built in Dajia in Taichung. Till 1770 (Yung Cheng Year of 35th) the little temple was changed to Hou Temple. In the Yung Cheng Year of 52nd (1778 A.D.), the temple was rebuilt. Afterwards the scholar gentry frequently raised reconstructs and change to become Zhenlan Temple. The temple with the statue of Mazu in Taiwan is more than five hundred and more.

Every year during the beginning of March of Chinese Year, territorial pilgrimage is a great celebration. There are hundreds of believers following the pilgrimage, and there are many celebrations for welcoming Mazu in every temple. The territorial pilgrimage of Zhenlan Temple of Dajia devolved hundreds of years. For every period, Ta An County will go aboard to the main Mazu temple in Meizhou to worship some holy spirit back for the statue. Whenever the people of pilgrimage several bulkiness and magnitude grandeur, it is praised and studied between the internal academic circle and mass communication border.

Zhenlan Temples has front palace, behind palace, south north palace, south north room, bell drum floor and so on all suffusion personality, flowers and birds, walk beast and so on sculpture carvings woodcarving, all essence carves are neat and beautiful. The inner part is the oblation of Mazu, and the south palace supplies the chastity Mazu. The chastity Mazu means the chastity workshop woman Ms. Lin. All of these are connected to each other. The views are bright and shine. But after many times of re-built, many of the ancient antiques were not found. Only one or two plaques that were written by Chien Lung and Kuang She emperors.

## Great Queen of Heaven Temple (Datianhou Temple, or Tainan Grand Matsu Temple)

TEL: +886-6-221-1178

Address: No.18, Ln. 227, Sec. 2, Yongfu Rd., West Central Dist., Tainan City 700, Taiwan (R.O.C.)

Datianhou Temple (Taina Grand Matsu Temple) is commonly known as a Mazu Temple of Tainan- the first Mazu Temple built by the government in Taiwan. The god worshipped in Datianhou Temple(Taina Grand Matsu Temple) is The Heaven God Mother, or widely called Mother Mazu, the most worshipped god in the Taiwanese society.

The Datianhou Temple (Taina Grand Matsu Temple) was originally the palace of Emperor Ningjing of the Ming Dynasty. In the 22nd year of Emperor Kang Si (in 1684), after admiral Hsih Long had occupied Taiwan, he found that Mazu was mostly worshipped by the Taiwanese people and as a way to easy their hard feeling towards foreign rule, he then reported to the emperor and requested to have the Ningjing Palace rebuilt into a Mazu Temple and promoted Mazhu to Tianhou, meaning the Heaven God Mother. Since then the Mazu temple is called Datianhou Temple (Taina Grand Matsu Temple).

Datianhou Temple (Taina Grand Matsu Temple) can be divided into 4 main parts : the San Chuan Hall, the Worship Hall, the Main Hall and the Back Hall. The lively large sized Mazu statue is the main feature of the Temple. It was the master piece of a sculptor from Chuan Chou about 300 years ago and is the representative work of Taiwan's sculpturing of its kind.

In all temples, there are door guarding gods. To shows its class, the door guarding gods in the Datianhou Temple (Taina Grand Matsu

Temple) are not by drawing but decorated by nails. Besides, owing to its unique status, there are numerous plates from well known scholars and VIP's and some of them even endorsed by emperors of different dynasties, making them of so much historical value. At the two sides on the walls of the Worship Hall there fitted two pieces of stone tablets. One of them was set up in the 24th year of Emperor Kang Si (year 1685) by admiral Hsih Long, laying down the whole invasion process of Taiwan as well as how to soothe and manage the people thereafter. This stone tablet is the earliest Qing tablet now being kept in Taiwan. Datianhou Temple (Taina Grand Matsu Temple) is full of architectural features as well as things of cultural heritage. Visitors just feel like walking into some ancient art exhibition halls. Everything is so valuable and worth studying.

The Datianhou (Great Queen of Heaven) Temple (Taina Grand Matsu Temple) was built in 1684 for the worship of Taiwan's most popular deity; Matsu, Goddess of the Sea. Mazu is the patron deity of fishermen, and her birthday on the 23rd day of the third lunar month (it falls in April or May) is celebrated each year with frenetic explosions of colorful activity.

The goddess is usually flanked by two guardians, Eyes that See a Thousand Miles and Ears that Hear on the Wind; these are said to have once been malevolent spirits who were reformed by Matsu's example and now use their powers to help her do good works. A secondary deity in this temple is the Old Man under the Moon, a sort of matchmaker god worshipped especially by unmarried men and women. They believe that all they need do is pray to the god for a red matrimonial thread or apply their rouge before him and they will quickly find a mate.

## Huangxi Academy (Huangxi Temple)

TEL: +886-4-2228-9111

Address: No.10, Wenchang 1st St., Dadu District, Taichung City

Huangxi Temple is located in Taichung City and it is also called Wenchang Temple. The temple was built in 1888 and the architecture was of late Qing style. The temple worships Wenchang Dijun, and scholars would gather here for discussion. During the Japanese occupation, the temple was forced to close. However, after World War II, people found that part of the property was sold and objects were stolen.

Huangxi Temple is a building of traditional southern Fujian style. The decoration is delicate and the brick works are refined. It is one of the most artistic buildings in Taiwan and is highly valued in architecture. The roof has five sections and six wallow tails. There are ventilators on the smaller roofs, which is both artistic and practical.

## Jiaoxi Xietian Temple

TEL: +886-3-988-2621

Address: No.51, Sec. 1, Zhongshan Rd., Jiaoxi Township, Yilan County

This temple, also known as Guandi Temple, can be reached by walking south from the railway station along Zhongshan Road for about one kilometer. Built in 1804, this is the largest and most important temple in northern Taiwan devoted to Guangong, the red-faced God of War.

The most important activities at this temple are the spring and autumn rites which take place on the 13th day of the first lunar month and the 24th day of the sixth lunar month, respectively. These are the times when images of all the "branch gods" that have been consecrated at Xietian Temple over the years are brought" back from all over Taiwan for communion with the 'senior' deity, and devotees flock into the temple in great crowds. The ceremonies involve offerings to the god and a ritual dance performed by primary school students acting as Guangong's soldiers. The spring rites also include turtles fashioned of sticky rice, which are offered to the god in thanks for services rendered or in supplication for help.

## Dharma Drum Mountain

TEL: +886-2-2498-7171

Address: No.14-5, Banling, Jinshan Dist., New Taipei City

The Dharma Drum Mountain (DDM) sits on a scenic hillside near the intersection of the North Coast Highway and Yangmingshan-Jinshan

Highway in Sanjie Village, Jinshan District, New Taipei City. Embraced by mountains and the Shuangxi River, the site looks out to the surrounding peaks and Green Bay in the distance.

The Dharma Drum Mountain World Center for Buddhist Education here was built through the collective effort of Buddhists brought together by Master Sheng Yen as a place for education, Buddhist practice, and culture.

The site could not have been more perfectly matched to the spirit of DDM. Facing south, the left side of the mountain resembles a green dragon with head raised or an ancient bell hanging in the sky, while the right side suggests a white tiger with head bowed. Viewed from above, the main part of the mountain looks a giant drum set lengthwise. The name of the village in which DDM is located also aptly reflects the "Three Realms" of existence in Buddhist belief, symbolizing the ability of the Dharma to overcome all and spread throughout the world.

## Lungshan Temple

TEL: +886-2-2302-5162

Address: No. 211, Guangzhou St., Wanhua District, Taipei City

Lungshan Temple is a famous old temple in Taiwan. It is for worshiping Guanshiyin Budda and other divine spirits. Lungshan Temple is facing the South. Its architecture is a three-section design in shape. There are the front hall, the rear hall and the right/left dragons protecting the middle hall. The layout is square and serene. The temple was built in Qianlong 5th year in Qing Dynasty. Due to natural disaster and damages caused by men, the temple was restored for several times. The doors, beams, and poles are beautifully decorated. There is a pair of bronze dragon poles in the front hall, four pairs of dragon poles in the middle hall. The sculptures are delicate. There are also exquisite wood sculptures. Among them, the well and Budda setting in the main hall are highly appreciated. The temple has many Chinese poems, verses and lyrics on signs. These add a touch of literature in addition to the religious and sightseeing value.

There are great decorative lamp fairs and temple activities on historical festivals. On each 1st and 15th day each month of lunar year, regular visitors will come to the temple for worship ceremony. The temple attracts many people. At normal times, there are domestic/foreign tourists visiting the temple. Lungshan Temple is not only a temple, a sightseeing attraction, but also a second-degree historical site. There are traditional streets/shops, antique shops, Buddhists article shops, and Chinese medicine shops surrounding the temple. These places are great to visit due to their richness in folk art.

## Tainan Confucius Temple

TEL: +886-6-220-0487

Address: No.2, Nanmen Rd., West Central Dist., Tainan City 700, Taiwan (R.O.C.)

The Confucius Temple in Tainan was built in 1666, it was the first Confucius Temple, before the end of Manchu Dynasty, it was the location of the highest official institute of higher learning in Taiwan. The Taiwan Palace of "Confucianism Study," it owned the incompatible position of culture and education, and was called "The Highest Institute." The Confucius Temple has been through more than thirty times of reconstruction, a part of the building was destroyed during the wars or ruined by nature disasters; the present scale of the Confucius Temple was the look after reconstructing during the time when Japanese were ruling (1917), its elegant and simple localization characteristic takes a distinctive attitude of its own among the Confucius Temples buildings in Taiwan. There are fifteen structures inside the Confucius Temple, the primary sacrifices in the palace is to Confucius divine tablet, on both sides, the sacrifices are to the sixteen pupils of Confucius.

Between the beams and pillars, there hang twelve horizontal described boards awarded by sovereigns of all dynasties since early Manchu Dynasty till today, it is the Confucius Temple in Taiwan to own the most complete royal horizontal described boards of all dynasties. Inside the temple, there are very old trees towering, classical elegant and tranquil, self-becoming a place of its own, the whole space presents a cultural breath, and is presently ranked among the national first-degree historic spots. Speaking of the preservation of the cultural articles in the Confucius, the inscriptional records through all times of repairs, the horizontal described boards awarded by sovereigns of all dynasties, and ceremony and musical instruments from early Manchu Dynasty till nowadays are still kept perfectly, and these are all very precious historical cultural articles that deserve to be carefully appreciated.

## Kaohsiung Rose Basilica

TEL: +886-7-221-4434

Address: No. 151, Wufu 3rd Rd., Lingya District, Kaohsiung City (by Love River)

Standing on Wufu 3rd Road, Lingya District, Kaohsiung City, the Kaohsiung Rose Basilica was established in the Xianfeng Reign Period of the Qing Dynasty and is commonly called Qianjin Cathedral. Rev. Fernando Sainz coordinated the fundraising and construction for this Gothic-style church. Madonna is enshrined and worshiped in the middle of the main hall. It is Taiwan's first Rose Basilica.

The church was established in the ninth year of Xianfeng Reign of Qing Dynasty (1859) when Spanish missionaries Rev. Terdirand and Rev. Angel Bofurull, o.p. came to Taiwan. It was reformed in 1860 and named Rose Basilica. Reformed again in 1928 into a Renaissance-style architecture, it became Taiwan's most representative church of decoration art with layers of decorative lines that display beautiful geometric patterns added for its arch ceilings, and the shrine and holy table on the altar that manifest the artistry of Chinese carving. The current Kaohsiung Rose Basilica was completed in 1931 and is an excellent place to visit.

## Tzu Chi Headquarters

Tzu Chi represents one of Taiwan's four major Buddhist sects, and its Still Thought Hall, located on Zhongyang Road in Hualien, includes a medical center, a temple, and a university. The temple is a Tang Dynasty-style three-tiered flying eaves structure, with classic corridors, round pillars, and a solemn atmosphere. Still Thought Abode is a simple white-walled, gray-tiled building; this is the cradle of the Tzu Chi sect, and contains displays that offer a window into an understanding of Tzu Chi. Together the two structures constitute a center of Tzu Chi Buddhist faith; and if you want to relieve yourself of worldly concerns and purify your spirit, this is the place to go.

## Eternal Fortress

TEL: +886-6-295-1504

Address: No.3, Guangzhou Rd., Anping District, Tainan City

Eternal Golden Castle was called "Anping Great Fort" or "Twice Fish Length Fort" in the ancient time, it was built to resist the Japanese troops who invaded Taiwan due to Peony Suffix Event. When Shern Bao-Tzen first arriving in Anping in 1874, he believed that Great Forts should be built to protect the city, therefore, the first western style fort was finally completed in 1876, which was designed by French engineers, it was the first port equipped with British Armstrong Cannon in Taiwan, moreover, it was a great step toward modernization of Taiwanese coastguard military defense.

On the construction form, Eternal Golden Castle is a square shape fort belongs to the western diamond type castle, with its four corners protruding, and its center indenting. There are fosses around the fort, and the fort is placed with big and small cannons, while the center of the port is used as exercising field; the shape is of integrity and complete, the scale is huge, supported with powerful fort, Eternal Golden Castle can be seen as the important epoch-making milestone among all forts in Taiwan. The fort was ruined later on, and was once neglected, but later it was ranked among one of the noted sights in the city and was carefully reserved. After the restoration, a major reconstruction was carried out, the shape and the materials were more or less changed.

But after the reconstruction, the original scale can generally be seen. Nowadays, its outer walls are about two meters high, the fosses are around the castle's walls, trees and woods are thickly growing, the bricks laying arched castle gate is 5 meters high, through the arched castle gate, what you can see is a carpet of green grass, flat and wide, there are also memorial brass sculpture of Shern Bao-Tzen and imitated ancient cannons.

## Anping Old Fort

TEL: +886-6-226-7348

Address: No.82, Guosheng Rd., Anping District, Tainan City

In 1624, Dutch built the first fort in Anping, Taiwan, called "Fort Zeelandia", now known as Anping Old Fort, where has been the administrative center of the Dutch regime, and the hub for trading. The building was originally constructed in square inner fortress and rectangle outer walls. In 1661, the fort was renamed as Anping to commemorate his home town when Guoxingye (Cheng Cheng-Kung) has driven the Dutch out of Taiwan. Therefore, Fort Zeelandia was also known as "King's Fort" or "Taiwan Fort", nicknamed Anping Old Fort.

In Kangxi Emperor's regime of Qing Dynasty, Taiwan was included in the empire that the political center was transferred to Tainan City, causing the decline of the Fort. The red bricks of the Fort have been taken for construction of Eternal Fortress. During the Japanese occupation, the Dutch style buildings in inner fortress were completely destroyed. A square red-bricked step platform was constructed with a western style house on the platform, being served as dormitory for Customs officials, where the memorial hall now is located. It was named Anping Old Fort after Restoration of Taiwan and become an attraction for tourists. The remaining more than 70 meters long south walls of the outer fort with worn-out red bricks, accompanied by the old banyan roots, chanted its odyssey. The fort is the very historical replica over three hundred years.

## Penghu Queen of Heaven Temple (Tianhou Temple)

TEL: +886-6-921-6521

Address: No. 1, Zhengyi St., Magong City, Penghu County

The Queen of Heaven Temple (Tianhou Temple) at Magong was built in 1592. It is Taiwan's oldest and finest temple. The temple survived for an age of 400 years and has become the worshipping center of Penghu residents. The architecture is the work of famous Tangshan artists. Every part of the temple is made with utmost refined style. Inside the temple are some prized Ching period arts. Its inside out is the extreme artistic presentation of styling and sculpture. There is also a tablet in memory of Yojong Sheng's success in persuading Dutch invaders to retreat, which is also the earliest tablet found in Taiwan.

## Fort San Domingo

TEL: +886-2-2623-1001

Address: No.1, Lane 28, Zhongzheng Rd., Tamsui District, New Taipei City

This is Tamsui's most prominent monument to foreign involvement in Taiwan. First built in 1629 by the Spanish, Fort San Domingo was intended to aid the imposition of Spanish rule over the local Chinese and aboriginal populations in northern Taiwan.

This fort was captured by the Dutch in 1642 when they drove the Spanish from the island. They replaced the Spanish-built stockade with a fort made of stone. The fort became known as the "Hongmao Castle" (Fort of the Red Heads) in reference to the colorful locks of its Dutch occupants.

In 1867, the British leased the fort and undertook massive renovations, which included the construction of the imposing British Consulate in the eastern section of the fortress compound. Its red brick verandah and red roof tiles complement the color scheme and design of the fort.

Hongmao Castle's position overlooking the mouth of the Tamsui River makes it a particularly attractive scenic spot, especially at sunset.

## Taipei Confucius Temple

TEL: +886-2- 2592-3934

Address: No.275, Dalong St., Datong Dist., Taipei City 103, Taiwan (R.O.C.)

The Taipei Confucius Temple is right across Dalong Street. This temple honors one of the greatest philosophers and teachers of all time,

Confucius, as well as other philosophers. Confucius valued simplicity, and simplicity is the dominant characteristic of his temple. Here you see none of the densely rich decor of many other temples; even the usual stone lions are missing from the entrance. The columns, doors, and windows here are also different, in that they bear no inscriptions.

This indicates, it is said, that nobody dares flaunt his literary prowess before the Master. Nor are there any images in this temple. In ancient times, Confucius temples contained images of the Sage, but different craftsman carved them in different likenesses. This lack of uniformity upset Emperor Tai Tsu (reigned 1368 A.D.) of the Ming dynasty, who decreed that all new Confucius temples would henceforth contain only memorial tablets and no images. Later on, during the reign of emperor Shi cong (1522-1586), it was decreed that all existing images of Confucius be replaced with memorial tablets. This rule is still followed today.

Standing outside of Dacheng Hall, the main hall of this temple, you can see a pair of upright cylinders in the center of the roof. These are called book-hiding barrels, and there is a story behind them. In ancient times, the first Emperor (reigned 246-214 B.C.) of the Qin dynasty wanted to keep his people illiterate so that they would not challenge his rule; he had books burned and scholars killed. To save their beloved books, students hid them in rooftop containers built to look like chimneys.

## Sacrificial Rites Martial Temple (Official God of War Temple)

TEL: +886-6-299-1111

Address: No.229, Sec. 2, Yongfu Rd., West Central District, Tainan City

This temple, along with the Confucius Temple, is known as one of the oldest and best-preserved temples in Taiwan. Just when it was originally built is not known, but according to legend it was during the Ming dynasty's Yungli reign, in the mid-17th century. During the Qing dynasty, this was where government officials offered sacrifices to the god.

The God of War (Guandi or Guangong) worshipped here holds a heavy sword and rides a swift horse. His mortal origin was as a general of the late Han dynasty (early 3rd century) who, because of his behavior, becomes a symbol of uprightness and loyalty to later generations and was finally deified. He is said to have been good at managing finances and to have invented a method of accounting, and so is also worshipped (by businessmen, especially) as the God of Commerce.

The entrance to this temple has a particularly high threshold, and for a reason. In the old days, it is said, women were banned from the temple and the high threshold was designed to keep them out.

## Fo Gunag Mountain (Fo Gunag Shan) Monastery

TEL: +886-7-656-1921

Address: No.153, Xingtian Road, Xingtian Village, Dashu District, Kaohsiung City

At the north-east of Dashu Township in Kaohsiung county on the left bank of the Gaoping (Kaoping) river, a famous tourist destination is located. Here you will find the Buddhist center of South Taiwan, established my Master Hsing Yun and his disciples. The architecture of the temples is very characteristic, and at the southeastern side of Fo Gunag Mountain (Gunag Shan) Monastery the most prominent landmark of the region is found: a huge golden statue of Buddha Amitaabha which measures some 120 meters.

The main square is surrounded by 480 standing Buddha's, while water and mountains form the magnificent scenery. The main structures consist of four temples, namely the Daxiongbao, the Dabei , the Dazhi and the Dashu shrines. The Daxiongbao shrine covers a large area and is the most imposing of all four shrines. The main god of worship here is Sakyamuni, while statues of Amitaabha is placed on the left and right sides. More than 10,000 Guanyin statues surround the temple. Buddha statues and lanterns of light rest in the 14,800 holes in the walls of the four shrines. The site counts more than a thousand Buddha statues, large and small.

## Qingshan Temple

TEL: +886-2-2382-2296

Address: No. 218, Sec. 2, Guiyang St., Wanhua District, Taipei City

Built in 1854, this temple is home to the god King Qingshan. According to legend, fishermen from Hui-an in mainland China brought the god's image to Taiwan; when they carried it past Old Street (today's Xiyuan Road) they suddenly found themselves brought to a halt; the god refused to move any further. Throwing the oracle blocks to find out what the matter was, the god's devotees discovered that he wanted to stay there, where they later built the temple. An epidemic was raging at the time, but prayers to King Qingshan were sure to bring a recovery; thus the god's grateful devotees increased, and they contributed money to build a new temple-the one that exists today.

The temple is home to two guardians, General Hsieh Pi-an and Fan Wu-ti. In the early days the chains in their hands were often heard clanging in the temple and the streets nearby, or the generals were seen patrolling the streets. Thus there were very few thieves in the neighborhood. The celebration marking the birthday of King Qingshan is held on the 22nd day of the 10th lunar month (Dec 10, 1998; Nov 29, 1999; Nov 17, 2000). On that day all of the other temples in the area also celebrate the occasion, helping make it one of the most interesting festivals in Mengjia. The approach to this temple takes you past some of Mengjia's most interesting architecture. Sec. 2 of Guiyang Street, which stretches between Qingshan Temple and

Qingshui Temple, is lined with red-brick shops in the Taisho-style. These were built during Japan's Taisho reign period (1912-1925), a time when Japan administered Taiwan as a colony.

## Lukang Longshan Temple

TEL: +886-4-777-2472

Address: No.81, Jinmen Lane, Lukang Township, Changhua County

Lukang is one of the important historical towns in Taiwan. It is the town for well preserved historical cites, old houses, old temples and folk arts. Longshan Temple is called the Forbidden City in Taiwan. It is the best among the 8 great scenes of Lukang. Longshan Temple in Lukang was originally a small temple in Lukang. Later it was remodeled by local residents to be the current larger scale. The temple was beautifully designed. It is seated facing the west with the back to the east. The layout is square.

The main building consists of four strata and three gardens. The format and design are inspired by Longshan Temple in Quanzhou (Chuanchow) of Taiwan. In the old days, there were 99 doors. The carving is magnificent in terms of the structure and the ornament. There is fine colorful painting. It has the reputation of being the Treasure of Chinese Architectural Art. The buildings are worthy of detailed observation. At the front gate, there is a pair of dragon poles made of granite. There are the ascending dragon and the descending dragon corresponding to each other. The design is simple and powerful and they are excellent art works.

At the end of front hall, there is a theater stage for traditional plays at festivals. There is an octagon well within the theater stage. Its colorful painting and the good technique reflect superb art works. In the past, the houses around Longshan Temple could not be higher than the temple. The buildings in Longshan Temple are getting higher and higher. It means ascending. There are many historical artifacts in the temple. For an example, there is an old bell from Ching Dynasty. It was made in Ninpo of Chekiang Province in China. It is the largest bronze bell in Taiwan. There is also a Guanshiyin Budda made of copper. The complexity of Longshan Temple in Lukang is amazing and the buildings in the temple are marvelous and rarely seen in Taiwan.

## Xingtian Temple

TEL: +886-2-2502-7924

Address: No. 109, Sec. 2, Minquan E. Rd., Zhongshan District, Taipei City

This very busy temple is devoted to Guan, a famous deified general who lived (A. D. 162-219) during the Three Kingdoms period. A man, who valued loyalty and righteousness above all things, Guangong is worshipped as the God of War; since he was adept at managing finances, he is also worshipped as the patron saint of businessmen.

This is young temple, built in 1967, with a simple and dignified appearance. In front of the hall is a censer with a somewhat unusual design, its two handles in the shape of flying dragons and its four sides adorned with dragons' heads stretching toward the sky. The courtyard of the temple is usually busy, with crowds of worshippers bowing their heads or kneeling in devotion.

On the main altar you will see offerings of only fresh flowers and tea, since the temple forbids the killing of offering of animals. The temple also discourages the burning of ritual paper money as an offering to the deities and the spirits of the deceased, the staging of operas for the gods, the presenting of gold medallions in gratitude to the deities, and the like. The temple supplies free candles, and there is no donation box-a first for traditional religion in Taiwan!

Many believers feel that this is a very efficacious temple, and it is frequently thronged with people praying for help and seeking divine guidance by consulting oracle blocks. Even the pedestrian underpass outside the temple is filled with fortune-tellers and vendors who take commercial advantage of the temple's popularity.

## Songshan Ciyou Temple

TEL: +886-2-2766-3012

Address: No. 761, Sec. 4, Bade Rd., Songshan District, Taipei City

This temple, built in the mid-18th century, is the cradle of development of the Songshan district. The story goes that a monk once roamed this area, carrying a gilded image of Mazu, Goddess of the Sea, as he begged for alms. One day at Xikou- the old name for this district- the monk came upon a number of people, all Mazu believers, from his old home. Together they planned construction of a temple to honor the goddess, and after raising funds for more than 10 years they were able to realize their dream. Construction started in 1753 and was completed in 1757.

The top of the temple roof is richly ornamented; in addition to human figures, there is also a flying dragon placed there because dragons were believed to have the power to prevent fires. Inside the temple are layer after layer of oil lamps lighted by devotees in the hope that Mazu will grant their wishes. The side altar to the right of the Mazu image enshrines the Earth God, who is protected on either side by flag-gearing Tiger Lords. The side altar to the left is devoted to Zhusheng Niang-niang, the Goddess of Birth. This goddess is normally accompanied by 12 female aides, but here she has 13. The extra aide is Duyu Niang; in life she was a midwife who never accepted money for helping women with childbirth, so after death she was deified because of her kindness and skill.

## Beigang Chaotian Temple

TEL: +886-5-783-0535

Address: No.178, Zhongshan Rd., Beigang Township, Yunlin County

The Chaotian Temple in Beigang was built in 1694 and is more than 290 years old. It used to be called Tianfei Temple or Tianhou Temple. In order to commemorate Mazu Temple (Chaotian Building) in Meizhou of China, it was thus re-named as Chaotian Temple. Because of the wide-spread reputation, Chaotian Temple has become the head temple for more than 300 Taiwan temples worshipping Mazu (the Goddess).The temple is grand and beautiful.

The temple is for worship of Tianshang Shengmu, Guanshiyin Buddha and spirits like Qianliyan (the spirit who can see very far) and Shunfeng'er (the Spirit who can hear very far). The poles and beams and wood carving are accomplished by famous artists. The four stone dragon sculptures forming the four poles outside the temple are majestic and lively. There is a traditional well in the form of arch web. The excellent craftsmanship is shown everywhere, from the facial expression of figures on windows to the grand dragon poles. It is indeed a classic combination of religion and arts.

Many people come to Chaotian Temple in Beigang for worshiping all year round. The greatest worship festival is on Chinese lunar new year to March of lunar year. Around the birthday of Mazu (March 19th of lunar year), many religious people and affiliated temples head toward Beigang for celebration. The scale of the activity is grand and there is parade in Beigang. The place is filled with sound of traditional Chinese instruments playing and many people. The parade is the highlight of celebration activities for Mazu. At the time, the whole Beigang is submerged in the religious atmosphere.

## Dalongdong Bao'an Temple

TEL: +886-2-2595-1676

Address: No. 61, Hami St., Datong District, Taipei City

Located at the confluence of the Tamsui and Keelung rivers, DaLong Cave (Longdong) developed very early. The center of worship here is Bao-an Temple, built in 1825. This is a large temple, and its construction was different; in addition, all of the wood and stone materials and even the artisans had to be brought over from mainland China. For these reason, the temple required a full quarter-century to complete.

This temple features the usual dragon pillars, and also a pair of stone lion that are not so usual. Normally, of the two lions (one male, one female) that guard a temple, the male has an open mouth and the female a closed mouth; here, however, both have open mouths. It is said that they are not lions at all but a "humane beast" and a "law beast," stationed there as an appeal to respect the law and carry out good government.

## Zhinan Temple

TEL: +886-2-2939-9922

Address: No.115, Wanshou Rd., Wunshan District, Taipei City

Zhinan Temple in the Wenshan District is one of the main religious institutions in Zhinan.

The name "Zhinan Temple" includes two important meanings: 1. that the god, Lu Enzhu resides at the Southern ("nan") temple in the Heavenly Court; and 2. that in order to determine who on Earth needs help, he uses a compass ("zhinan").

In the same area, there is also Fude Temple, dedicated to the land god. In front of the temple, there is Qixing (Seven Stars) Pond, which was designed according to fengshui principles and also serves as a receptacle for believers to place their monetary contributions. Taking the stone steps, it is possible to reach Zhinan Temple Corridor, as well as see the entire Muzha tea farm landscape.

This temple is known to foreigners as "the Temple of a Thousand Steps." This is no exaggeration there are actually around 1,200 stone steps up to the temple and there is a saying, "live an extra 20 seconds for each step you climb." If this is true, you can add more than six hours to your life by climbing all of the steps.

The main deity in this temple is Lu Tunpin, one of the Eight Immortals of Chinese legends. He is a well-loved deity, despite a reputation for somewhat randy behavior. He is said to return frequently to the mortal world to bring salvation to the faithful.

Zhinan Temple sits on Monkey Mountain and, in addition to the steps, is accessible by a paved road. But the stone steps are worth a trip in themselves; they are flanked by rows of stone posts topped by stone lanterns that were donated by devotees during the period of Japanese occupation (1895-1945).

## Chikanlou

TEL +886-6-299-1111

Address: No.212, Sec. 2, Minzu Rd., West Central District, Tainan City

Tainan Chikanlou（Chihkanlou）is built by the Dutch in 1652. It was originally called Provintia. In Dutch it means eternity. The Chinese called the building "Chikanlou（Chihkanlou）", "Fanzailou" or "Honmaolou". Although Chikanlou（Chihkanlou）has gone through Ming Dynasty, Qing Dynasty and the Japanese Colonization Period, it basically still maintains its original look.

Chikanlou（Chihkanlou）has been an administration center from the Dutch's occupation period. In 1661, when the Chinese General Cheng Chengkung repelled the Dutch, Provintia was changed to be Chentien governor's mansion. In the early stage of Qing Dynasty when Taijiang River was still running, the tides could reach Chikanlou ( Chihkanlou ) directly. "The sunset in Chikanlou ( Chihkanlou " was one of the eight famous scenes in Taiwan. In front of Chikanlou ( Chihkanlou ) there are nine sets of stone turtles carrying plates. There were made in Qing Dynasty and were removed from elsewhere to be located here. The legend says that the stone turtle is one of the dragon's nine sons. It shifted into a turtle because it loved to endure heavy objects. There is also a stone horse with broken legs. The legend says that the stone horse's legs were broken by force because it shape-shifted into a monster at night and harassed the residents. Later, Chikanlou ( Chihkanlou ) declined due to damages caused by civilian upheaval and lack of management. Chinese style building was added to the original Dutch architectural body. For a time the place hosted the worship for Guanshiyin Budda. During the Japanese colonization period, Chikanlou ( Chihkanlou ) was changed to be army hospital. There were some restoration and repair. After Taiwan was returned to R.O.C., the wooden structure was changed into steel concrete structure. The main entrance was changed. Thus they created the look of Chikanlou ( Chihkanlou ) today.

## The Red House

TEL: +886-2-2311-9380

Address: No.10, Chengdu Rd., Wanhua District, Taipei City

The Red House, a Western-style red-brick octagonal structure in Taipei's Ximen space built in 1908, is Taiwan's first public market and the most well preserved historical site. Designed by Kondo Juro, a western-styled architect in the prefectural civil engineering office at the time, the market entrance, incorporating both octagonal and cruciform shapes, was paralleled by no other in the east and west. The market entrance also took on the "eight trigrams (bagua)" design considered boldly creative then. Octagon Building, Cruciform Building, and the adjacent South-North Square are now collectively known as the Red House.

In November, 2007, Department of Cultural Affairs commissioned Taipei Culture Foundation to manage The Red House. It underwent a series of cultural transformation including: at Octagon Building 2F Theater, Central Display Area, The Red House Tea Shop, The Red House Select Shop, at Cruciform Building 16 Workshops, Cultural Arts Exhibition Platform, Riverside Live House, Market for Artists & Designers located by North Square and Outdoor Café located by South Square. These changes provided better services to the general public, created a space of creativity, attracted crowds, and expanded the domain of overlapping cultural arts. The Red House has successfully transformed into a new cultural & creative industries development center in Taipei City. In 2008, it was awarded The 7th Urban Landscape Award in Historical Space Redevelopment Category.

## Guandu Temple

TEL: +886-2-2858-1281

Address: No.360, Zhixing Rd., Beitou District, Taipei City

About a 15-minute walk from Guandu MRT Station is the Guandu Temple. The temple, first built in 1661, is dedicated to Mazu, goddess of the sea. Beside the temple is a kind of Buddhist chapel dedicated to the Buddhist goddess of mercy, Guanyin of Thousand Arms and Eyes. Outside the temple there are numerous stalls selling products such as spirit money used in religious observances, as well as snack foods and souvenirs.

The hillside above the temple provides excellent views of the river and the mangrove swamps. The dike that stretches from Guandu in both directions toward Taipei and Tamsui is an ideal place to take a stroll or enjoy the scenic beauty afforded by the wide expanse of the river. Founded in 1661, this is the oldest Mazu (goddess of the sea) temple in northern Taiwan; its original name was "Ling-shan (Mt. Ling) Temple," since it is located atop Mt. Ling. According to legend, in 1895 three old banyan trees standing at the temple's entrance died suddenly during the same night; local residents believed that this might have been a message from Mazu warning of impending disaster- and sure enough, the area was soon occupied by the Japanese.

Guandu temple is filled with exquisitely carved dragon pillars, stone lions, and wall sculptures. Even the door gods are in the form of relief carvings, in contrast to the usual paintings. The rafters and beams are also beautifully carved and painted. On the main altar sits an image of Mazu, the benign expression on her face in sharp contrast to the fierce visages of the guardians who flank her, Eyes that See a Thousand Miles and Ears that Hear on the Wind.

To the right of the temple is an 80 meter Buddha cave, at the entrance of which is a symbolic mortar that is supposedly able to suppress all evil. The sides of the cave are lined by 28 devas, and at the rear is a thousand armed, thousand-eyed Guanyin, or goddess of Mercy. To the rear of Guanyin is the cave's exit and a fine river view.

## Baimiweng Fort (Holland Castle)

TEL: +886-2-2428-7664 (Keelung City Visitor Information

Address: End of Lane 37, Guanghua Road, Zhongshan District, Keelung City

TheBaimiweng Fort (Holland Castle) is located on the upland at the west bank of Keelung Port. It was probably installed more than 300 years ago during the Spanish and Holland colonial periods and is thus also known as the "Gun Emplacement of Fort Holland." It was once occupied by French troops during the Sino-French War. The Japanese colonial government remodeled the place to become the way it looks today.

Among all the gun emplacements still exist in Taiwan, this is the only one that has a shape of a rectangular platform and is listed one of the country's third-class historical sites. However, there is no cannon at the site today. The vestiges of four platforms and fragments of wall are all that is left. While the command post at the left side of the emplacement has been remodeled, the observation post at the right side can be reached by taking the stone steps next to a pavilion. The view up here is magnificent, with the earth and sky spreading out to form a harmonious picture.

## Hsinchu City God Temple

TEL: +886-3-522-3666

Address: No.75, Zhongshan Rd., North District, Hsinchu City

Hsinchu City god Temple (Chenghuang Temple) is regarded as the highest-ranking of all City God temples in Taiwan, due to the superior spiritual power of its City God in protecting the town.

In front of the temple is a market with a lot of small stalls selling delicious Taiwanese snacks, including rice noodles, meat balls, thick cuttlefish broth, and Zhuqian Biscuit (Zhuqian is the original name of Hsinchu).

Hsinchu is famous for a number of specialty foods, especially Hsinchu rice noodles, which are produced in Nanshr Village, Hsinchu City. Another famous product of Hsinchu is shiangfen, a traditional cosmetic powder which was used by women throughout Taiwan before the arrival of foreign-style cosmetic products. The powder is also used in offerings to Qiniangma, the guardian spirit of children. Only one store, run by the Tsai Family in Julian Street, still produces this powder. Although there are many stalls from which Hsinchu meatballs can be purchased, many are concentrated around the Chenghuang Temple. The famous Peanut Butter is sold mainly along Dongda Road, and if you want to try Zhuqian Biscuits, you should go to the Shinfujen Cake Shop at No.26 Beimen Street.

## Yanshui Wu Temple

TEL: +886-6-652-1264

Address: No.87, Wumiao Rd., Yanshui District, Tainan City

Yanshui Beehive Firecracker

The lantern festival in Taiwan is characterized by sky lanterns in the north and beehive firecrackers in the south. Customarily, it is believed that bad luck would go away after one is bombed with beehive firecrackers. Hence, the Yanshui Beehive Firecracker attracts tens of thousands enthusiastic participants, and even foreign media and visitors are attracted to the event.

People in Yanshui feel most proud on the 14th and 15th day of the first month on the Lunar Calendar because these are days to play beehive firecrackers. Wherever the god's sedan chairs go, town residents light firecrackers, and beehives, fireworks, and sparklers of all kinds shot up through the sky with loud thundering sounds, coming with beautiful misty smokes and lighting up the night sky in a magnificent festive fashion. The streets of entire town of Yanshui are so densely covered with scarps of firecracker paper that the surface of the asphalt road is hardly seen. Visitors from every corner of the nation and abroad are eager to see for themselves the thrilling and exciting scenery on the evening of Lantern Festival.

Yanshui Wu Temple

The temple is also named "Guandi Temple," and was first established in the Yongli Reign Period. In the fourth year of the Jiaqing Reign Period (1799), Lin Wun Jyun of Lugang came to Tainan (which was then the capital town of Taiwan) for a legal case. When he was released, he felt greatly thankful for Lord Guandi's (Guangong) blessings and provided capital to refurbish the temple, laying the foundation for the temple's scale today.

The custom of lighting beehive firecrackers is said to be deeply linked with the Wu Temple. Legend has it that a plague once occurred in the

Yanshui area during the Guangxu Reign Period and the staggering number of people dying every day caused great panic among the residents. Not knowing what to do with the disease, they had no alternative but to ask gods and Buddha for a solution. Lord Guandi had always been very efficacious in the local area, so they prayed to him for safety. Lord Guandi answered to their plea just as expected. He ordered the residents to carry sedan chairs on the evening of the Lantern Festival with Jhou Cang He at the front of the parade team and his statue at the very back and firecrackers lit along the way through every street and lane along the border the Yanshui area until dawn.

After the night of Lantern Festival, the Yanshui area became safe and the local people decided to make the firecracker parade an annual custom to remember with gratitude the blessings from Lord Guandi. The custom continued to develop and became the current beehive event on the 14th and 15th day of the first month in the Lunar Calendar every year. Today, the event is hosted by the Wu Temple and considered an annual grand occasion of folk art in the Yanshui area, leaving glorious records on the history of Yanshui.

For the past one hundred years, the local residents have had the belief that the more firecrackers one is bombed with, the luckier he or she is in the coming new year. So remember to wear a helmet, mask, and transparent eye pads. Raincoats and plastic boots also come as part of the standard garments for the event. Arrive at the Yanshui Wu Temple well ahead of time, and be ready to enjoy this one-of-a-kind beehive carnival.

## Recreational Areas

### Daxueshan National Forest Recreation Area

TEL: +886-4-2587-7901

Address: No.18, Xueshan Rd., Heping Dist., Taichung City

Long an important logging area in central Taiwan, Daxueshan National Forest Recreation Area retains few virgin stands and the current forest ecology is composed mainly of second-growth temperate and warm zone species, forming a typical mixed coniferous-broadleaf forest.

The upper level of the forest is dominated by Taiwan cryptomeria, red cypress, Taiwan yellow cypress, Taiwan spruce, hemlock and Taiwan red pine. The local hemlocks are huge and have broad-reaching boughs. The forest is also the most abundant mid-elevation bird habitat in all of Taiwan.

Daxueshan maintains an average year-round temperature of 12 degrees centigrade, making it a popular summer destination. The spring blooms, autumn maples and winter frosts complete the area's seasonally changing scenic attraction. The view of the evening sky and cloud formations set against the mountain ranges is a sight that is hard to surpass anywhere on the island.

## Fuyuan National Forest Recreation Area

TEL: +886-3-881-2377

Address: Guangdong Rd., Fuyuan Village, Ruisui Township, Hualien County

The Fuyuan National Forest Recreation Area is located in the mountain foothills three kilometers to the west of Fuyuan Village in Ruisui Township. In addition to having the largest stand of camphor trees of any recreation area in Taiwan, its 190 hectares also features a butterfly valley (where the butterflies swarm from March to August) and scenic waterfalls.

As you stroll along the footpath through the camphor forest, you can learn all about the area's insects, birds, trees, and other vegetation from the explanatory plaques that are positioned there.

Fuyuan Stream, which runs through the recreation area, offers an abundance of boulders in interesting shapes as well as intermittent hot springs. Following the stream upwards into the gorge, and you will soon come to a series of waterfalls that cascade over sheer cliffs

## Hehuanshan National Forest Recreation Area

TEL: +886-49-280-2732

Address: Hehuanshan National Forest Recreation Area, Ren-ai Township, Nantou County

Taiwan's mountains are attracting the attention of hikers from all over the world for their height, which rivals the Alps and the Rocky Mountains, and their beautiful alpine scenery. While some of the highest peaks require considerable time and effort to reach, there is one place on the island that gives an instant overview of what Taiwan's mountains have to offer.

Mt. Hehuan, despite its altitude of more than 3,000 meters, has a road that goes right across it, making access very convenient. It is the best place to see snow in the tropics, and escape from the summer heat. In as little as one day, you can travel the highest road in East Asia, and take the many hiking paths that lead off the main road. These are usually short and always safe. Mt. Hehuan, Taiwan's "tourist mountain," rivals the island's other high peaks in scenery and atmosphere, yet it is easily reachable by car or on foot.

Accommodation is offered at Hohuan Cottage. At the same time, it is the starting point for one of Taiwan's most challenging and exciting treks, Chilai Ridge, a two-day "ultimate experience" that involves negotiating a knife-edge ridge with many dizzying pinnacles. Although the road scares away many of the birds and animals for which Taiwan is known, a short walk along the trails leading off the main road, particularly those in the direction of Chilai, will reveal their presence."

## Yehliu Ocean World

TEL: +886-2-2492-1111

Address: No. 167-3, Gangdong Rd., Wanli Dist., New Taipei City

The Yehliu Ocean World is the first ocean world in Taiwan; you can see different marine animal or oceanic species and many different shows such as dolphin show or sea lion show, except the shows, the springboard diving and the ocean tunnel takes you to a trip to enjoy the amazing ocean world and to see how those special creation lives under the world. You can totally enjoy your time and have an unforgettable oceanic experience in this great ocean world.

Ocean World is located along the beautiful North Coast near Yehliu, a scenic area with abundant natural resources. There is a plan for a performance auditorium with a capacity of over 3,000. There are startling, high-jumping water presentations held at irregular intervals, cute and smart dolphins, mischievous sea lions and other spectacular performances!

And in the Sea Animal Exhibition Hall, there are the original forms of many sea ecological environments. The Sea Animal Museum also stores samples of many precious sea animals and employs simple language to explain to everyone basic information about the sea.

## Taipingshan National Forest Recreation Area

TEL: +886-3-980-9806

Address: Taiping Village, Datong Township, Yilan County

Taipingshan is situated in the northern county of Yilan and is one of Taiwan's three major national forest recreation areas. With a moist climate and abundant rainfall, it has nurtured an environment rich in ecological resources. The forests that cover the area consist of such valuable trees as Taiwan cypress, Taiwan hemlock, and Japanese cypress.

The area is also blessed with geothermal energy at the Renze Hot Springs, the largest alpine lake on the island (Cuifeng Lake), and a variety of other enchanting scenery. One of the prime tourist spots here is the Taipingshan primeval forest park, which you reach via flights of stone steps lined with purple-leafed maple trees that become especially rich in color between the months of March and November. This used to be a major logging area, and traces of the old logging equipment can still be seen here-the old forestry railroad, ruins of a cable car up the mountain, motorized carts, trestles.

Visitors here can also savor the constantly changing sight of the "sea of clouds," the brilliant sunrise, forest waterfalls, and other alluring scenes. No wonder that this is a favorite vacation spot for the people of Taiwan! Entry to the Taipingshan National Forest Recreation Area requires a B-class mountain permit, and an A-class permit is needed to proceed on to Cuifeng Lake. You can get your permit to the national forest recreation area by presenting your ID card or passport at the Taipingshan inspection post.

Taipingshan Forest Park is located in Datong, Yilan County, 12,000 hectares in area. The park covers the Nanhu Mountain, Sanxing Mountain and Dabajian Mountain. There are abundant cypress and pine trees and it used to be one of the three major forestry centers in Taiwan. Scenery here differs with the seasons. Visitors can come here to appreciate the flowers in spring, the sunrise and clouds in autumn. Vegetation here differs with the altitude.

Scenic spots here include Renze Hot Spring, Forest Park, Forest Tour Track, Wildlife Conservation area and Cuifeng Lake. The plants that change colors, such as maples, have brought Taipingshan beautiful views. Cherry blossoms, plum blossoms and apricot blossoms make the park exquisite scenery.

## Qilan Forest Recreation Area

TEL: +886-3-980-9606

Address: No. 6, Sec. 4, Taiya Rd., Datong Township, Yilan County

The Qilan Forest Recreation Area is located about 38 kilometers up the Northern Cross-Island Highway, at the intersection with the highway's Li Mountain (Lishan) Branch. There is a terraced nursery here for cryptomeria trees, a cottage once used by the late President Chang Kai-shek, a forest foot-path, and a little Tarzan forest playground. Qilan Villa provides accommodation in hotel rooms as well as wood cottages. In its restaurant, the specialty of the house is the locally grown monkey-head mush-room.

This area, surrounded by primeval forest at the 12-kilometer mark of the Qilan Forestry Road, features 51 huge red cypress and Japan cypress trees thousands of years old. Each of the 51 is named after a famous personage from Chinese history, chosen because its age approximates the time when the historical figure lived. One, of course, is named for Confucius, who lived over 2,000 years ago. This linkage with history makes a visit to the Chinese Historic Men Arboretum educational as well as fun.

A Tour of the Ancient Forest

Tours are arranged by, and depart from, the Qilan and Mingchi (Mingchih) forest recreation areas and go to the Chinese Historic Men Arboretum, the natural cypress forest renewal area, and the Forestry By-Products Center.

## The Great Roots Forestry Hot Spring & Spa Resort

TEL: +886-2-2674-9228

Address: No.79, Chajiao Village, Sanxia District, New Taipei City

The Great Roots Forestry Hot Spring & Spa Resort is located in the Dabao River basin in Sanxia District, New Taipei City. The resort covers a 20-hectare site that was formerly Taiwan's biggest tea-processing plant during the Japanese colonial period. The facilities of the nearly century-old resort include a vacation villa formerly used by the Japanese royal family, as well as gardens, fishponds and forest trails. The grounds also include the only low-elevation primitive tropical rain forest in Taiwan, with rare century-old tabular root (buttress root) trees. Veined/mountain figs (Ficus nervosa), Ficus variegata and tree ferns from the dinosaur age are among the nearly 500 species of plants in the rain forest. The forest is also home to more than 4,000 kinds of insect and over 30 kinds of bird, among them the blue - winged pitta—a globally protected species. These entire rare natural wonders wait along with the healthy and relaxing essences of the forest at the resort.

In addition to enjoying the natural scenery, visitors can take a soothing and skin-pampering soak in the carbonic hot springs at the resort.

Many species of tree in tropical rain forests have tabular roots that help keep the soil from washing away in the rain. Such roots grow at a pace of only about one centimeter a year, and are thus extremely precious. The radial tabular roots growing on steep slopes, like those at the Great Roots Forestry Spa Resort, are especially rare in Taiwan.

## Dongshih Forest Garden

TEL: +886-4-2587-2191

Address: No.6-1, Shilin St., Dongshi District, Taichung City

Dongshi Forest Garden is located in the northeast corner of Dongshi District in Taichung City. Known as the Yangmingshan of central Taiwan, the park covers an area of 225 hectares at an elevation of 500 to 700 meters above sea level. This ecologically rich area and seasonally changing park is well equipped for family recreations and company training retreats. The park facilities include vacation cabins, playgrounds, camping and barbecue areas, conference rooms, and hiking trails.

In recent years, Dongshi Forest Garden has enhanced forest management and planted flowers to ensure year-round blooms. The plum blossoms come out January, the cherry blooms and azaleas from January to March, the azaleas, and the paulownia flowers from April to May. From November to January, visitors can also enjoy the fall colors as the maples blush with brilliant reds. The forest park is also a popular firefly viewing area during the months of March to September. And there are park guides on hand to introduce visitors to all of the many of Dongshi Forest Garden.

## E-Da Theme Park

TEL: 0800-588887

Address: No. 10, Sec. 1, Xuecheng Rd., Dashu Dist., Kaohsiung City

An integration of Greek-style environment consisting of major attractions like The ancient Greek temple, The blue and white city of

Santorini with an imagination of being at the Aegean Sea and The Trojan castle.

It has a pristine atmosphere with a touch of breathtaking elements.

It has the largest entertainment theatre and the biggest indoor recreation center in Taiwan.

Enjoy the country's first roller coaster ride in a complete pitch-black surrounding, watch the charming magical water show, see the soaring erupting volcano show and the spectacular view from the biggest ferris wheel in Taiwan.

A place where dreams comes alive. A place of laughter and hope. An exciting adventure that will definitely stimulate your senses.

## Atayal Resort

TEL: +886-49-246-1311

Address: No.56-2, Beiyuan Rd., Guoxing Township, Nantou County 544, Taiwan (R.O.C.)

Atayal Resort lies in Nantou County, between the Guandao Mountains and Beigang River. The resort was planned and established by people who loved the Atayal Aboriginal Tribe. There were a lot of Atayal indigenous living in Nantou County in the past; thus, Nantou is full of characteristics of Atayal. The resort features the natural environment,

Atayal culture and recreation. Visitors can take a good rest and learn more about the Atayal Tribe after visiting Atayal Resort.

Atayal Resort places great emphasis preserving aboriginal culture. There are aboriginal museum, sculptures and dance shows in the resort. Aboriginal houses, such as Wandashe, Balashe and Atayal, are recreated in the resort. The museum exhibits historic objects and introduces the traditional Atayal lifestyle.

## Shangrila Paradise

TEL: +886-37-561-369

Address: No.15-3, Rugushan, Zaoqiao Township, Miaoli County

Shangrila is located in Miaoli. It is a large-scale amusement park that combines entertainment and culture. There is a Hakka culture village in the park, presenting the traditional Hakka buildings and foods. In addition, visitors can camp and barbeque in the park. Thus, schools often hold extracurricular activities in Shangrila. The night view in Shangrila is also attractive.

Shangrila has a European garden, water fountain and a restaurant that can serve 1000 guests. Tourists can have fun in the amusement park and walk along the forest track. The Hakka village, the wax figures and sculptures have been quite popular among the tourists. It is a place suitable for families.

## Wanpi World Safari Zoo

TEL: +886-6-781-0000

Fax: +886-6-781-0460

Address: No. 75-25, Dingjhou, Sangching Neighborhood, Syuejia Township, Tainan County 726, Taiwan (R.O.C.)

Located in Tainan City, Leopard King Safair Zoo was established in 1994. It is the first wildlife zoo in Asia and is the first zoo that received tourism medal. The zoo focuses on research, conservation, entertainment and education. 20 hectares in area, the zoo keeps over 300 animals from all over the world. There are performances by trained animals.

The zoo has the largest amphibious reptile collection in the world, with more than 200 amphibious reptiles from all over the world. In addition, there are raccoons, pandas and many other endangered animals in the zoo. The trained animal performances are entertaining and shorten the distance between visitors and the animals.

## Manyueyuan National Forest Recreation Area

TEL: +886-2-2672-0004

Address: Sanxia District, New Taipei City

Manyueyuan Park is famous for its waterfalls. The special geography has helped for spectacular waterfalls in the park. The hills and mountains are of different heights, altitude ranging from 300 to 1700 meters. Flora and fauna in the park are diversified and there are abundant birds here. In addition, along the Ruizai River, there are groups of butterflies. Hikers can enjoy the forests, watch the birds, and appreciate the waterfalls in the park.

Manyueyuan Park has abundant cryptomeria trees, which was introduced from Japan in 1896. It is reported that the trees are good for health, especially for respiratory tract. There is a tour track as long as 1,210 meters, along which visitors can appreciate the maple leaves and beautiful birds. There are 16 guide boards, explaining the natural environment in Manyueyuan Park.

## Shuangliu National Forest Recreation Area

TEL: +886-8-870-1393

Address: No.23, Danlu 2nd Ln., Shizi Township, Pingtung County

Shuangliu National Forest Park is situated next to the southern highway and features the beautiful rivers. The origin of Fenggang River is inside the park and Shuangliu Waterfall is over 20 meters in height. The pounding sound and dense mist of the waterfall are the most famous scene in the park. There are thick forests in the park, making it a perfect place to expose oneself to the nature. There are pavilions and stone chairs along the track for visitors to take a rest.

The track from the entrance to the waterfall has beautiful scenery and is suitable for recreational activities. There are chairs, pavilions and trash cans. Maozi Mountain is the highest point in the park, 650 meters in altitude; standing here, you can overlook the mountains, the Pacific Ocean and the Taiwan Strait. Shuangliu Waterfall is 3,650 meters away from the entrance and is the origin of Fenggang River. Visitors can enjoy the fresh water, the butterflies and the beautiful scenery in the park.

## Aowanda National Forest Recreation Area

TEL: +886-49-297-4511

Address: No.153, Da'an Rd., Ren'ai Township, Nantou County

Aowanda is famous for maples. It is canyon in the west of the convergence of Danan River and Wanda River, which are the origin of Wushe Reservoir. Every autumn, maple leaves in Aowanda turn red and flutter in the air. Aowanda has different faces in different seasons. From February to September, tourists can enjoy the comfortable weather, the forests and the flowers. In May, there are many fireflies shining at night. Autumn and winter are the seasons to appreciate the beautiful maple leaves and plants. Aowanda is perfect for hiking, bird-watching, and contacting the nature.

Aowanda is famous for its beautiful maple leaves. Every autumn, the maple leaves would turn red or orange. With the river running in the woods, the scenery is tranquil and peaceful. Coreopsis has been introduced in recent years, attracting more tourists. Besides the maple trees, Aowanda also provide Aowanda Hot Spring, Wandanan River Hot Spring, and Wandapei River Hot Spring.

## Neidong National Forest Recreation Area

TEL: +886-2-2661-7358

Address: Xinxian Village, Wulai District, New Taipei City

Neidong Forest Park was established in 1984. It is located in Wulai, Taipei, and is also known as Wawagu. It has the best conserved ecology in northern Taipei. The magnificent mountainous scenery and canyons are connected with Wulai. There are many waterfalls in the park and the most famous is Xinxian Waterfall, which has 3 levels. Along the tour track, visitors can enjoy the dense forests, the birds and the butterflies. Flora and fauna in the park are conserved very well. In addition, the park has different views in different times of the year and is worthy to visit.

Nanshi River runs across the Neidong Forest Park and in the south there is Neidong River. The rivers form many waterfalls in the park. The most famous is the 3-level Xinxian Waterfall, which presents a grand spectacle. The rail-cart, which was used for transporting timber, is now a tourist attraction. The distance between Lansheng Bridge to Wulai Waterfall is 1.6 km and it takes about 3-5 minutes on a rail-cart to finish the trip.

## Guanwu National Forest Recreation Area

TEL: +886-3-727-2917

Address: between Hsinchu County Wufeng District and Miaoli County Tai-an Township

Guanwu Park is located on the border of Wufeng District, Hsinchu and Tai'an Township, Miaoli. As the mists here are very thick and dense, it is also called the country of clouds. Entering Guanwu Park from Zhudong, Hsinchu County, the scenery along the road is fascinating with special clouds and mountainous views. Guanwu Park has an altitude of 1,800 meters and is the entrance to Dabajian Mountain. The Hsinchu Forest Bureau has built many tour tracks, leading to ancient trees as old as 2000 years old, forests and waterfalls. In addition, the forests also have several species of mountain birds, endangered plants and animals.

The most famous scene in Guanwu Park is the Zhenshan Track, along which are tall trees. The track is 4,130 meters long and it takes about 3 to 4 hours to finish the track. Climbing up to the top of Zhenshan, 2,439 meters in altitude, visitors can appreciate and admire the spectacles of the Xue Mountains and the Daba Mountains.

## Formosan Aboriginal Culture Village

TEL: +886-49-289-5361

Address: No. 45, Jintian Lane, Dalin Village, Yuchi Township, Nantou County

Formosa Aboriginal Culture Village was established in 1986; total area is 62 hectares. The culture village features aboriginal cultures, combining tourism, culture and educational functions. It is located in Yuchi, Nantou County, near Sun Moon Lake. The culture village has made great efforts in updating the amusement facilities and services and has shown the vigorous spirits of the aboriginal tribes.

Formosa Aboriginal Culture Village has five theme parks: the European Gardens, the Aladdin Plaza, the Aboriginal Villages, Amusement Isle and Ti Ka Er Rainforest. Amusement facilities in these five theme parks include joy ride, cultural square, artistic fountain, museums, 3-D theater, aboriginal dance show, etc. The Culture Village is entertaining and educational, perfect for families on holidays.

## Zhiben National Forest Recreation Area

TEL: +886-89-510-961

Address: No.290, Longquan Rd., Wenquan Village, Beinan Township, Taitung County

Located in the middle reaches of the Zhiben River, this forest recreation area is rich in natural scenery including hot springs, waterfalls, many-rooted banyan trees, and tropical forests. From the deep-red 80-meter bridge that spans the river and gives access to the recreation area, you can look into the riverbed and see its wild primitive nature.

The "Tough Man Slope" here is named for the steepness of its incline. It is only 320 meters long, but it rises 150 meters and has 792 steps, making it a fine place to test your stamina. The recreation area contains forests with many types of trees, including camphor and fir as well as bamboo; and along the shaded pathway, of course, you can see the awe-inspiring "thousand-root banyan."

## Chinan National Forest Recreation Area

TEL: +886-38-641-594

Address: Jinan (Chinan) Village, Shoufeng Township, Hualien County

The Jinan (Chinan) National Forest Recreation Area is located on the mountain slopes to the east of Liyu Pond. Its attractions include verdant forests, enchanting mountain vistas, and a pavilion area which provides excellent views of the lake. Facilities include a visitor center, forest paths, a grass-skiing slope, and a children's playground.

A cableway, railway engine, and other old equipment are preserved and provided with explanatory plaques to illustrate how this area once operated as a logging camp. In addition, there is a small forestry museum with exhibits, multimedia shows, and old photographs that illuminate the development of the forestry industry in Taiwan.

Chinan National Forest Recreation Area lies in Shoufeng, Hualien County, established in 1981. It is in the south of the Liyu Pond and is 5 hectares in area. It was a transportation center for the logging industry in the past. Therefore, there is a timber museum in the park, exhibiting the machines and history of the logging industry in Taiwan. This park overlooks the Liyu Pond and has very beautiful scenery.

The rails, carts and tools for the logging industry are still preserved in the forest. The timber museum is located in the center of the park and it has a complete collection of historic documents, introducing the development of the logging industry in Taiwan. The cable car used for transportation of timber in the past is now used to transport tourists. Tourists can camp, barbeque and fish in the park.

## Bada Forest Paradise

TEL: +886-8-789-8822

Address: No. 800, Chaozhou Rd., Chaozhou Township, Pintung County

The origin of Bada Elf Paradise was Chiaochow Vacation Park. In 1998, Japanese financial group invested the money to manage. It turned successfully into Bada Elf Paradise. It will make the tourists feel like placing in the nursery tale-dreaming center. The whole area of Bada Elf Paradise is about 17 hectare. It is constituted by two thousands more mahoganies with the tree age over 80 years old. The forest is full of abound fresh fragrance air. You can take forest bathe, barbeque, and get some information about the forest. The entire parkland is taking the English chateau style design. It can satisfy visitor to the fancy of nursery tale. And the main theme "Green forest castle" was divided into eight chateaus. The eight themes are designed with story type to make cascade. All the animals and plants were named and personify with a new life to let the tourists enjoy the fun with the characters in the fairy stories. Creative and new designs make Bada Elf Paradise the special amusement park in Taiwan.

The Flora Forest is the administrative center of Green forest castle. There planted a lot of flowers. Visitors can take pictures with the white pigeon flying and dancing in the sky. The food forest is the populace good dinner fabricator area of Green forest castle and it plants every style of delicious botanically. The amusement equipments are established in the machine forest of Green forest castle. There are ten kinds of machine amusement equipments in the park. It is the machine of magnitude kingdom in south Taiwan. Another part is about the nature biome. The garden designs outer insect biome education area and beautiful water world. The nature wild biome is shown in front of you. You can get many kinds of knowledge about the animals. The visitors can touch and feel the animals with the great fun.

## Lihpao Land

TEL: +886-4-2558-2459

Address: No. 8, Fullon Rd., Houli District, Taichung City

The Lihpao Land is located at 115 Anmei Rd. in Taiching county Houli village. It was originally a ranch belonging to the Taiwan Sugar Corporation. Many amusement facilities have already been completed since year 2000, including the Wave which is the first large-scale open-air artificial wave pool to appear in the entire south-east Asia, that creates waves that are 2.4 meters high. The main attractions in the Lihpao Land are live performances, gift shops, restaurants, food stalls, the gourmet alley, and rides. The Resort is planned to become similar to international amusement resorts such as Tokyo Disneyland, the Miazaki Sea Gaia in Japan, Hong Kongs Ocean Park, and Koreas Ever land.

Lihpao Land Discovery World is 25 hectares wide, and it encompasses 6 live performing groups, 10 gift shops, 20 restaurants, 8 food stalls, and 23 amusement rides. Future World, Magical Castle, the Enchanted Forest and the Fairytale Village all have their own exclusive merchandise for customers. The objective of the Resort is to let visitors experience the fun of water in an exotic atmosphere, along with the service of trained staff. The Central Garden boasts a 6 dimensional Crystal Palace Restaurant, which offers 6-stage shows at Disneyland standards. A combination of western-style and Chinese-style drama is performed, and there are also parades and large-scale stage shows. Visitors can now enjoy Disney-standard performances without having to go abroad.

## Literature and Art

Perhaps the best thing about experiencing the endless variety of Taiwan's cultural and artistic wonders is that whatever you like, whether it be folk festivals, religious practices, traditional skills, or modern art, everything is right at hand. You can find expressions of the country's rich and varied arts on every street and lane, and in the lives of the people. And every part of Taiwan - north, center, south, and east, and even the offshore islands - presents its own unique local characteristics, profoundly different yet centered on a common cultural core. This is the source of Taiwan's magnetic allure.

Glove Puppetry

Glove puppetry is one of the most important traditional performing arts in Taiwan, an art form that incorporates literary motifs, music, and voice acting.

The puppets are expertly crafted with carved wooden heads, elaborate attire, and other trimmings that make them works of art in their own right. Their faces have no obvious expression; the liveliness of the figurines depends entirely on the puppetry skills of the puppeteer. The carvings and paintings of the puppet stage further add to the delight of the show.

Oil Paper Umbrellas

Oil paper umbrellas play an important role in the life of the Hakka people. In addition to providing shelter from sun and rain, they are also a symbol of good fortune. The Hakka town of Meinong in southern Taiwan is renowned for its oil paper umbrellas. It is a custom among the townspeople to give umbrellas away as a gesture of good luck. It is common to see people in Meinong walking through the town streets holding an oil paper umbrella on a rainy day. The umbrellas represent not only the locals' love for their hometown, but also pride in their skill and art.

Meinong Folk Village: +886-7-681-7508

Dough Figures

The making of dough figures is a traditional folk art in Chinese culture. The figures are fashioned from steamed sticky rice and flour dough and so are also called "rice sculptures." Most dough figures are made into characters from legendary stories or are shaped like beasts, flowers, or birds.

Nowadays, some dough figures are shaped into cartoon and comic story characters as well. Since they are brightly colored, dough figures are popular among and loved by children. Dough figures were often sold at temple fairs. Today, they are considered as art works to be collected and appreciated rather than items offered at an altar to the dead or deities in temples, as they once were.

## Blowing Sugar Figurines

A sugar figurine is made by first melting malt sugar in a pot, then taking it out when it becomes semi-colloid and blowing it into a hollow round ball with a long and thin tube. When the ball cools down, it becomes solid while the lump of elastic sugar remains soft and warm in the hand. At that point, the sugar blower pulls, rolls, and pinches the ball while blowing into the tube. In less than a minute, a figure takes shape. Although it is not difficult to learn the basics of blowing sugar figurines, it takes much time and practice to do it well.

## Chinese Knots

In earlier times, knots were used not only to fasten objects, but also to record facts. In Chinese culture, they have long served a decorative function as well.

The knots have a symmetrical design and subtle beauty that exemplifies traditional Chinese aesthetic values. Today they are called "Chinese knots," or "Chinese macrame."

## Scented Sachets

It is customary in Taiwan to make and wear scented sachets (pomanders) during the Dragon Boat Festival, celebrated on the 5th day of the fifth lunar month of the Chinese calendar. In the past when medicine was less advanced, people ground up realgar (arsenic mineral ore) and artemisia and calamus plants into fine powders, and wrapped them in a small piece of cloth to make a sachet that could be worn around the neck. The sachets gave out a scent that kept away insects and bacteria; this is the origin of today's scented sachets.

While these auspicious symbols are no longer used to ward off evils or cure illnesses, they still retain a cultural value and are appreciated for their decorative beauty.

Spinning Tops

"Spinning tops" is a game dating from ancient times which still enjoys great popularity today.

This special type of folk sport is well preserved in the town of Daxi in Taoyuan City, where many residents begin whipping tops from a very young age. The largest "king top" displayed at the Furen Temple weighs 120kg, and is played with a cord thicker than your thumb. The next time you visit this enchanted town to see its historical streets, appreciate the wooden furniture, and shop for tofu, don't forget to see the tops as well!

Kites

Traditional kites in Taiwan are made of narrow bamboo strips and cotton paper, which is light, easy to paint, and not so easily damaged as paper made from wood pulp. Today's kites are mostly made of plastic or nylon and are durable even in rain. In terms of style, there are regular flat kites and sculptural kites in the shapes of dragons, centipedes, and other fanciful figures.

Diabolos

A diabolo is a juggling prop whirled and tossed on a string connected to two sticks, one held in each hand. As the diabolo accelerates, it issues a low humming sound. Experienced performers can simultaneously spin multiple diabolos and send them high through the air. Diabolos are also incorporated into dances and other riveting performances.

Calligraphy

Calligraphy is the most appreciated form of all Chinese arts. Some say it embodies the essence of Chinese culture.

Calligraphy comes in many styles. The characters may be carefully and neatly written, or described with flourish. The characters may also be presented to emphasize their meaning. A work of calligraphy evokes a different response from each viewer. Calligraphy is said to bring peace of mind and inner tranquility, elevate one spiritually, and promote the ability to observe and make judgments. It is also said to enhance perseverance and willpower.

# Natural Environment

Formosa ("Beautiful Island")

Formosa is what the Portuguese called Taiwan when they came here in the 16th century and saw the verdant beauty of the island.

Located off the southeast coast of the Asian Continent at the western edge of the Pacific Ocean, between Japan and the Philippines and right in the center of the East-Asian island arc, Taiwan forms a vital line of communication in the Asia-Pacific region. It covers an area of approximately 36,000 square kilometers (14,400 square miles) and is longer than it is wide. Two-thirds of the total area is covered by forested mountains and the remaining area consists of hilly country, platforms and highlands, coastal plains and basins. The Central Mountain Range stretches along the entire country from north to south, thus forming a natural line of demarcation for rivers on the eastern and western sides of the island. On the west side, lies the Yushan (Yu Mountain) Range with its main peak reaching 3,952 meters, the highest mountain peak in Northeast Asia.

The Mountains

Taiwan has been abundantly endowed with mountains; over 200 of its peaks are more than 3,000 meters high, making Taiwan geographically unique. As mountains can be found anywhere, mountain climbing is a popular leisure activity in Taiwan. One can choose to hike the mountains on the outskirts of the city or accept the challenge of climbing one of the numerous high mountains, following the course of streams and valleys, tracing back to the source of rivers, or crossing entire mountains. In any case, lush scenery will unfold your eyes and it will not take too long for you to be convinced of the beauty of Taiwan's mountains.

In addition, there are nine national parks which offer a variety of distinct topographic landscapes: the Taroko National Park, focused on a narrow ravine created by a river which has cut through the mountains; Yushan National Park, containing the highest landmark of Taiwan and also the highest peak in Northeast Asia; Shei-pa National Park, featuring dangerously steep slopes; Yangmingshan National Park, with its volcanic craters and lakes; Kenting National Park, encompassing the only tropical area in Taiwan which breathes a truly Southeast Asian atmosphere; Kinmen National Park, which greets visitors with white coral and shell beaches and other geological wonders. Finally, both culture and natural attrations await your discovery at Taijiang National Park.

Sea World

Taiwan has a very rich marine ecology. You can see a groups of bottlenose dolphins, spinner dolphins, Risso's dolphins, and pan tropical spotted dolphins jumping out of the Pacific Ocean along the east. Azure seas and magnificent coral reefs can be found in Kending (Kenting) at the southern tip of Taiwan, and on Green Island and the Penghu Archipelago. This is a place for you to discover and be amazed.

Eco-park

Taiwan has a warm and humid climate and a variety of terrain, including sandbars, plains, basins, hills, plateaus, and mountains. As a result, the country is home to abundant animal and plant life, including various endemic species, and can therefore be regarded as one gigantic eco-park. Because of the formation of mud flats and mangroves along the coast, large numbers of migratory birds from around the world are attracted to Taiwan, where they use these coastal areas as a temporary shelter and rest area before they resume their journey. In spring and summer time, there are the birds that leave the tropics behind to spend this season in Taiwan, such as the eye-catching fairy pitta, known in Chinese as the eight-color bird. During autumn time, birds from colder northern areas come to Taiwan to spend the winter, such as the black-faced spoonbill. The gray-faced buzzard will be right on time to participate in the Double Ten celebrations (Taiwan's national day) in October each year, and there are also countless other migratory birds that use Taiwan either as a stopover or as their final destination, one way or the other adding exuberant vitality to the island's wildlife.

## Climate

If you are from a low-latitude country, you will certainly revel in the comfortable warmth of Taiwan's sun. The coolness that hangs in the air will be a welcome change from the simmering heat of your native country.

You can do some hiking in the mountains, immersing yourself in the beautiful trees of the forest while inhaling the pure and fresh air that blows across the island of Taiwan. If you are from a high-latitude country, you can leave your winter coat behind when coming to Taiwan and enjoy the pleasant warmth of the sun. If you'd rather experience the carefree sensation of healthy beads of sweat running down your forehead, then you should visit the beach at Kending (Kenting) in southern Taiwan, where it is summer all year round. Don't worry too much about getting burned by the dazzling sun, so long as you take prudent precautions; the sun may not be as stinging hot as it seems. Furthermore, the country is surrounded by the ocean; and the ocean breezes, which are the reasons for Taiwan's humid weather, will surely make you completely forget the dry cold back home.

Taiwan enjoys warm weather all year round. Weather conditions fluctuate during spring and winter, while in summer and autumn the weather is relatively stable. Taiwan is extremely suitable for traveling, as the annual average temperature is a comfortable 22 degrees Celsius with the lowest temperatures on the lowlands generally ranging from 12 to 17 degrees Celsius (54-63 Fahrenheit). Therefore, with the exception of a few mountain areas where some traces of snow can be found during winter, no snow can be seen in Taiwan. During raining season (March to May), continuously drizzling rain will sometimes fall on Taiwan. When visiting Taiwan during this period, remember to carry an umbrella at all time. Although it might seem romantic to have a stroll in the rain, it is no fun to travel when you're soaking wet. During the summer time (June to August), typhoons sometimes approach or hit the country.

We suggest you keep an eye on weather reports, because weather conditions are often severe and unpredictable when typhoons hit Taiwan. In addition, the roaring waves along the coast are not to be regarded as one of Taiwan's tourist scenes. During the autumn (September to November), you can wholeheartedly enjoy the cool and comforting weather, while Taiwan's relatively warm and short winters (December to February) are the time for you to appreciate the beautifully colored maple trees. The cold fronts that reach Taiwan sporadically are greatly favored by the island's hot-spring lovers. In short, Taiwan, where it always seems to be spring, is your perfect travel destination!

# Before You Go

## Arrival & Departure

### Visas

Foreign travelers may obtain tourist visas if they hold foreign passports or travel documents valid for more than six months in the Republic of China for purposes of sightseeing, business, family visits, study or training, medical treatments, or other legitimate activities.

Visa requirements included one completed application form, incoming and outgoing travel tickets, one photo, documents verifying the purpose of the visits, and other relevant documents. The Visitor Visa Application Form can be downloaded from the site of the Bureau of Consular Affairs, Ministry of Foreign Affairs. The completed form should be submitted to an Embassies and Mission Abroad of the Republic of China for visa issuances.

30-day visa-free privileges are afforded to citizens of 31 countries and30-day landing visas are afforded to citizens of 3 countries. For any further information, please visit the site of the Bureau of Consular Affairs, Ministry of Foreign Affairs. For any further questions about visa application, please contact: e-mail: post@boca.gov.tw TEL: +886-2-2343-2891 or +886-3-398-2629.

Traveler Luggage Clearance

Foreign Currencies: value over US$10,000 should be declared.
New Taiwan Currency: under NT$100,000. A traveler should apply for the permission to the Central Bank for amounts over such value. There is no restriction on the amount of gold that a traveler can bring out of Taiwan; however, a traveler should declare to the customs office. When carrying out gold valued over US$20,000 out of Taiwan, a traveler should apply for an export permit to the Board of Foreign Trade, MOEA (Tel : +886-2-2351-0271 ext. 352) and apply for customs clearance to the customs office.

NB: A traveler should register at the customs office counter when bringing out of Taiwan gold, foreign currencies or New Taiwan currency in excess of the said amount. ( Tel: +886-3-398-2308, +886-3-398-3222 )

## Tax Refund

### VAT Refund Guidelines for Foreign Travelers

Eligible Applicants:

Foreign travelers who enter the R.O.C. with the following documents and stay for no more than 183 days from the date of Arrival:

1. Passport of a country other than the R.O.C.
2. R.O.C. passport without personal ID No. recorded.
3. Travel documents.
4. Exit & Entry permit.
5. Temporary entry permit (Note: only eligible for use in claims made at an international airport or port, not applicable for on-site or designated tax refund service outside of airports or ports).

Requirements for VAT Refund:

Foreign travelers, with the entry document, who make purchases of at least NT$2,000 on the same day from the same designated stores with the "Taiwan Tax Refund"-label are eligible to request the "Application Form for VAT Refund." To claim the refund, they must apply at the port of their departure from the R.O.C. within 90 days following the date of purchase, and they must take the purchased goods out of the country with them.

Where to claim your refund:

1. The Tax Refund Service at Airports/port terminals: Tax Refund Service Counters located at the airport/ seaport.
2. On-site Small-amount Tax Refunds: Authorized "Taiwan Tax Refund"-labeled stores.
3. Designated Counter for Tax Refund Service: Designated Counters for Tax Refund Service.

Procedures of Claiming Tax Refunds:

1. Before your luggage check-in, please take your passport and Tax Refund Claim Form to the E-VAT Refund machine or Tax Refund Service Counter, to prove your foreign identity and check the Tax refundable receipts. The Tax refund system will instruct you if the goods need to be examined by the Customs or not.

2. If your goods need to go through the Customs, the machine will print out a checklist. Please visit the customs counter with the following documents and the checklist:
    - The checklist (printed by the E-VAT Refund machine)
    - "Tax Refund Claim Form."
    - Personal documents (passport, travel documents, entry/exit permits or temporary entry permit.
    - The uniform invoices noted with "tax-refundable goods" or "the last 4 digits of your passport number."
    - The goods you purchased.
3. Please obtain the receipt "Tax Refund Assessment Certificate for Eligible Goods Purchased by Foreign Travelers" printed out by the machine or given by the Service Counter and go to the designated banks or cash counters located at departure airports/ seaports for your tax refund.

# Emergency

## Useful Phone Numbers

| Contact | Telephone No. |
|---|---|
| Emergency Numbers(Free Service)-Police | 110 |
| Emergency Numbers(Free Service)-Fire, Ambulance | 119 |

| | |
|---|---|
| Emergency Numbers(Free Service)-Emergency Call (For Bad Cell Phone Reception) | 112 |
| Overseas Operator | 100 |
| Chinese Local Directory Assistance | 104 |
| Chinese Long Distance Directory Assistance | 105 |
| English-language Directory Assistance | 106 |
| Telephone Repair | 123 |
| Time | 117 |
| Weather | 166 |
| Traffic | 168 |
| Tourist Information Hotline | +886-2-2717-3737 |
| 24-Hour Toll-Free Travel Information Call Center | 0800-011-765 |
| International Community Service Hotline | 0800-024-111 |
| Taiwan Taoyuan International Airport Terminal 1 Service Counter, Tourism Bureau | +886-3-383-4631 |
| Taiwan Taoyuan International Airport Terminal 2 Service Counter, Tourism Bureau | +886-3-398-3341 |
| Tourist Service Center, Kaohsiung International Airport, Tourism Bureau | +886-7-805-7888~9 |
| Board of Foreign Trade | +886-2-2351-0271 |
| Taiwan External Trade Development Council (TAITRA) | +886-2-2725-5200 |
| Taiwan Visitors Association | +886-2-2594-3261 |
| Ministry of Foreign Affairs | +886-2-2348-2999 |
| Police Radio Station | +886-2-2388-8099 |

# Hospitals

| Region | Hospital | Address | Telephone No. |
|---|---|---|---|
| Taipei | Taiwan Adventist Hospital | No. 424, Sec. 2, Bade Rd., Taipei City | +886-2-2771-8151 |
| | Taipei Chang Gung Memorial Hospital | No. 199, Dunhua N. Rd., Taipei City | +886-2-2713-5211 |
| | Mackay Memorial Hospital | No. 92, Sec. 2, Zhongshan N. Rd., Taipei City | +886-2-2543-3535 |
| | National Taiwan University Hospital | No. 7, Zhongshan S. Rd., Taipei City | +886-2-2312-3456 |
| | Cathay General Hospital | No. 280, Sec. 4, Ren-ai Rd., Taipei City | +886-2-2708-2121 |
| | Taipei City Hospital | No. 145, Zhengzhou Rd., Taipei City | +886-2-2552-3000 |
| | Taipei Show Chwan Hospital | No. 1, Lane 116, Guangfu S. Rd., Taipei City | +886-2-2771-7172 |
| | Far Eastern Memorial Hospital | No. 21, Sec. 2, Nanya S. Rd., Banqiao District, New Taipei City | +886-2-8966-7000 |
| | Taipei Veterans General Hospital | No.201, Sec. 2, Shipai Rd., Beitou District, Taipei City, | +886-2-2871-2121 |
| Taichung | China Medical University Hospital | No. 2, Yude Rd., Taichung City | +886-4-2205-2121 |
| | Taichung Veterans General Hospital | No.1650, Sec. 4, Taiwan Blvd., Xitun Dist., Taichung City | +886-4-2359-2525 |

| Kaohsiung | Kaohsiung Chang Gung Memorial Hospital | No.123, Dabi Rd., Niaosong District, Kaohsiung City | +886-7-731-7123 |
|---|---|---|---|
| | Kaohsiung Medical University, Chung-Ho Memorial Hospital | No.100, Shiquan 1st Rd., Kaohsiung City | +886-7-312-1101 |
| | Kaohsiung Veterans General Hospital | No. 386, Dazhong 1st Rd., Kaohsiung City | +886-7-342-2121 |
| Hualien | Buddhist Tzu Chi General Hospital | No. 707, Sec. 3, Zhongyang Rd., Hualien County | +886-3-856-1825 |

# Getting Around

## Transport Info

Taiwan High Speed Rail has made Taiwan's public transport system more convenient, because it brings cities and towns closer. Today, passengers can even travel between Taipei and Kaohsiung in one day. Along the "Western Corridor" of Taiwan are 12 THSR stations: Nangang, Taipei, Banqiao, Taoyuan, Hsinchu, Miaoli, Taichung, Changhua, Yunlin, Chiayi, Tainan and Zhuoying. Moving among the corridor's stations at 300km per hour the fastest, THSR offers truly convenient rides.

THRS Customer Service:

International Calls: +886-2-4066-3000 | Local: 4066-3000

Miaoli area: 4266-3000

Taitung and Kinmen areas: 4666-3000

Matsu areas and mobile phones: +886-2-4066-3000 (Note: Calls are not toll-free.)

Ticket Purchase

There are a few ways to purchase a THSR ticket either of the day or for a later date, such as by the ticket counter or at a ticket vending machine. Payment may be made in cash or with a credit card. The customer may also purchase the ticket or print a pre-ordered ticket in most of the convenience stores in Taiwan. Please find the multi-media machine in the convenience store and follow instructions shown on the screen. Get the order sheet and have the ticket printed at the counter in 10 minutes, or otherwise the order will become invalid. Not that at convenience stores only cash payment is accepted.

Ticket Price and More

THSR offers three types of tickets: business class, standard and non-reserved ones. Both holders of business-class and standard tickets would have reserved seats. Those with non-reserved seats may choose any available seat in the non-reserved cars on the date of travel. Early-bird discounts are provided, and so are multi-ride, senior citizens' and children's tickets. Each type of ticket is sold at a slightly different price. Please pay attention to the dates within which you must print your ticket. Pre-orders must be paid within three days

How to Take a THSR Train

1. Insert the ticket from the right of the gate and get it back after you pass through it. Be sure to go through the gate from the left. Wait for the train on the waiting area of your platform. Please present your ticket when the conductor wants to check it.

2. Wait for the train in the waiting area of your platform. Please present your ticket when the conductor wants to check it.

3. When leaving the station, insert the ticket from the right of the gate. The ticket will not be returned this time. If you use a ticket issued by a convenience store, please swipe the code.

## Intercity Buses

Highway Bus

Taiwan's long-distance highway buses are mostly run by private companies such as Kuo-Kuang Motor Transport, Ubus, Southeast Bus, Aloha Bus and Ho-hsin Bus. These buses take passengers to all parts of Taiwan through national and provincial highways.

Many buses depart daily, traveling among the country's major cities. It is therefore a convenient transport to take. Some routes even operate 24 hours a day. Besides, the cost is usually cheaper than taking a flight or a train. All such makes highway bus a heavily utilized transport means in Taiwan. For safety reasons, however, please do not take any bus offered by an unregistered company.

A highway bus trip allows one to relax and enjoy the scenery along the way, and even get to know the local lifestyle more. Generally speaking, no reservations are needed for non-rush hour buses. During holidays, including the New Year vacation, as well as when highway traffic gets congested, it is recommended to book tickets in advance or simply choose another transport, just to save time.

Bus Station

Taipei Bus Station

Add: No.209, Sec. 1, Civic Blvd., Datong Dist., Taipei City 103, Taiwan (R.O.C.)

Tel: +886-2-77335888

Transfer among MRT, city bus and highway bus is provided.

Taipei City Hall Bus Station

Add: No.6, Sec. 5, Zhongxiao E. Rd., Xinyi Dist., Taipei City 110, Taiwan (R.O.C.)

Tel: +886-2-87806252

Transfer among MRT, city bus and highway bus is provided.

Other Bus Station

1. Banqiao Bus Station

2. Yuanlin Bus Station
3. Yilan Transfer Station
4. Luodong Transfer Station
5. Chiayi Transfer Station
6. Taipei Songshan Airport Bus Station
7. Taiwan Taoyuan International Airport Bus Station

## Taxi

Visitors can find convenient taxi services in most of Taiwan's cities. The starting and meter rates vary depending on each city, according to local laws. But the difference is rather small. Most drivers do not speak English, however. Therefore we advise that you ask a hotel staff to write down the destination in Mandarin and the estimate charge first, so that you can hand it over to the driver later. Keep a note of the info of the hotel you stay with in Mandarin, too.

Fare

Taxi fare is charged slightly differently throughout the country. For instance, in Taipei, the first 1.25km is NT$70. From that point on, every additional 200m is NT$5. Night cab charges NT$20 more per ride. Cross-town long-distance taxi does not charge by the meter.

Please discuss the fee with your taxi driver first. (For more info, please visit the site of the transportation bureau of your destination city.)

Complaints

In case your taxi driver asks for an unreasonably high charge or performs any other inappropriate behavior, please note down his name and his car number, and file a complaint to a local motor vehicles office or a police station with a foreign affairs division, including time, location and details of the incident.

1. To file a complaint in Taipei City:

   Department of Transportation, Taipei City Government: +886-2-2720-8889 ext.6888

   Traffic Division, Taipei City Police Department: +886-2394-9007

   Taipei City Public Transportation Office: +886-2-2759-2677

2. To file a complaint at Taiwan Taoyuan International Airport:

   To file a Taxi-related complaint: +886-3-383-4499

3. To file a complaint in Taichung City:

   Taichung Motor Vehicle Office, Directorate General of Highways, MOTC: +886-4-2691-3464

4. To file a complaint in Kaohsiung City:

   Transportation Bureau, Kaohsiung City Government: +886-7-229-9865

## Car Rental

Taiwan has a highly developed and well maintained highway network, consisting of National Highways 1 and 3 go across the main island and various local highways and roads. With this network, from city to town, visitors can freely explore. Renting a car is a great option for those wanting more flexibility while traveling.

Renting a car is fairly easy in Taiwan. Car rentals can be found by the major airports and train stations. In larger cities, such companies are not few. Together they offer a vast range of vehicles for customers to choose from, and one can thus be assured with a relaxing and fun car trip. Most companies give special discounts, too, and the client may get the car in place A and return it in place B, with a small extra fee. Please ask the company if the rent includes insurance and if there is anything additional to be paid.

Visitors not familiar with the roads in Taiwan may consider renting a car and hiring a driver at once. At international-level hotels, you may even ask the hotel staff to help find a rental. For those only needing an airport pick-up or a few hours' drive, rental services provided by a hotel may be a more convenient and economical choice.

Driving and Laws

In Taiwan, all cars must drive on the right side of a road. Both the driver and passengers must fasten their seatbelts. If you plan to take a car trip in Taiwan, please check our traffic rules first and get a valid international driver's license before hitting the road.

## Railway

Taiwan's trains go through big cities and small towns, providing passengers with a safe and comfortable travel experience. There are several types of passenger trains, such as intercity, Fuxing, Juguang and Ziqiang. Depending on time, budget and destination, visitors are free to make a choice. Advance reservations for weekend and holiday trains are recommended in case tickets are sold out.

24-hour Customer Service Hotline (for general inquiries and customer complaints):

0800-765-888 (Landline Only)

+886-2-2191-0096 (Landline, Cellphone)

How and Where to Buy Tickets

Visitors may purchase tickets by the station windows or vending machines. They may also book tickets online and get the tickets at a train station, post office or convenience store. Payment may be made in cash or with credit card. If getting the tickets at a convenience store, please use the store's multi-media machine. Follow instructions, key in booking info, and have the order sheet printed. Pay by the counter in 10 minutes or the sheet will become invalid (but may be printed again).

After booking tickets online or via phone, please complete payment in two days after the order, either at physical ticket point or online. If the tickets are booked two days or less from the departure day, payment must be made at least one day prior to departure. If the tickets are booked on the day of departure, payment must be made at least 30 minutes before the train leaves.

Pre-orders start 12 days prior to the day of departure. No particular tickets are reserved for on-site passengers. Please pay for and get the tickets with a valid ID and order No. at a train station or post office. Please make sure the date, train number, ticket number, and amount of payment are correct on site, when getting the tickets.

Price and More

(A) Single-journey tickets: Full, children's, elderly, and disabled fare.
(B) Return tickets: A return ticket means the passenger returns to the departure station when taking the home-coming ride, and that the outbound and inbound routes and seat and train types are the same.

(C) Taiwan Railways Multi-card System: Multi-cards, such as Easy Card, iPass and Taiwan Smart Card, may be used to take the trains. A 10% discount is given to different train rides such as Juguang, Fuxing and intercity trains, depending on railway sections..

(D) TR-pass: There are TR-passes for students and general passengers. The passes may be purchased at each station's ticket windows. Please present a valid student ID of one's own when purchasing a student pass. The TR-pass holder may take intercity and Juguang trains unlimitedly during the valid dates. No reservations may be made when taking Fuxing and Juguang trains, however.

(E) Day Pass for 3 Branch Lines (Pingxi, Neiwan and Jiji):

1. Prices:

   (1) Pingxi / Shen'ao Line (National Museum of Marine Science & Technology Jingtong): Full fare is NT$80 and discount fare is NT$40.

   (2) Neiwan Line (Hsinchu Neiwan): Full fare is NT$95 and discount fare is NT$50.

   (3) Jiji Line (Ershui Checheng): Full fare is NT$90 and discount fare is NT$45.

2. Rules for use:

   (1) The pass may only be used on the day of validation. It may not be used without a validation stamp.

   (2)The pass holder may hop on and off the trains as many times freely within the designated zones.

How to Take a Train

Please present your ticket or swipe your Easy Card at the gate. Scan the ticket by the ticket-reading gate if there is one. The ticket will be retrieved once inserted when you make an exit.

# Festival

## Chinese New Year

The Chinese New Year, also known as the Spring Festival, is celebrated from the first to the fifth day of the first month of the Chinese lunar calendar. Literally, Chinese people refer to this festival as "passing the year," which means shooing out the old and welcoming the new; it is considered the most important Chinese holiday of the year. There are a number of related customs and traditions that go along with the festival. Normally, on the 23rd or 24th day of the last month of the Chinese lunar calendar, people sacrifice to the Hearth God and send him off on his annual journey to Heaven; this signals the start of the Chinese New Year holidays.

On the Chinese New Year's Eve, families complete their spring cleaning, signifying the sweeping away of the misfortunes of the previous year. After the spring cleaning, a New Year's cake is made (the cake is a symbol of "reaching new heights"). The second to last day of the last month of the Chinese lunar calendar is when families stick up spring couplets and New Year's prints on their doors and windows to bring good luck. On the last day of the last month of the Chinese lunar calendar, families gather together for a New Year's Eve dinner, called the "Gathering around the stove." Adults then give the younger members of the family, particularly children, red envelopes with cash inside. This monetary gift is thought to bring peace and good fortune to the recipients. Then there is the "Keeping of the Year," which is seeing the old year out and the New Year in by staying up on New Year's Eve. This starts after the family has finished eating the New Year's Eve dinner. Once the clock strikes midnight, people set off firecrackers to welcome the arrival of the New Year.

Chinese New Year activities also include the practice of going around to friends and relatives to offer New Year's greetings on the 1st day of the Chinese New Year, visiting the wife's family on the 2$^{nd}$ day, welcoming the God of Wealth on the 4$^{th}$ day, and reopening business on the 5$^{th}$ day.

## Taiwan Lantern Festival

The Lantern festival is also known as the "little New Year." Aside from the usual worship of the gods, the occasion involves guessing lantern riddles, eating rice-flour dumplings, and releasing lanterns into the sky in New Taipei City's Pingxi Township. The Yanshui Beehive Rocket Festival in Tainan County is another major event during the Lantern Festival. Colorful lanterns of all sizes and shapes have always been main attractions of the Lantern Festival, which is celebrated with a grand national festival and other major festivals in Taipei and Kaohsiung.

The Taipei Lantern Festival is held for several days at the Taipei Expo Park, reaching its peak on the day of the Lantern Festival itself. There are many traditional lanterns, electromechanical lantern displays, and large themed lanterns sponsored and designed by different companies.

The Kaohsiung Lantern Festival is held along the Love River. During the festival period, both sides of the river, as well as Wufu Rd., Heping Rd., Guangzhou St., and other thoroughfares, have lantern exhibitions. There are also musical performances, helping to throw the whole city into a festive mood.

The Tourism Bureau has been holding the Taiwan Lantern Festival for years to attract visitors and raise the international profile of the cultural attractions of Taiwan. Traditionally, the festival has been celebrated by carrying hand lanterns. The Taiwan Lantern Festival adds a high-tech touch to this traditional custom and brings the event to the international stage. From the theme lantern displays to folk arts and performances, the festival has become a favorite of both locals and foreign visitors.

Taipei & Kaohsiung Lantern Festivals

Colorful lanterns of all sizes and shapes have always been the main feature of the Lantern Festival, which is celebrated with a grand national festival and major festival in Taipei and Kaohsiung.

The Taipei Lantern Festival is held for several days at the Taipei Expo Park, reaching its peak on the day of the Lantern Festival itself. There are many traditional lanterns, electromechanical lantern displays, and large themed lanterns sponsored and designed by different companies.

The Kaohsiung Lantern Festival is held along the Love River. During the festival period, both sides of the river as well as Wufu Rd., Heping Rd., Guangzhou St., and other thoroughfares have lantern exhibitions. There are also musical performances, helping to throw the whole city into a festive mood.

Pingxi (Pingsi) Sky Lantern Festival

The Pingxi Sky Lantern Festival is one of the most colorful activities of the Lantern Festival. Pingxi is a remote hillside town. In the past, those who worked or farmed in the mountains faced the risk of being robbed or killed, and they used lanterns to inform their families they were safe. The lanterns do not function as signals anymore, but are now used as symbols of peace and good fortune.

Yenshui Fireworks Festival

The fireworks display at the God of War Temple in Yanshui, Tainan City, is one of the most popular and anticipated events of the Lantern Festival.

The display starts one day before the Lantern Festival, when the deity tours the town in his sedan chair, accompanied by the discharge of firecrackers and bottle rockets. The noise, lights, and rituals that follow the god continue well into the following morning.

Bombing of Master Han Dan

The Lantern Festival is celebrated on the 15th day of the first month of the Chinese lunar calendar with a series of activities throughout Taiwan. Among the highlight events at this time is the inspection tour of the deity Master Han Dan in Taitung City. As guardian of the celestial treasury, Master Han Dan is revered today as a God of wealth, but people believe that he was once a real person named Zhao Gong-ming. When the Master Han Dan makes his annual inspection tour of the earthly world, crowds turn out to pray for his blessing and for good fortune. On the day of the festival, Master Han Dan is joined on his tour of the community by gods from, other temples in Taitung and surrounding townships.

Households along the route of the divine procession prepare offerings of fresh flowers and fruit, and light strings of firecrackers to welcome the Master Han Dan. The person representing the Master Han Dan on the tour wears only a headscarf, mask and pair of red short. He stands courageously amid the fusillade of firecrackers, protected only by a tree branch. There are several stories as to why the people throw firecrackers at Master Han Dan. In one version, Master Han Dan is the god of hooligans and his power grows with the loudness of the explosions. A less widely accepted explanation is that Master Han Dan is afraid of the cold, so the people throw firecrackers at him to keep him warm and win his blessing. Integrates religious, cultural, sporting, and other events that display Taiwanese artistry and innovation

## Dragon Boat Festival

Together with the Chinese New Year and the Mid-Autumn Moon Festival, the Dragon Boat Festival is one of Taiwan's three major annual traditional holidays. Because of its origins and customs, it is closely related to the remembrance of Qu Yuan, a poet who lived during the Warring States Period. That is why, from ancient times, people have also referred to the Dragon Boat Festival as the" Poet's Festival."

At the time of the Dragon Boat Festival, the most common customs are holding dragon boat races and eating glutinous rice dumplings called zongzi. Legend has it that when the poet Qu Yuan jumped to his death in the Miluo River, the local people rowed their boats to and fro in search of him. Later, this practice slowly evolved into the dragon boat races. Today, dragon boat races are a popular activity in Taiwan and abroad, and many local areas in Taiwan hold their own races. Every year, there is also an international dragon boat race with competing teams from Taiwan and abroad.

The practice of making zongzi came from the people who tried to save Qu Yuan from being eaten by fish by stuffing rice into bamboo sections and throwing them into the river to feed the fish. Today, the dumplings are wrapped in bamboo leaves and eaten by people.

## Zhongyuan Festival

The seventh month of the Chinese lunar calendar is Ghost Month. Traditionally, it starts from dawn on the first day of the month, when the gates of the netherworld open, and ends on the 29th day of the month, when the gates close. During the festivities of the month, which reach a peak on the 15th day, people hold rituals to solicit salvation from disaster and misfortune.

Zhongyuan Universal Salvation Ceremonies

Traditionally, on the day of Zhongyuan Festival every household has to prepare meat, fruit, fresh flowers, and other sacrificial items, which they offer to the "hungry ghosts" at temples or on temporary altar tables set up in front of their homes. They also ask monks to say prayers for their deceased loved ones as well as those lost souls who have no living descendants left on earth. This is known as Zhongyuan Pudu, or Universal Salvation.

The ceremonies take place in temples and on streets. On the afternoon of Pudu, local residents prepare offerings and carry them to the main altar at a temple to join in the ceremonies there. For the street festivities, local residents prepare chicken, duck, and fish as offerings in front of their homes in a ceremony known as "doorway worship."

Launching of the Water Lanterns

The launching of water lanterns is a longstanding custom. The purpose is to help light the way for the lost souls in the water, call the souls to come on land to enjoy the offerings prepared for them, and pray for the early reincarnation of these souls. It is also said that the further a lantern floats on the water, the better the fortune that the clan it represents will enjoy in the coming year.

Grappling with the Ghosts

Grappling with the Ghosts is a pole-climbing competition held during Ghost Month. In Taiwan, it is carried out only in Toucheng, Yilan County and Hengchun, Pingtung County. Of these two locales, Toucheng has the larger celebration.

In the early days, people migrating to Yilan from Guangdong and Fujian provinces were beset by natural disasters, accidents, and diseases, and many of them died. They were afraid that nobody was going to be left alive to make offerings after they were gone, and that their souls would have nowhere to go. Therefore, they held pole-climbing ceremonies to commemorate those who had passed away during the year. Since Toucheng was the first city to be developed in the Yilan area, residents of its eight major districts jointly organize the

Universal Salvation ceremony. On the last day of the month - the day when the gates of the netherworld close they also hold a big Grappling with the Ghosts pole-climbing competition.

## Mid-Autumn Festival

The Mid-Autumn Festival, also called the Moon Festival, is the holiday with the most romantic atmosphere. Because this holiday occurs during the autumn, when the harvest season is over, people in earlier days chose this day to make offerings and thank the gods for the bountiful harvest. The celebration has become a time for families to get together. The most familiar myth concerning this festival is that Chang-e flying to the moon after secretly drinking her husband's elixir of life. Aside from this, there are also tales of the Jade Rabbit and of "Wu Gangchopping down the cassia tree."

Because most of the activities held on this holiday are related to the moon, it has come to be known as "Moon Day." Important activities at this time include eating moon cakes, which symbolize unity and togetherness; strolling under the full moon; and eating pomelos, since the Chinese term for pomelo sounds like "care and protection." The barbecuing that is so popular in Taiwan on this holiday is a recent custom is in which families and friends get together and enjoy a meal.

Integrates religious, cultural, sporting, and other events that display Taiwanese artistry and innovation.

## Religious Activities

Dajia Mazu Pilgrimage

Mazu, the Goddess of the Sea, migrated to Taiwan with the people of Fujian Province in the 17th century to become one of the most revered deities on the island, where today about 870 temples are dedicated to her worship. Mazu's birthday falls in the third month of the Chinese lunar calendar, and at that time temples all over the island hold birthday activities including the burning of incense and tours of the deities around their domains. Some of the largest of the celebrations take place at Dajia’s Zhenlan Temple in Taichung City, Lugang’s Tianhou Temple in Changhua County, Chaotian Temple in Yunlin County, Datianhou Temple in Tainan City, and Fengtian Temple in Chiayi County. Zhenlan Temple’s is the largest celebration of all, and also has the longest history.

The pilgrimage from Dajia's Zhenlan Temple takes place during the third month of the Chinese lunar calendar, around the time of Mazu’s birthday. All sorts of festive activities are arranged at this time, including puppet stand theater performances, displays of embroidered banners, float parades, dragon and lion dances, and other events as the procession passes by. The nine-day procession passes through Changhua and Yunlin counties, and terminates at Fengtian Temple in Xingang, Chiayi County. Many devotees walk the whole trip.

The Mazu image which the pilgrims carry along with them is warmly welcomed at Fengtian Temple. The devotees prepare meat, fruit, and vegetables as offerings; firecrackers are discharged, and incense is burned. Another climax of the activities occurs when Mazu returns home to Dajia in her palanquin; along the route, one can see hundreds of thousands of devotees holding parties for friends, relatives, and the returning pilgrims.

Neimen Songjiang Battle Array

Origins of the Songjiang Battle Array

1. Some people trace the origins of the battle array to Song Jiang, a fictional bandit in the Song novel The Water Margin, otherwise known as All Men Are Brothers. According to this view, Song Jiang developed this type of martial art, with a focus on formation and a lesser emphasis on individual fighting, to train his followers for combat. The battle array is said to have been formed of 36 Tiangang star gods and 72 Disha star gods.

2. Another version is that the battle array is a boxing branch of the Shaolin School of martial arts handed down from the period of the Shaolin Shantao boxing, lion formation, and sword lion formation.

3. Some people believe that the Songjiang Battle Array in Taiwan was a type of training used by Zheng Cheng-gong (Koxinga) to prepare his troops to defend the coastal areas of Taiwan during the late Ming Dynasty. At that time, Song Jiang had a deep influence on popular respect for morally courageous revolutionaries. In their campaign to overthrow the Qing government and restore the Ming Dynasty, Zheng Cheng-gong and his army from Fujian were compared to the heroes of Liangshan (Liang Mountain) Marsh of The Water Margin. The martial arts skills used by the army became the prototype of the Songjiang Battle Array.

Composition of the Songjiang Battle Array: The original Songjiang Battle Array was composed of 108 heroes who were said to be transformed from the 36 Tiangang star gods and 72 Disha star gods. Today, the Songjiang Battle Array is generally composed of 36 members. The reduced size is due to social changes in Taiwan and the belief that 108 is an inauspicious number. In Taiwan, the traditional Songjiang Battle Array is active in Kaohsiung City, with a large number of battle array groups in Dashu District and Neimen District; in terms of related temple activities, however, Neimen District occupies a central place in the Songjiang Battle Array in Taiwan. Originally known as "Luohanmen," Neimen has a population of less than 30,000, but there are 15 Songjiang Battle Array groups in the township. This is due largely to the dedication of the temple committees of Neimen's Zizhu Temple and Nanhai's Zizhu Temple keeping this colorful tradition alive and bringing it to the international stage.

Burning of the Plague God Boat in Donggang

The burning of the plague god boat is a folk ritual practiced by fishermen in southwestern Taiwan. The original purpose of this ritual was to send the Plague God out to the sea, taking disease and pestilence along with him. Today, it has become an activity whose purpose is to solicit peace and good fortune. In Donggang, Pingtung County, the festival is held once every three years, around the ninth month of the Chinese lunar calendar, at Donglong Temple. There is also another festival, held in the middle of the fourth month, at Qing'an Temple in Xigang, Tainan County. Generally, the Donggang event is larger. These celebrations include large-scale temple activities which climax with the burning of the plague god boat on the last day.

The Donggang boat-burning celebration runs for eight days and seven nights. According to custom, first the boat is set on fire by devotees as other participants prepare goods for the symbolic trip. Then a big fire is made to force any bad spirits and the Plague God to go aboard) and the boat is finally burned as the devotees pray for peace.

Kunshen Wangye's Salt for Peace Festival

The salt industry enjoys a long history along the southwest coast of Taiwan, dating back to the Ming and early Qing dynasties. The industry was based on solar evaporation of seawater using complex and highly skilled techniques, and it was one of Taiwan's biggest industries for nearly 340 years. It contributed significantly to the country's economic development and provided an essential product for the people's daily life. Although Taiwan has not been a major salt producer since 2002, the Southwest Coast National Scenic Area Administration maintains a traditional working salt field to preserve the history of this important industry in Taiwan.

Late fall to early winter is the best season for observing sea-salt production, thanks to strong coastal winds and scarce rainfall. Several salt-themed activities are held at this time, including the Kunshen Wangye's Salt for Peace Festival at Nankunshen's Daitian Temple and in Beimen, a center of the traditional salt industry. These events take visitors back to an earlier time when salt was the spice of life on the southwest coast of Taiwan.

## Indigenous Ceremonies

The mysterious customs and traditions of the indigenous tribes, Taiwan's indigenous people, such as the Harvest Festival (Smatto), the Worship of Hunting (Mabuasu), spiritual rituals, totemism, and snake worship, give an extra dimension to Taiwan's culture. The indigenous tribes of Taiwan form the most northern branch of the Austronesia language group, and ethnically belong to the Malay race. Most indigenous tribes have retreated into the mountains; but although many are faced with assimilation, still some 16 different tribes that have their own languages, traditions, and tribal structure can be distinguished: the Amis, the Atayal, the Paiwan, the Bunun, the Puyuma, the Rukai, the Tsou, the Saisiyat, the Yami (Tao), the Thao, the Kavalan, the Truku, the Sakizaya, the Sediq, the Kanakanavu and the Hla'alua.

Mayasvi Ceremony of the Tsou tribe

The Mayasvi is the holiest of all the religious ceremonies of the Tsou tribe. In the early years, it was held before a battle or hunt; today, it is held annually in February and is alternately organized by the communities of Dabang and Tefuye in Chiayi County. The ceremony is held at the tribal gathering house for men (Kupah).

The tribe's war ceremony includes the rites of triumph, rites for the heads of the enemies, and welcoming rites for the gods.

The Ear-shooting Festival of Bunun tribe

The Ear-shooting Festival is the most important celebration of the Bunun people. Held at from the end of the April and to the beginning of the May, the celebration is divided into sowing rites, hunting rites, and ear-shooting rites; pig roasting, apportioning the meat, and storing the meat; work celebrations, witch inductions, and other major activities.

The traditional ear-shooting ceremony starts well before the celebration itself when the young men of the tribe go into the mountains and hunt. Then they cut off the ears of their kills, sticking the ears on a pole or a tree branch for the village men to shoot with arrows. Little children, accompanied by their fathers and older brothers, also practice shooting arrows, hoping that this will enable them to become good hunters.

Flying Fish Festival of the Yami (Tao) tribe

The lives of the Yami (Tao) people are closely intertwined with the Flying Fish Festival. Each year the flying fish come with the Kuroshio Current from January to June, and this brings a rich harvest of fish for the Yami (Tao) living on Orchid Island. That is why the tribe's people believe that these fish are gifts from the gods, and why they treasure this natural resource. Some of the tribe's social customs and taboos are also closely associated with the coming and going of the flying fish.

The Flying Fish Festival consists of ceremonies that begin in the second or third month of the lunar calendar and run for approximately four months. The festival is divided into different parts, including the blessing of the boats, praying for a bountiful catch, summoning the fish, first-fishing night ceremony, fish storing ceremony, and fishing cessation ceremony. The men of the tribe wear loincloths, silver helmets, and gold strips, and face the sea to pray for a bountiful catch. Participation is restricted to men.

Harvest Festival of the Amis tribe

The Harvest Festival is the largest festival of the Amis tribe. Different villages hold separate festivals during July and August; the festival has three stages, including welcoming the spirits, feasting the spirits, and sending the spirits off. In modern times, the ceremony has been shortened and the religious ceremonies simplified. Several activities have been added, including a race, tug-of-war, and arrow shooting competition. The festivities, once limited to tribal participation, are now open to the general public.

Sacrifice to the Short Spirits Saisiat tribe

The Sacrifice to the Short Spirits is the most important traditional rite of the Saisiyat tribe, with a smaller ceremony every two years and a large one every 10 years. The festival is held around the 15th day of the 10th lunar month, at the end of the harvest season, and lasts for four days and three nights.

The first day of the festival starts with welcoming of the spirits, when tribal elders offer wine and meat and then, facing to the east, pray to welcome the Short Spirits. The second day is for entertaining the spirits, which is the centerpiece of the entire festival. The tribe's people engage in festivities and dancing to commemorate the Short Spirits. On the last day, rites for sending off the spirits off are performed. At the appropriate time, the tribes throw sheaves of grass and hazelwood sticks toward the east, signifying that the Short Spirits have already departed. After that, the rice wine, pork, and rice cakes that were offered to the spirits are given to the participants, bringing the festival to an end.

New Year Ritual of the Puyuma tribe

The Monkey Ceremony and Hunting Ceremony are together referred to as the Annual Festival of the Puyuma tribe.

The Puyuma were traditionally the most warlike of Taiwan's indigenous peoples. Every year toward the end of December, the tribe holds the Monkey Ceremony, a unique ritual that serves as a rite of passage that marks the entry of tribal boys into adulthood. Many call it the Monkey Piercing Ceremony as young men of the tribe go through a series of strict trials, the most important of which is the piercing of a monkey (today, the monkey is made of straw) with a bamboo staff. This is thought to build courage and cooperation among the young people. Participants have to complete four levels of trials, after which they are allowed to take part in the hunting ceremony. This requires a young boy to be able to hunt down a wild animal within five days. After this, the young boy is considered a man eligible for marriage.

## Hakka Cultural Activities

Tung Blossom Festival

Take a trip to the Hakka Tong Blossom Festival and prepare to be touched by the forests and mountains, covered with Tung flowers, and engulfed in Hakka art and culture. Don't forget to take these impressions home with you!

National Yimin Festival

During the Lin Shuangwen incident in the late Qing dynasty, Lin Xiankun of Liuzhangli Village (present day Zhubei) led a group of soldiers and joined forces with other leaders from Guangdong including Wang Tingchang, Chen Ziyun, and Liu Chaozhen to bravely resist invaders. Over 200 men sacrificed their lives in the battle, winning them an imperial decree declaring their loyalty. Later, Lin Xiankun enlisted the aid of local leaders such as Liu Chaozhen, Wang Tingchang, Huang Zongwang, and Wu Ligui in constructing a temple to memorialize the dead. Traditional ceremonies of the Yimin Festival include raising lantern poles, releasing water lanterns, carrying shoulder poles, returning black banners to the woman's parents' home, and Da Shi Ye. 15 villages in Hsinchu and Taoyuan take turns hosting the event, which has a history over 220 years.

These ceremonies became a unique form of belief for the Hakka people and turned Yimin Ye into one of Taiwan's main deities. Since the festival occurs during the seventh month of the lunar calendar, it is often organized along with the Ghost Festival, combining the spirit of compassion for departed spirits with respect for those who gave their lives in defense of their homeland. During the seventh month, Taiwan's Yimin Temples organize events to pay the proper respects, and as Xinpu Yimin Temple is the country's main one, it represents the Hakka's religious center. The worship ceremonies organized here have a long history, are held on a large scale, are representative of Taiwan, and are overall highly regarded. The branch temples will gather and return to the woman's parents' home, carrying on Yimin Ye's spirit of loyalty and righteousness.

## Specially Industry Activities

Hsinchu International Glass Art Festival

The establishment in 1999 of the Hsinchu Municipal Glass Museum, the first glass museum in Taiwan, was designed to promote Hsinchu's glass industry by integrating the resources of culture and tourism. Its main functions are to conduct research into Taiwan's glass-manufacturing technology, and collect and display glass artworks. In addition, glass workshops with live glass-making demonstrations are organized to help visitors learn to appreciate the artworks and how to make, paint, and reuse glass. And there are symposiums, led by experts, artists and scholars from Taiwan and abroad, for visitors who work in the glass industry. Since the glass festival was first organized by the Hsinchu City Government in 1995, it has provided an opportunity for the exchanges of glass arts. Artists from different countries share their experiences and ideas, providing exception opportunities for the local glass art industry to promote its achievements.

## Sanyi Wood-Carving Festival

The town of Sanyi, situated in the southern part of Miaoli County, is known internationally as the center of wood carving in Taiwan. The town's wood-carving industry originated back in the 1920s and, in those days, concentrated on oddly shaped pieces of natural wood. The golden age of wood carving in the area came in the 1970s, when most of the products were exported. Facing the recession in the 1980s caused by the global energy crisis, the wood-carving industry had the opportunity to think about how to elevate its products from commodities to artworks. The establishment of the Museum of Wood Sculpture in 1995 prompted numerous wood carvers from other places to gravitate to Sanyi and develop their own styles of artistic creation; Sanyi quickly became known as a specialized wood-carving area. The Sanyi Wood-Carving Festival has been held in May yearly since 1990, attracting visitors from all over the country and abroad. The festival has allowed local wood-carving artists to exchange ideas and techniques, and to develop unique styles that have become known even in international circles. The success of the festival has brought the development of cultural and tourism resources. The activities include wood-carving exhibitions, color wood-carving DIY, a wood-carving market, and a series of Hakka life and culture shows.

## Taiwan Hot Spring & Fine-Cuisine Carnival

The gradual arrival of winter formally announces that Taiwan's peak hot spring season has begun! Taiwan abounds in the gifts of nature—cold springs, hot springs, mud springs, submarine springs—it is a world-famous scenic spot for springs of every variety. Beginning in 2007 the Tourism Bureau, Ministry of Transportation and Communication combined two touristic resources the unique healthcare aspects of thermal springs and the demand for a modern, healthy diet to integrate Taiwan's "thermal springs" and "gourmet cuisine" for a plan to launch a "Taiwan Hot Spring Fine-Cuisine Carnival." This event takes center stage throughout Taiwan at the same time each year, with one of Taiwan's 17 thermal spring areas chosen as the year's kick-off location. Not only is the Carnival an opportunity for Taiwanese tourists to soak up the pleasures of thermal springs throughout the country and receive merchandise discounts, overseas tourists are also fascinated and attracted, and the Carnival is a driving force behind the annual autumn/winter Taiwan hot spring tourist boom. During this period, hot spring areas throughout the country hold a series of hot spring/fine-cuisine events and pull together hundreds of county and municipal companies, introducing the scenic beauty of the springs, the local cultural landscape, and special products.

Yunlin International Puppets Arts Festival

Shadow puppetry, glove puppetry, and marionette were introduced to Taiwan, blended with local customs and beliefs, and had developed into a unique art form of puppetry since, becoming three treasures of Taiwan. As time goes by, regardless of a vivid performance in the hands of the masters, an incidental music of live musicians' pragmatic responses, or an audience of different generation, or even the purpose of performance switched from offering thanks to the gods to entertaining people, the significance of puppetry arts has been gradually changing. Yunlin International Puppet Arts Festival was founded in 1999, and Yunlin becomes puppets' hometown in Taiwan, creating a variety of performing schools. To establish the International Puppet Arts Festival is to realize Yunlin as a cultural county, to carry forward the traditions of fine art, and to promote international cultural exchanges. The festival activities include inviting international puppet teams to perform, and sponsoring the Golden Palm Award to encourage skill contests and competitive performances of classic and innovative plays. In addition, it combines with exhibitions of arts, cultural and creative works, and installation art of agricultural product puppets, and promoting, encouraging, teaching and experiencing glove puppetry to enable sustainable development and to pass on the heritage of glove puppetry culture.

## The End

Made in United States
Troutdale, OR
08/14/2024